D1591260

SONG OF SONGS RABBAH
An Analytical Translation
Volume One

Program in Judaic Studies
Brown University
BROWN JUDAIC STUDIES
Edited by
Jacob Neusner
Wendell S. Dietrich, Ernest S. Frerichs, William Scott Green,
Calvin Goldscheider, David Hirsch, Alan Zuckerman

Project Editors (Projects)

David Blumenthal, Emory University (Approaches to Medieval Judaism)
William Brinner (Studies in Judaism and Islam)
Ernest S. Frerichs, Brown University (Dissertations and Monographs)
Lenn Evan Goodman, University of Hawaii (Studies in Medieval Judaism)
William Scott Green, University of Rochester (Approaches to Ancient Judaism)
Norbert Samuelson, Temple University (Jewish Philosophy)
Jonathan Z. Smith, University of Chicago (Studia Philonica)

Number 197
SONG OF SONGS RABBAH
An Analytical Translation
Volume One
by
Jacob Neusner

SONG OF SONGS RABBAH
An Analytical Translation
Volume One

SONG OF SONGS RABBAH TO SONG
CHAPTERS ONE THROUGH THREE

by

Jacob Neusner

Scholars Press
Atlanta, Georgia

SONG OF SONGS RABBAH
An Analytical Translation

© 1989
Brown University

Library of Congress Cataloging in Publication Data

Midrash rabbah. Song of Solomon. English.
 Song of Songs rabbah : an analytical translation / by Jacob
Neusner.
 p.   cm. -- (Brown Judaic studies ; no. 197-198)
 Translation of: Midrash rabbah, Song of Solomon.
 ISBN 1-55540-418-9 (v. 1. : alk. paper). -- ISBN 1-55540-419-7 (v.
 2 : alk. paper)
 1. Bible. O.T. Song of Solomon--Commentaries--Early works to
1800. I. Neusner, Jacob, 1932-   . II. Title. II. Series.
BM517.M72A3   1989
296.1'4--dc20   89-24055
                                                   CIP

Printed in the United States of America
on acid-free paper

I DEDICATE MY TRANSLATION
OF THIS BEAUTIFUL SONG OF LOVE
AS THE ONLY SUFFICIENT METAPHOR
OF GOD'S BOND TO ISRAEL, THE HOLY PEOPLE,

IN MEMORY OF
THE FATHER OF MY FRIEND
AND THE FATHER-IN-LAW OF MY COLLEAGUE
BETSY BROWN DIETRICH AND WENDELL DIETRICH

FREDERICK WILLIAM BROWN

1907-1989

WHO, IN HIS FIFTY-SEVEN YEARS OF MARRIAGE,
LIVED OUT WHAT THROUGH THE HOLY SPIRIT OUR POETS IN THIS
SONG HAVE CELEBRATED FOR ETERNITY,

AND

WHO HAS LEFT AS HIS LEGACY
AN ENDURING MODEL AND MEMORY OF LOVE.

Table of Contents

Volume One

Part One
PARASHAH ONE

Part Two
PARASHAH TWO

Part Three
PARASHAH THREE

Preface

Concluding my sustained project of translating or retranslating every document of the canon of the Judaism of the Dual Torah that reached closure by the seventh century, I proceed to Song of Songs Rabbah, one of the Midrash compilations of the sixth century. This Midrash compilation forms part of a group assigned to the late fifth or early sixth centuries, the others being Lamentations Rabbah, Esther Rabbah I, and Song of Songs Rabbah. In many ways, I think Song of Songs Rabbah is the greatest intellectual achievement of our sages,[1] because it surmounts the most formidable challenge of all of Scripture: understanding the Song of Songs as a metaphor. So far as our sages work out the meanings of the *is* in response to the messages of the *as-if*, in these pages we see with great clarity the outer limits of their labor. For here the *is* is the love of man for woman and woman for man, and the *as-if* is the love of God for Israel and Israel for God. But that is leaping from metaphor to metaphor, and that is precisely what our sages have done: like a hart, like a gazelle. In my language, they attain here that level of abstraction that fully exposes the deepest layers of sensibility within.

So real and concrete is that poetry that understanding its implicit meanings, identifying its hidden messages as an account of the lovers,

---

[1] Admittedly, I have reached the same judgment of every rabbinic document I have studied, in order and in sequence, falling in love with each in its day, then finding the next still more engaging. Still, now that I have completed my translation of all or large parts of every document produced by the Judaism of the Dual Torah – that is, the entire canon, from the Mishnah through the Bavli – I see this last one as in many ways the climax of the whole. From the laconic philosophy of the Mishnah through the erotic sensibility of Song of Songs Rabbah a single path moves always upward, from the concrete to the most abstract. And the road from the Mishnah down there to Song of Songs Rabbah up here surely is from this world and the everyday to the transcendent height attained in the pages of the document before us. So my profession of admiration for the compilers and authors whose work is before us is not merely the enthusiasm of the commited moment.

God and Israel, and the urgency of their love for one another – these represent a triumph of the *as-if* mentality over the mentality of the merely *is*. But, we rapidly realize, the poem is the metaphor, the reality, the tangible and physical and material love of Israel for God and of God for Israel: the urgent, the never fully satisfied desire. Given the character of the Song of Songs, our sages power to grasp its wholly other meanings and plausibly to state them attests to the full givenness of their affirmations of God and Israel as the principal figures in contention – as the lover and the beloved must always contend – in this world.

For the text, I follow the standard printed edition, there being no alternative so far as I know. For the date I am guided, as always, by what seems to me the established consensus of the moment, which I find in Moses D. Herr, "Midrash," *Encyclopaedia Judaica* 11:1511. Herr places Ruth Rabbah in the fifth century, along with Genesis Rabbah, Leviticus Rabbah, and Lamentations Rabbah; he lists as sixth-century compilations Pesiqta deRab Kahana, Esther Rabbah I, and Song of Songs Rabbah. In due course in this sequence of translations I shall turn to the last-named item. If the consensus shifts, all hypotheses of interpretation deriving from context will of course fall away. But nothing in my work of exposition and analysis will change, since I concentrate on the intrinsic traits of form and logic, rather than on extrinsic pieces of evidence, such as contents. The indicative characteristics of a document will not be altered by the assignment of a different date from the present one; they only will be seen in a different context.

Herr describes the whole group of later fifth and sixth century compilations of scriptural exegeses as follows: "These Midrashim all consist of a collection of homilies, sayings, and aggadot of the amoraim (and also of the tannaim) in Galilean Aramaic and rabbinical Hebrew, but they also include many Greek words. It seems that all these Midrashim, which are not mentioned in the Babylonian Talmud, were edited in Erez Israel in the fifth and sixth centuries C.E. Two types can be distinguished: exegetical and homiletical. The exegetical Midrash (Genesis Rabbah, Lamentations Rabbah, et al.) is a Midrash to one of the books of the Bible, containing comments on the whole book – on each chapter, on every verse, and at times on every word in the verse. The homiletical Midrash is either a Midrash to a book of the Pentateuch in which only the first verse...of the weekly portion is expounded... (e.g. Leviticus Rabbah), or a Midrash that is based only on the biblical and prophetic reading of special Sabbaths....in which, also, only the first verses are expounded (e.g., Pirkei deRav Kahana). In both cases in contrast to the exegetical Midrashim, the homiletical Midrashim contain almost no short homilies or dicta on variegated topics, but each chapter...constitutes a collection of homilies and sayings on one topic that seem to combine into one long homily on the specific topic" ("Midrash," p. 1510).

It remains to explain why I have done this large-scale project of Midrash-translation, since my interests have moved far beyond the literary problems that engaged me when I originally turned to the earlier Midrash compilations. The place of this work in my larger program of present inquiry requires explanation. I am in process of exploring the requirements of the social description of a religion, with special interest in the philosophy, politics, and economics that a religious system lays out (or, may lay out) as its statement of the social order. That program, of course, carries forward the inquiry of Max Weber, founder of social science in the study of religion. In the preface of my *Ecology of Religion* (Nashville, 1989: Abingdon), I explain in some detail my reframing of the program of Max Weber. My aim is to set forth religion as an independent variable and so a primary component in the study of society.

Within the sequence of my own researches, now completing my third reading of the entire canon of formative Judaism, the work is readily situated. Since I have already demonstrated that documents are to be read as autonomous statements, not only in connection with other documents and also as part of a continuity of all canonical writings, I determined to describe the politics, philosophy, and economics of the Mishnah and its associated writings, then to turn to what I have already shown is an autonomous, but connected, corpus, the Yerushalmi and its friends, particularly Genesis Rabbah and Leviticus Rabbah, and finally, at the third phase, to take up the Bavli and its colleagues. These, by all accounts, are Lamentations Rabbah, Esther Rabbah I, Ruth Rabbah, and Song of Songs Rabbah. In preparation for the third phase of my inquiry, therefore, I addressed these documents. As I have provided introductions to all of the earlier documents in the canon of formative Judaism, so I plan to introduce these in the proper way, following the model of my *Sifré to Deuteronomy. An Introduction* (Atlanta, 1987: Scholars Press for Brown Judaic Studies).

A further factor explains the particular timing of this work. Planning to begin the second phase – the economics, politics, and philosophy of the Yerushalmi and associated writings – at The Institute for Advanced Study in 1989-1990, I found that I had come to an end of the work on the first phase when, in 1988-1989, I closed *The Philosophy of Judaism: The First Principles*. The interval between the conclusion of the one stage and the commencement of the next seemed a good time to turn to the initial work, and thought, concerning the third, and that explains the occasion for studying the late Rabbah compilations at just this time. I see no doubt whatsoever that in rhetoric and logic, these Rabbah compilations fall well within the circle of the Bavli, and in my introductions, I shall explain why.

My thanks go to Oxford University Press for permission to reprint the Revised Standard Version translation of the Song of Songs and to Professor Andrew M. Greeley for permission to reprint his rendition of the same poetry. In the Introduction I explain why I think both responses to the poetry should be read side by side. It is appropriate, also, to call attention to the generous support for my research provided by Brown University, which has paid the costs of formatting this book for the preparation of camera-ready copy; and to the conscientious and elegant presentation of the work by Mr. Joshua Bell, Verbatim, Inc., Providence, Rhode Island, and his staff. The constant improvement in the aesthetic quality and accuracy of my books is owing to him and his proofreaders and formatters.

I acknowledge with real thanks the everyday help of Rabbi and Professor Bernard Mandelbaum, who was kind enough to read every line of my translation and criticize it. I have always benefited from his comments. This work could not go forward without the generous gift of his great learning. He is an ornament to The Jewish Theological Seminary of America, where he received his rabbinical education and served for decades in successive posts of great responsibility, including the Chancellorship. I greatly value his criticism and appreciate his friendship.

JACOB NEUSNER

September 1, 1989

The Institute for Advanced Study
Princeton, New Jersey 08540 USA

Introduction

The sages who compiled Song of Songs Rabbah, read the Song of Songs as a sequence of statements of urgent love between God and Israel, the holy people. Their remarkable document provides the single best entry in all canonical literature of Judaism into the symbolic system and structure of the Judaism of the Dual Torah. The reason is that, over and over again, the compilers of the document as a whole and also the authors of the components they have chosen appeal to a highly restricted list of implicit meanings, calling upon some very few events or persons, repeatedly identifying these as the expressions of God's profound affection for Israel, and Israel's deep love for God. The message of the document comes not so much from stories of what happened or did not happened, assertions of truth or denials of error, but rather from the repetitious rehearsal of sets of symbols.

The implicit meanings are always few and invariably self-evident; no serious effort goes into demonstrating the fact that God speaks, or Israel speaks; the point of departure is the message and meaning the One or the other means to convey. To take one instance, time and again we shall be told that a certain expression of love is God speaking to Israel about [1] the Sea, [2] Sinai, and [3] the world to come; or [1] the first redemption, the one from Egypt; [2] the second redemption, the one from Babylonia; and [3] the third redemption, the one at the end of days. The repertoire of symbols covers Temple and schoolhouse, personal piety and public worship, and other matched pairs and sequences of coherent matters, all of them seen as embedded within the poetry. Here is poetry read as metaphor, and the task of the reader is know that for which each image of the poem stands. So Israel's holy life is metaphorized through the poetry of love and beloved, Lover and Israel.

This highly restricted vocabulary – some might call it a symbolic vocabulary, in that messages are conveyed not through propositions but through images, whether visual or verbal – shows us that Scripture supplied a highly restricted vocabulary; meanings were few and to be repeated, not many and to be cast aside promiscuously. We do not find endless multiple meanings[1] but a highly limited repertoire of a few cogent and wholly coherent meanings, to be replayed again and again. It is the repetitious character of discourse, in which people say the same thing in a great many different ways, that characterizes this document. The treatment of the Song of Songs by our sages of blessed memory who compiled Song of Songs Rabbah shows over and over again that long lists of alternative meanings or interpretations end up saying just one thing, but in different ways. The implicit meanings prove very few indeed.

Not only so, but I maintain, in Song of Songs Rabbah, the repertoire of meanings is provoked by the Song of Songs itself, its power and its appeal. That explains why, in order to show the dimensions of meaning that inhere in the Song of Songs itself, I begin by presenting two versions of the poem. The first is the excellent and flawless translation of the Revised Standard Version.[2] This shows us the Hebrew text in English. The second is the poetic and interpretative translation by Father Andrew Greeley, which captures the richness and deeply erotic quality of the exchange of love – God's for Israel, Israel's for God – that the Song has the power to convey. Greeley provides one example, among many, of how the Song of Songs weaves its spell of enchantment over a careful and appreciative reader. Accordingly, in setting RSV and Greeley side by side, I mean to underline the power of the Song itself, and that seems to me amply to justify the response to that power captured in the astonishing document before us. No one can read the Song of Songs without seeing the poetry as analogy for the love he or she holds most dear. Here we see how deeply and unreservedly our sages loved Israel and loved God, and so found self-evident the messages of the Song of Song that stood for metaphors for that love. In this way I mean to show the opportunity that the sages of Judaism recognized and underline the magnificence of their theological achievement.

---

[1]Cf. William Scott Green, "Romancing the Tome: Rabbinic Hermeneutics and the Theory of Literature," *Semeia* 1987, 40:147-169, = *Text and Textuality*, ed. Charles Winquist, with special reference to p. 163: "If it is doubtful that rabbis ascribed 'endless multiple meanings' to scripture, it is no less so that rabbinic hermeneutics encouraged and routinely tolerated the metonymical coexistence of different meanings of scripture that did not, and could not, annul one another."

[2]Translation: *The Oxford Annotated Bible with the Apocrypha. Revised Standard Version*. Edited by Herbert G. May and Bruce M. Metzger (N.Y., 1965: Oxford University Press), pp. 815-821. © 1962 by Oxford University Press. Reprinted by permission.

Since this is the second translation of Song of Songs Rabbah, at the outset let me explain why I have found it necessary to undertake the thankless (if also rewarding) labor of retranslating what we already have – in a quite accurate and reliable version as a matter of fact – in the English language. For my translation is second to, and closely follows, the excellent one of Maurice Simon, *Song of Songs*, in H. Freedman and Maurice Simon, eds., *Midrash Rabbah* (London, 1939: Soncino Press), Volume IX.[3] Not only so, but to begin with I express much admiration for Simon's translation.[4] In the body of my translation, when I use Simon's translation verbatim, I signify in this way: [Simon, p. 00:]. What follows is then his translation, word-for-word or nearly so, until the opening of a new unit of thought. I also cite his notes verbatim, so indicating throughout. Simon's translation seems to me beyond serious complaint for the content of the compilation. His notes are learned and always interesting. Even when I do not follow Simon verbatim, I try to give credit for what I have learned from him. Where I translate in my own words but follow the sense given by Simon, I signify that fact as well, e.g., by inserting the words, [following

---

[3]Like Simon, I translate the standard printed text. There is no other at this time. I have never conceived that the task of a translator begins with the establishment of "the critical text." Let the text-scholars give us their superior versions, with adequate commentaries as to variants and also meanings of words and parallel versions, and we shall happily (re)translate the documents quite faithfully.

[4]And that of all of the other translators of the Soncino Talmud, Midrash Rabbah, Zohar, and the like. It was a heroic work, and, in the context of the 1930s and 1940s when they did it, they affirmed life. I do not believe that the Soncino scholars have received sufficient thanks from the English-speaking world for their achievements, under the most difficult material and psychological circumstances. When, moreover, we remember that in the world of the scholars who claim to know these writings, translation is deemed an act of legerdemain (not to say, *lèse majesté* in the case of some of them!), we recognize the full meaning of their work. The yeshiva- and seminary-world then took, and now takes, the view that the documents are not comprehensible outside of the political framework defined by those institutions; and they further say that "if you know the original, you don't need the translation, and if you don't know the original, you can't understand the translation and will get nothing out of it." The former misses the simple point that a translation by definition is a commentary, and the commentaries/translations produced by the Soncino translators form a précis of a vast received exegetical literature. The latter criticism has to be weighed with reference to the translation to which it is addressed. I think the Soncino translations of Midrash-compilations are quite accessible. Those of the Bavli, by contrast, are somewhat less readily entered. But these were the pioneers, and everything they did was far superior to anything done prior to their own work, where there was anything available for comparison to begin with.

Simon, p. 00]. Finally, very often I absorb, with ad hoc revisions, his versions of scriptural verses or copy his translation of verses verbatim.

But, as I explain in more general terms in my *Translating the Classics of Judaism. In Theory and in Practice* (Atlanta, 1989: Scholars Press for Brown Judaic Studies), his translation – in common with all others of those classics of Judaism that reached closure in late antiquity – is without use for any purpose other than reference as to the contents of the document. Simon tells us what is in Song of Songs Rabbah, but he does not help us study the document in any important way. That is to say, his descriptive translation, lacking all analytical indicators, makes possible no study of the indicative traits of the document, no definition of the compilation, no analysis of the patterns of rhetoric and logic that characterize this particular piece of writing. Mine makes possible all of these analytical studies. By isolating the smallest whole units of thought and then showing how they comprise propositional discourse, and also by highlighting through fixed formulas in English the formal traits of the original, my translation allows for critical inquiry that a translation lacking a reference system does not.

While, therefore, this is the second translation of Song of Songs Rabbah into English, it is as a matter of fact the first analytical translation. By that I mean a simple thing. Unlike Simon and all prior translators of all rabbinic documents of late antiquity into all languages, I offer the text not as a sequence of undifferentiated columns[5] of words. Rather, I represent the Hebrew as a set of distinct and discrete compositions, put together in one way, rather than in some other, and bearing formal and rhetorical traits of a particular sort, rather than some other. Furthermore, in my commentary I take up, item by item, the indicative traits of each entry and, further, the principles of composition and redaction of one entry with the others fore and aft. In this way I set the stage for analytical studies of the document, such as cannot be carried on, and have not been carried on, on the basis of the earlier translation.

An analytical translation is one in which – as explained in terms of my system of enumeration – I make immediately visible to the naked eye the principal and indicative literary traits of the Hebrew, so highlighting the distinctive character of rhetoric and logic of the original. I paragraph the whole units of thought, from the smallest building blocks of discourse upward, and indicate the larger

---

[5]Or purposelessly differentiated, e.g., by mere page and line references, which convey on their own no further information than where, in a document, I can find a passage; but even that kind of reference system is rare!

compositions, their beginnings and endings. On the basis of that presentation, readers may perform their own form-analyses, inquiries into modes of logical discourse, and other studies that tell us, in aesthetics as much as in theology, the authorship's message and meaning. For any distinction between method and message, form and meaning, obliterates the power of discourse attained in this compilation – as in any other component of the canon of Judaism.

Since I find Simon's translation so suitable as to meaning, why have I retranslated the document? It is to make possible research into this text that we cannot undertake on the strength of what he has given us. To explain: questions of inquiry into the traits of the constituents of the compilation and the plan and program of composition, the types of form and patterning of language and syntax, the logics of cogent discourse, even the topical and propositional program – none of these indicative traits can be analyzed in a text that consists of long columns of undifferentiated type, broken up into unmarked paragraphs. But that is all he gives us; his reference system is not sequential; not differentiated as to completed units of thought; not informative as to the distinct components of a given composition. The problem is not only that Simon, like all my predecessors without exception, supplied no reference system whatsoever. Among them all, he has also presented an utterly undifferentiated text, so that it is difficult to conduct such studies as require differentiation between and among sizable constituents of the whole.

Nor on the basis of his translation[6] can we tell where he thinks one unit of thought ends and another begins or why one unit of completed thought has been set next to another, rather than somewhere else. In order to make possible a variety of descriptive and analytical studies of a variety of documents, therefore, I found it necessary to translate many of them once again. I do not claim to have improved in any important way on the exegetical and philological work of most of my predecessors (though some reviewers have suggested that I indeed have done so, and others have not agreed).[7] Overall, wherever I had

---

[6]I repeat, or any other translation of any classic of Judaism in its formative age!

[7]In various components of my *Garland Library of Formative Judaism* (N.Y., 1990: Garland Publishing Co.), in twenty-one volumes, I have reproduced the sometimes violent and even irrational reviews of books of mine. Read all together, they offer welcome guidance as to areas that can stand improvement. It would make matters somewhat clearer if reviewers would differentiate between out and out error, which is to be corrected, and differences of opinion, which may be negotiated or allowed to stand; but that is asking what is rarely given. The mode of discourse deemed plausible in these writings need not detain us; readers will readily realize that that mode is conventional and not

access to prior work on documents, I have found it admirable, but only on the re-presentation of the document in a more suitable way.

Accordingly, on the basis of Simon's genuinely admirable translation, no analytical studies of this document are possible. Indeed, the more I reflect upon the character of all prior translations, the more I wonder what earlier scholars could have had in mind in presenting the text as they did: without a trace of a reference system, without the slightest attention to the indicative marks of style and form and even beginnings and endings of sentences, paragraphs, and completed arguments ("chapters"). And I conclude, they had nothing more in mind than to present the contents of the text, nothing more.

But there is much more to be known about any rabbinic writing, and through correct, which is to say, analytical, translation, the indicative traits of style and form can make clear, even to the naked eye, much of the inner structure and program of the rabbinic writings. Questions of inquiry into the traits of the constituents of the compilation and the plan and program of composition, the types of form and patterning of language and syntax, the logics of cogent discourse, even the topical and propositional program – none of these indicative traits can be analyzed in a text that consists of long columns of undifferentiated type, broken up into unmarked paragraphs. The problem is not only that Simon supplies no reference system whatsoever.

Simon also presents an utterly undifferentiated text, so that it is difficult to conduct such studies as require differentiation between and among sizable constituents of the whole. Nor on the basis of his translation can we tell where he thinks one unit of thought ends and another begins or why one unit of completed thought has been set next to another, rather than somewhere else. In order to make possible a

---

specific to the books under discussion or particularly provoked by them. Indeed, that convention of uncivil discourse has deplorably denied these hostile reviews much of a hearing outside of very narrow circles of like-minded persons, most of them in a few isolated places. But, since in all cases I was able to absorb and make use of the important criticism (for instance, in my *In the Margins of the Yerushalmi. Glosses on the English Translation* [Chico, 1983: Scholars Press for Brown Judaic Studies]), what was productive in the writings about my books, including my translations, of Zeitlin, Lieberman, and some rather junior scholars in Jerusalem and in the yeshiva-world, has assuredly been taken into account and used. These reviews should not be dismissed as crackpot merely because they are cranky. There is much of value in them, as I explain in *In the Margins*. That is why, when given the chance to reprint them all together in one place, I of course did so. The established fact that no translation pleases those who know both the original language and the language of the translation has been lost on those (few) who take seriously the ad hominem and malicious *obiter dicta* of a Lieberman and a Zeitlin.

variety of descriptive and analytical studies of this document, I have found it necessary to translate it once again. I do not claim to have improved in any important way on the exegetical and philological work of Simon, which I have found admirable, but only on the re-presentation of the document in a more suitable way.

While taking full advantage of Simon's reading of the document, therefore, I have found it necessary to retranslate the entire composition. My intent here is to offer a clear account of the basic statement of the authorship of Song of Songs Rabbah, together with an identification of the components of their writing classified from the smallest whole units of discourse on upward to completed and coherent statements. That program accounts for my analytical system, which marks each smallest whole unit of thought with a letter, completed propositions of thought (which we might call "paragraphs") with an Arabic numeral, and entire cogent statements or arguments with a Roman numeral. In addition to contributing the first usable analytical marking system for every sentence, I also supply a numbering system in sequence, beginning to the end of the document, for every completed unit of thought ("*petihta*" and "*parashah*" as well), simply by enumerating every chapter in sequence, beginning to end. Now people do not have to find a passage identified only as "see *Petihta* 9" – which may run on for pages!

The foundation of my analytical translation is the reference system. My reference system allows identification of each complete unit of thought or other irreducible minimum of discourse, e.g., a verse of Scripture. On that basis we may clearly perceive the formal traits of each composite or composition (as the case may be). Until now, to refer to our document we had to use a rather complex system, which distinguished *petihtaot* from *parashiyyot*, and, within *parashiyyot*, relied on chapter and verse and then a number, thus I.I.16 stood for the sixteenth among all of the comments in Song of Songs Rabbah on Song of Songs 1:1. This seemed to me not felicitous, since the representation of a text by a reference system should number in one and the same way all of the document's components. Hence I have divided the whole into chapters, whether a short *petihta* or a very long *parashah*. I further divided the *parashiyyot* into chapters by reference to the verse that is treated, e.g., Song of Songs Rabbah on Song of Songs 1:1 forms a single chapter, then Song of Songs Rabbah on Song of Songs 1:2 likewise. I formed the whole into a single undifferentiated system, as the table of contents makes clear.

The real issue is internal to these chapters. Once I have my Roman numeral, that is, for a given complete unit of material, how do I divide it up? I signify with a small (lower-case) Roman numeral the principal components of a given chapter, of which there may be only one or two. That is indicated by an Arabic numeral, thus **XIII:i.1** alludes to the first major division of the thirty-fifth chapter of the book. The Arabic numeral then identifies what I conceive to be a complete argument, proposition, syllogism, or fully worked out exegetical exercise (a whole thought). Finally, I point to what I maintain is the smallest whole unit of thought – e.g., a sentence or a major component of a sentence, a verse of Scripture, a constituent clause of a complex thought, and the like. This is indicated by a letter. Hence **I:I.1.A** alludes to the opening whole unit of thought, in the case at hand, the citation of the base verse, deriving from what happens to be *Petihta* One.

By indicating in a thorough way the divisions of discourse, from the smallest whole unit of thought upward, I make possible referring to each component of the document, short of individual words or incomplete clauses, and therefore analyzing the building of each complete thought, proposition, and the like. Everything else rests upon this system. Its utility for form-analysis has been amply demonstrated in all my prior works, listed in the preface. In the planned introduction to this compilation, all analysis rests on the complete, detailed account of what I conceive to be all the building blocks of discourse and thought, smallest to largest.

A mark of the primitive stage at which we stand in the study of the entirety of the rabbinic corpus out of late antiquity is the necessity, at the end of two hundred years of the so-called *Wissenschaft des Judenthums*, to provide a useful system of identifying each sentence of each paragraph of each chapter of each document, something that, for Scripture, we have had for many centuries. The system of identifying the sentences, paragraphs, and chapters that I have devised now applies to nearly the whole of rabbinic literature of late antiquity, that is, from the Mishnah through the Bavli, with successive tractates of the Bavli coming out in our *The Talmud of Babylonia. An American Translation* (Scholars Press for Brown Judaic Studies), alongside the now nearly complete *Talmud of the Land of Israel. A Preliminary Translation and Explanation* (University of Chicago Press). I anticipate that, however the exegesis of the text may improve upon my basic translation and philological progress revise and correct details of sense imputed to words and phrases, the fundamental analytical structure I have identified and presented will endure, as it has for every other document in the rabbinic canon translated by me.

So far as I know, no other reference system has been offered to compete with mine. To be sure, even now, rabbinic texts are presented, in Hebrew, German, and English, lacking any reference system beyond "chapter" and translation page number. But that only confirms my claim to have invented the only useful and simple reference system. I am not surprised that others may find their own reference systems; that is to be encouraged. I am astonished that, this late in the history of modern scholarship on Judaism, texts still appear from otherwise reputable publishers without even a pretense at a reference system. A work to which in my *Translating the Classics of Judaism* I devote considerable attention,[8] Hammer's *Sifré to Deuteronomy*, published by Yale University Press, is a case in point. But similar, retrograde attitudes prevail among supposedly "scientific" translators into the Western languages: German, French, English, and now, even Spanish.

It remains to acknowledge the sources of biblical verses. I consulted the translations of either *The Oxford Annotated Bible with the Apocrypha. Revised Standard Version,* ed. by Herbert G. May and Bruce M. Metzger (New York, 1965: Oxford University Press), or *Tanakh. A New Translation of The Holy Scriptures According to the Traditional Hebrew Text* (Philadelphia, 1985: The Jewish Publication Society of America). Many of the translations are my own. Still more are Simon's, where he has rendered a verse in a way that immediately makes clear the intent of the exegete. So the translations of biblical verses are eclectic.

Since my near-term goal is the comparative study of Midrash compilations, I have included in the appendix of this book a sustained theoretical statement of what I mean to do, with some attention to what I have already done, in (re)defining the field of learning that is called Comparative Midrash. This statement will place the present document into its larger context of sustained inquiry. It also shows what is at stake in the analytical translation, since, without translating in precisely the way that I do, the comparative studies I work out are not possible. The analytical translation in the historical and religious study of canonical writings forms the counterpart to the biologist's preparation of specimens. Everything depends upon that preliminary and not always compelling phase of the work.

I near the end of eight years of work on the Midrash compilations, undertaken after twelve years of sustained work of description, analysis, and interpretation, of the Mishnah, Tosefta, Talmud of the Land of Israel, and Talmud of Babylonia – after ten years of prior work on these same documents for narrowly-defined historical purposes. In all, I have finished thirty years of everyday study, from the completion of my doctoral degree in 1960, and, in that time, three go-arounds through the entire canon. I have now covered, for purposes of my address to the relationship between religion and society in the

---

[8]Because I find it exemplary of what is at fault in all other translations.

context of the Judaism of the Dual Torah, most of the documents (and all of the important ones) of that Judaism in its formative age, the first seven centuries of the Common Era. I plan to translate the remaining Midrash compilations generally assigned to late antiquity (the period between the Mishnah and the Bavli). These are few, and the work will not be long postponed.

This work finds its particular place, within my *oeuvre*, among other studies of mine on the documentary character of Midrash compilations and the comparison of one Midrash compilation with another. Indeed, in the introduction, when I compare the prevailing logic of this Midrash compilation to the logic of the Mishnah, readers will understand full well that the comparison of documents of all types, not only of one type, e.g., Midrash compilation, is really the goal of my endeavor. Readers may find it convenient to see the present translation of a document focused upon the written Torah in the context of the other such translations I have completed (I do not list my translations of the Mishnah and its succession of writings, Tosefta, Yerushalmi, and Bavli).[9] My other translations of Midrash compilations are as follows:

> Leviticus Rabbah: *Judaism and Scripture: The Evidence of Leviticus Rabbah.* (Chicago, 1986: The University of Chicago Press).
>
> *Genesis Rabbah. The Judaic Commentary on Genesis. A New American Translation.* Atlanta, 1985: Scholars Press for Brown Judaic Studies. I. *Genesis Rabbah. The Judaic Commentary on Genesis. A New American Translation. Parashiyyot One through Thirty-Three. Genesis 1:1-8:14.*
>
> *Genesis Rabbah. The Judaic Commentary on Genesis. A New American Translation.* Atlanta, 1985: Scholars Press for Brown Judaic Studies. II. *Genesis Rabbah. The Judaic Commentary on Genesis. A New American Translation. Parashiyyot Thirty-Four through Sixty-Seven. Genesis 8:15-28:9.*
>
> *Genesis Rabbah. The Judaic Commentary on Genesis. A New American Translation.* Atlanta, 1985: Scholars Press for Brown Judaic Studies. III. *Genesis Rabbah. The Judaic Commentary on Genesis. A New American Translation. Parashiyyot Sixty-Eight through One Hundred. Genesis 28:10-50:26.*
>
> *Sifra. The Judaic Commentary on Leviticus. A New Translation. The Leper. Leviticus 13:1-14:57.* Chico, 1985:

---

[9]These are catalogued in *Translating the Classics of Judaism.*

Scholars Press for Brown Judaic Studies. [With a section by Roger Brooks.] Based on *A History of the Mishnaic Law of Purities. VI. Negaim. Sifra.*

Sifré to Numbers. An American Translation. I. *1-58.* Atlanta, 1986: Scholars Press for Brown Judaic Studies

Sifré to Numbers. An American Translation. II. *59-115.* Atlanta, 1986: Scholars Press for Brown Judaic Studies. [III. *116-161:* William Scott Green.]

The Fathers According to Rabbi Nathan. An Analytical Translation and Explanation. Atlanta, 1986: Scholars Press for Brown Judaic Studies.

Pesiqta deRab Kahana. An Analytical Translation and Explanation. I. *1-14.* Atlanta, 1987: Scholars Press for Brown Judaic Studies.

Pesiqta deRab Kahana. An Analytical Translation and Explanation. II. *15-28. With an Introduction to Pesiqta deRab Kahana.* Atlanta, 1987: Scholars Press for Brown Judaic Studies.

For Pesiqta Rabbati, *From Tradition to Imitation. The Plan and Program of Pesiqta deRab Kahana and Pesiqta Rabbati.* Atlanta, 1987: Scholars Press for Brown Judaic Studies.

Sifré to Deuteronomy. An Analytical Translation. Atlanta, 1987: Scholars Press for Brown Judaic Studies. I. *Pisqaot One through One Hundred Forty-Three. Debarim, Waethanan, Eqeb, Re'eh.*

Sifré to Deuteronomy. An Analytical Translation. Atlanta, 1987: Scholars Press for Brown Judaic Studies. II. *Pisqaot One Hundred Forty-Four through Three Hundred Fifty-Seven. Shofetim, Ki Tese, Ki Tabo, Nesabim, Ha'azinu, Zot Habberakhah.*

Sifré to Deuteronomy. An Introduction to the Rhetorical, Logical, and Topical Program. Atlanta, 1987: Scholars Press for Brown Judaic Studies.

Sifra. An Analytical Translation. Atlanta, 1988: Scholars Press for Brown Judaic Studies. I. *Introduction* and *Vayyiqra Dibura Denedabah* and *Vayyiqqra Dibura Dehobah.*

Sifra. An Analytical Translation. Atlanta, 1988: Scholars Press for Brown Judaic Studies. II. *Sav, Shemini, Tazria, Negaim, Mesora,* and *Zabim*

Sifra. An Analytical Translation. Atlanta, 1988: Scholars Press for Brown Judaic Studies. III. *Aharé Mot, Qedoshim, Emor, Behar,* and *Behuqotai.*

Uniting the Dual Torah: Sifra and the Problem of the Mishnah. Cambridge and New York, 1989: Cambridge University Press.

Sifra in Perspective: The Documentary Comparison of the Midrashim of Ancient Judaism Atlanta, 1988: Scholars Press for Brown Judaic Studies.

Mekhilta Attributed to R. Ishmael.   An Analytical Translation. Atlanta, 1988: Scholars Press for Brown Judaic Studies. I. *Pisha, Beshallah, Shirata, and Vayassa.*

Mekhilta Attributed to R. Ishmael.   An Analytical Translation. Atlanta, 1988: Scholars Press for Brown Judaic Studies. II. *Amalek, Bahodesh, Neziqin, Kaspa and Shabbata.*

Mekhilta Attributed to R. Ishmael.   An Introduction to Judaism's First Scriptural Encyclopaedia. Atlanta, 1988: Scholars Press for Brown Judaic Studies.

Lamentations Rabbah.   An Analytical Translation. Atlanta, 1989: Scholars Press for Brown Judaic Studies.

Esther Rabbah.   An Analytical Translation. Atlanta, 1990: Scholars Press for Brown Judaic Studies.

Ruth Rabbah.   An Analytical Translation. Atlanta, 1990: Scholars Press for Brown Judaic Studies.

So far as I now see things, this is the last of the Midrash compilations concluded prior to the Muslim conquest, according to the standard article on the subject.   At some later time I plan to continue my (re)translation of the Bavli; the five tractates that I have completed, as well as the several now done by former students of mine, have served for the probes for which I needed to make those translations.

My analytical studies of these Midrash compilations have set forth some of the results of the comparison of one Midrash compilation to another, that is, comparative Midrash in redactional context.   I have further shown that a variety of Midrash compilations constitute well-crafted and cogent documents, each with its distinctive medium, method, and message.   These studies include the following:

The Integrity of Leviticus Rabbah. The Problem of the Autonomy of a Rabbinic Document. Chico, 1985: Scholars Press for Brown Judaic Studies.

Comparative Midrash: The Plan and Program of Genesis Rabbah and Leviticus Rabbah. Atlanta, 1986: Scholars Press for Brown Judaic Studies.

From Tradition to Imitation. The Plan and Program of Pesiqta deRab Kahana and Pesiqta Rabbati. Atlanta, 1987:

Scholars Press for Brown Judaic Studies. [With a fresh translation of Pesiqta Rabbati *Pisqaot* 1-5, 15.]

Canon and Connection: Intertextuality in Judaism. Lanham, 1986: University Press of America *Studies in Judaism* Series.

Midrash as Literature: The Primacy of Documentary Discourse. Lanham, 1987: University Press of America *Studies in Judaism* Series.

Invitation to Midrash: The Working of Rabbinic Bible Interpretation. A Teaching Book. San Francisco, 1988: Harper & Row.

What Is Midrash? Philadelphia,1987: Fortress Press.

Judaism and Story: The Evidence of The Fathers According to Rabbi Nathan. Chicago, 1990: University of Chicago Press.

The Foundations of Judaism. Method, Teleology, Doctrine. Philadelphia, 1983-5: Fortress Press. I-III. I. *Midrash in Context. Exegesis in Formative Judaism.* Second printing: Atlanta, 1988: Scholars Press for Brown Judaic Studies.

The Oral Torah. The Sacred Books of Judaism. An Introduction. San Francisco, 1985: Harper & Row. Paperback: 1987. Bnai Brith Jewish Book Club Selection, 1986.

Editor: *Scriptures of the Oral Torah. Sanctification and Salvation in the Sacred Books of Judaism.* San Francisco, 1987: Harper & Row. Jewish Book Club Selection, 1988.

Judaism and Christianity in the Age of Constantine. Issues of the Initial Confrontation. Chicago, 1987: University of Chicago Press.

Writing with Scripture: The Authority and Uses of the Hebrew Bible in the Torah of Formative Judaism. Philadelphia, 1989: Fortress Press.

Why No Gospels in Talmudic Judaism? Atlanta, 1988: Scholars Press for Brown Judaic Studies.

Genesis and Judaism: The Perspective of Genesis Rabbah. An Analytical Anthology. Atlanta, 1986: Scholars Press for Brown Judaic Studies.

Christian Faith and the Bible of Judaism. Grand Rapids, 1987: Wm. B. Eerdmans Publishing Co.

Beyond this work, it should be self-evident, I plan the following:

The Midrash Compilations of the Sixth and Seventh Centuries. An Introduction to the Rhetorical Logical, and Topical Program. I. Lamentations Rabbah. Atlanta, 1990: Scholars Press for Brown Judaic Studies.

The Midrash Compilations of the Sixth and Seventh Centuries: An Introduction to the Rhetorical Logical, and Topical Program. II. Esther Rabbah I. Atlanta, 1990: Scholars Press for Brown Judaic Studies.

The Midrash Compilations of the Sixth and Seventh Centuries: An Introduction to the Rhetorical Logical, and Topical Program. III. Ruth Rabbah. Atlanta, 1990: Scholars Press for Brown Judaic Studies.

The Midrash Compilations of the Sixth and Seventh Centuries: An Introduction to the Rhetorical Logical, and Topical Program. IV. Song of Songs Rabbah. Atlanta, 1990: Scholars Press for Brown Judaic Studies.

Comparative Midrash. Volume II. *The Plan and Program of Lamentations Rabbah, Esther Rabbah I, Song of Songs Rabbah and Ruth Rabbah.* Atlanta, 1990: Scholars Press for Brown Judaic Studies.

That work will introduce all four late fifth- or sixth-century documents and place them into the broader literary context in which they find their natural location.

In methodological inquiry, it seems to me self-evident, we have to reconsider what we mean by "the dating of a document," and how we go about proposing and testing hypotheses on that matter. For, ultimately, the goal of the work of comparison of document to document, the analysis of how each stands autonomous of the others, each is connected to others, and all form a single continuum, depends upon the (re)definition of "the dating of documents." Precisely what we can mean by "dating" a document, or a component of a document, requires rigorous reconsideration. Only at the end of my re-presentation of the classics of Judaism and my analytical and comparative studies of them shall I set forth what I conceive to be the correct method of "dating sayings" or "dating writings," with all that those commonly used phrases contain and convey.

It goes without saying that, while this problem has occupied my mind for many years, it is at this moment premature to set forth my ideas on the matter, but I have been thinking about it since the late 1960s, as remarks in the prefaces of my *History of the Jews in Babylonia* Volumes IV and V attest.[10] The beginning of my work on the Mishnah, Tosefta, Yerushalmi, and Bavli was in studies of the state of the question; with my students of that time, I reread the received and then-

---

[10]Not to mention *Development of a Legend. Studies on the Traditions Concerning Yohanan ben Zakkai* (Leiden, 1971: E. J. Brill)!

definitive accounts of the problem of the Mishnah and the Bavli in particular. These readings yielded *The Formation of the Babylonian Talmud. Studies on the Achievements of Late Nineteenth and Twentieth Century Historical and Literary Critical Research* (Leiden, 1970: E. J. Brill), *The Modern Study of the Mishnah* (Leiden, 1973: E. J. Brill), and *Soviet Views of Talmudic Judaism. Five Papers by Yu. A. Solodukho* (Leiden, 1973: E. J. Brill). Along these same lines, I have in due course to reread such literature as we have in hand on the dating of Midrash compilations. My impression is that while "we all know" what we are doing, no one has put pen to paper to spell out the theory of dating these writings in the way in which for the *halakhic* counterparts a theoretical literature of some consequence was created in the nineteenth and twentieth centuries.[11] But colleagues will have to wait until the remainder of the preliminary studies of all of the classics, and the comparison of document to document, have come to conclusion. Then we may begin the work. Until then, everything is merely preliminary. And all beginnings are hard.

---

[11]I did assign to a then-junior colleague, Professor Richard S. Sarason, the task of conducting a graduate seminar on "the dating of Midrash," but the seminar did not produce a single publishable paper and nothing came of the work. Nor has Sarason continued it, so far as I have read.

The Song of Songs
in the Revised Standard Version

[Translation: *The Oxford Annotated Bible with the Apocrypha. Revised Standard Version.* Edited by Herbert G. May and Bruce M. Metzger (New York, 1965: Oxford University Press), pp. 815-821. © 1962 by Oxford University Press. Reprinted by permission.]

The Song of Songs Chapter One

1:1   *The Song of Songs, which is Solomon's.*

1:2   *O that you would kiss me with the kisses of your mouth!*
       For your love is better than wine.

1:3   *Your anointing oils are fragrant,*
       your name is oil poured out;
       therefore the maidens love you.

1:4   *Draw me after you, let us make haste.*
       The king has brought me into his chambers.
       We will exult and rejoice in you;
       we will extol your love more than wine;
       rightly do they love you.

1:5   *I am very dark, but comely,*
       O daughters of Jerusalem,
       like the tents of Kedar,
       like the curtains of Solomon.

1:6   *Do not gaze at me because I am swarthy,*
       because the sun has scorched me.
       My mother's sons were angry with me,
       they made me keeper of the vineyards;
       but my own vineyard I have not kept!

1:7   *Tell me, you whom my soul loves,*
       where you pasture your flock,
       where you make it lie down at noon;
       for why should I be like one who wanders
       beside the flocks of your companions?

1:8   *If you do not know,*
       O fairest among women,
       follow in the tracks of the flock,
       and pasture your kids

17

> beside the shepherds' tents.

1:9   I compare you, my love,
      to a mare of Pharaoh's chariots.

1:10 Your cheeks are comely with ornaments,
      your neck with strings of jewels.

1:11 We will make you ornaments of gold,
      studded with silver.

1:12 While the king was on his couch,
      my nard gave forth its fragrance.

1:13 My beloved is to me a bag of myrrh,
      that lies between my breasts.

1:14 My beloved is to me a cluster of
      henna blossoms,
      in the vineyards of En-gedi.

1:15 Behold, you are beautiful, my love;
      behold, you are beautiful;
      your eyes are doves.

1:16 Behold, you are beautiful, my beloved,
      truly lovely.
      Our couch is green;

1:17 the beams of our house are cedar,
      our rafters are pine.

The Song of Songs Chapter Two

2:1   I am a rose of Sharon,
      a lily of the valleys.

2:2   As a lily among brambles,
      so is my love among maidens.

2:3   As an apple tree among the trees of the wood,
      so is my beloved among young men.
      With great delight I sat in his shadow,
      and his fruit was sweet to my taste.

2:4   He brought me to the wine cellar,
      and his banner over me was love.

2:5   Sustain me with raisins,
      refresh me with apples;
      for I am sick with love.

2:6   O that his left hand were under my head,
      and that his right hand embraced me!

2:7   I adjure you, O daughters of Jerusalem,
      by the gazelles or the hinds of the field,
      that you not stir up nor awaken love
      until it please.

2:8   The voice of my beloved!
      Behold he comes,
      leaping upon the mountains,
      bounding over the hills.

2:9   My beloved is like a gazelle,
      or a young stag.
      Behold, there he stands
      behind our wall,

gazing in at the windows,
looking through the lattice.

2:10　My beloved speaks and says to me,
"Arise, my love, my fair one,
and come away;

2:11　"for lo, the winter is past,
the rain is over and gone.

2:12　"The flowers appear on the earth,
the time of singing has come,
and the voice of the turtledove is heard in our land.

2:13　"The fig tree puts forth its figs,
and the vines are in blossom;
they give forth fragrance.
"Arise, my love, my fair one,
and come away.

2:14　"O my dove, in the clefts of the rock,
in the covert of the cliff,
"let me see your face,
let me hear your voice,
"for your voice is sweet,
and your face is comely.

2:15　"Catch us the foxes,
the little foxes,
that spoil the vineyards,
for our vineyards are in blossom."

2:16　My beloved is mine and I am his,
he pastures his flock among the lilies.

2:17　Until the day breathes
and the shadows flee,
turn my beloved, be like a gazelle,
or a young stag upon rugged mountains.

The Song of Songs Chapter Three

3:1　Upon my bed by night
I sought him whom my soul loves;
I sought him, but found him not;
I called him, but he gave no answer.

3:2　"I will rise now and go about the city,
in the streets and in the squares;
I will seek him whom my soul loves."
I sought him but found him not.

3:3　The watchmen found me,
as they went about in the city.
"Have you seen him whom my soul loves?"

3:4　Scarcely had I passed them,
when I found him whom my soul loves.
I held him and would not let him go
until I had brought him into my mother's house,
and into the chamber of her that conceived me.

3:5　I adjure you, O daughters of Jerusalem,
by the gazelles or the hinds of the field,

	that you not stir up nor awaken love
	until it please.
3:6	*What is that coming up from the wilderness,*
	like a column of smoke,
	perfumed with myrrh and frankincense,
	with all the fragrant powders of the merchant?
3:7	*Behold it is the litter of Solomon!*
	About it are sixty mighty men
	of the might men of Israel,
3:8	*all girt with swords*
	and expert in war,
	each with his sword at his thigh,
	against alarms by night.
3:9	*King Solomon made himself a palanquin,*
	from the wood of Lebanon.
3:10	*He made its posts of silver,*
	its back of gold, its seat of purple;
	it was lovingly wrought within
	by the daughters of Jerusalem.
3:11	*Go forth, O daughters of Zion,*
	and behold King Solomon,
	with the crown with which his mother crowned him
	on the day of his wedding,
	on the day of the gladness of his heart.

The Song of Songs Chapter Four

4:1	*Behold, you are beautiful, my love,*
	behold you are beautiful!
	Your eyes are doves
	behind your veil.
	Your hair is like a flock of goats
	moving down the slopes of Gilead.
4:2	*Your teeth are like a flock of shorn ewes*
	that have come up from the washing,
	all of which bear twins,
	and not one among them is bereaved.
4:3	*Your lips are like a scarlet thread,*
	and your mouth is lovely.
	Your cheeks are like halves of a pomegranate
	behind your veil.
4:4	*Your neck is like the tower of David,*
	built for an arsenal,
	whereon hang a thousand bucklers,
	all of them shields of warriors.
4:5	*Your two breasts are like two fawns,*
	twins of a gazelle,
	that feed among the lilies.
4:6	*Until the day breathes*
	and the shadows flee,
	I will hie me to the mountain of myrrh
	and the hill of frankincense.

4:7   You are all fair, my love;
       there is no flaw in you.
4:8   Come with me from Lebanon, my bride;
       come with me from Lebanon.
       Depart from the peak of Amana,
       from the peak of Senir and Hermon,
       from the dens of lions,
       from the mountains of leopards.
4:9   You have ravished my heart, my sister, my bride,
       you have ravished my heart with a glance of your eyes,
       with one jewel of your necklace.
4:10   How sweet is your love, my sister, my bride!
       how much better is your love than wine,
       and the fragrance of your oils than any spice!
4:11   Your lips distill nectar, my bride;
       honey and milk are under your tongue;
       the scent of your garments is like the scent of Lebanon.
4:12   A garden locked is my sister, my bride,
       a garden locked, a fountain sealed.
4:13   Your shoots are an orchard of pomegranates
       with all choicest fruits,
       henna with nard,
4:14   nard and saffron, calamus and cinnamon,
       with all trees of frankincense,
       myrrh and aloes,
       with all chief spices —
4:15   a garden fountain, a well of living water
       and flowing streams from Lebanon.
4:16   Awake, O north wind,
       and come, O south wind!
       Blow upon my garden,
       let its fragrance by wafted abroad.
       Let my beloved come to his garden,
       and eat its choicest fruits.

The Song of Songs Chapter Five

5:1   I come to my garden, my sister, my bride,
       I gather my myrrh with my spice,
       I eat my honeycomb with my honey,
       I drink my wine with my milk.
       Eat, O friends, and drink;
       drink deeply, O lovers!
5:2   I slept, but my heart was awake.
       Hark! my beloved is knocking.
       "Open to me, my sister, my love,
       my dove, my perfect one;
       for my head is wet with dew,
       my locks with the drops of the night."
5:3   I had put off my garment,
       how could I put it on?
       I had bathed my feet,

how could I soil them?

5:4   *My beloved put his hand to the latch,*
      and my heart was thrilled within me.

5:5   *I arose to open to my beloved,*
      and my hands dripped with myrrh,
      my fingers with liquid myrrh,
      upon the handles of the bolt.

5:6   *I opened to my beloved,*
      but my beloved had turned and gone.
      My soul failed me when he spoke.
      I sought him, but found him not;
      I called him, but he gave no answer.

5:7   *The watchmen found me,*
      as they went about in the city;
      they beat me, they wounded me,
      they took away my mantle,
      those watchmen of the walls.

5:8   *I adjure you, O daughters of Jerusalem,*
      if you find my beloved,
      that you tell him
      I am sick with love.

5:9   *What is your beloved more than another beloved,*
      O fairest among women!
      What is your beloved more than another beloved,
      that you thus adjure us?

5:10 *My beloved is all radiant and ruddy,*
      distinguished among ten thousand.

5:11 *His head is the finest gold;*
      his locks are wavy,
      black as a raven.

5:12 *His eyes are like doves,*
      beside springs of water,
      bathed in milk,
      fitly set.

5:13 *His cheeks are like beds of spices,*
      yielding fragrance.
      His lips are lilies,
      distilling liquid myrrh.

5:14 *His arms are rounded gold,*
      set with jewels.
      His body is ivory work,
      encrusted with sapphires.

5:15 *His legs are alabaster columns,*
      set upon bases of gold.
      His appearance is like Lebanon,
      choice as the cedars.

5:16 *His speech is most sweet,*
      and he is altogether desirable.
      This is my beloved, and this is my friend,
      O daughters of Jerusalem.

The Song of Songs Chapter Six

6:1   *Whither has your beloved gone,*
O fairest among women?
Whither has your beloved turned, that we may seek him with
    you?

6:2   *My beloved has gone down to his garden,*
to the beds of spices,
to pasture his flock in the gardens,
and to gather lilies.

6:3   *I am my beloved's, and my beloved is mine;*
he pastures his flock among the lilies.

6:4   *You are beautiful as Tirzah, my love,*
comely as Jerusalem,
terrible as an army with banners.

6:5   *Turn away your eyes from me,*
for they disturb me –
Your hair is like a flock of goats,
moving down the slopes of Gilead.

6:6   *Your teeth are like a flock of ewes*
that have come up from the washing,
all of them bear twins,
not one among them is bereaved.

6:7   *Your cheeks are like halves of a pomegranate,*
behind your veil.

6:8   *There are sixty queens and eighty concubines,*
and maidens without number.

6:9   *My dove, my perfect one, is only one,*
the darling of her mother,
flawless to her that bore her.
The maidens saw her and called her happy;
the queens and concubines also,
and they praised her.

6:10   *"Who is this that looks like the dawn,*
fair as the moon, bright as the sun,
terrible as an army with banners?"

6:11   *I went down to the nut orchard*
to look at the blossoms of the valley,
to see whether the vines had budded,
whether the pomegranates were in bloom.

6:12   *Before I was aware, my fancy set me*
in a chariot beside my prince.

6:13   *Return, return, O Shulammite,*
return, return that we may look upon you.
Why should you look upon the Shulammite,
as upon a dance before two armies?

The Song of Songs Chapter Seven

7:1   *How graceful are your feet in sandals,*
O queenly maiden!

> *Your rounded thighs are like jewels,*
> *the work of a master hand.*

7:2   *Your navel is a rounded bowl,*
> *that never lacks mixed wine.*
> *Your belly is a heap of wheat,*
> *encircled with lilies.*

7:3   *Your two breasts are like two fawns,*
> *twins of a gazelle.*

7:4   *Your neck is like an ivory tower.*
> *Your eyes are pools in Heshbon,*
> *by the gate of Bath-rabbim.*
> *Your nose is like a tower of Lebanon,*
> *overlooking Damascus.*

7:5   *Your head crowns you like Carmel,*
> *and your flowing locks are like purple;*
> *a king is held captive in the tresses.*

7:6   *How fair and pleasant you are,*
> *O loved one, delectable maiden.*

7:7   *You are stately as a palm tree,*
> *and your breasts are like its clusters.*

7:8   *I say I will climb the palm tree*
> *and lay hold of its branches.*
> *O, may your breasts be like clusters of the vine,*
> *and the scent of your breath like apples,*

7:9   *and your kisses like the best wine*
> *that goes down smoothly,*
> *gliding over lips and teeth.*

7:10   *I am my beloved's,*
> *and his desire is for me.*

7:11   *Come my beloved,*
> *let us go forth into the fields,*
> *and lodge in the villages;*

7:12   *let us go out early to the vineyards,*
> *and see whether the vines have budded,*
> *whether the grape blossoms have opened*
> *and the pomegranates are in bloom.*
> *There I will give you my love.*

7:13   *The mandrakes give forth fragrance,*
> *and over our doors are all choice fruits,*
> *new as well as old,*
> *which I have laid up for you, O my beloved.*

The Song of Songs Chapter Eight

8:1   *O that you were like a brother to me,*
> *that nursed at my mother's breast!*
> *If I met you outside, I would kiss you,*
> *and none would despise me.*

8:2   *I would lead you and bring you*
> *into the house of my mother,*
> *and into the chamber of her that conceived me.*
> *I would give you spiced wine to drink,*

       the juice of my pomegranates.

8:3   *O that his left hand were under my head,*
       and that his right hand embraced me!

8:4   *I adjure you, O daughters of Jerusalem,*
       that you not stir up nor awaken love
       until it please.

8:5   *Who is that coming up from the wilderness,*
       leaning upon her beloved?
       Under the apple tree I awakened you.
       There your mother was in travail with you,
       there she who bore you was in travail.

8:6   *Set me as a seal upon your heart,*
       as a seal upon your arm;
       for long is strong as death,
       jealousy is cruel as the grave.
       Its flashes are flashes of fire,
       a most vehement flame.

8:7   *Many waters cannot quench love,*
       neither can floods drown it.
       If a man offered for love
       all the wealth of his house,
       it would be utterly scorned.

8:8   *We have a little sister,*
       and she has no breasts.
       What shall we do for our sister,
       on the day when she is spoken for?

8:9   *If she is a wall,*
       we will build upon her a battlement of silver;
       but if she is a door,
       we will enclose her with boards of cedar.

8:10   *I was a wall,*
       and my breasts were like towers;
       then I was in his eyes
       as one who brings peace.

8:11   *Solomon had a vineyard at Baal-hamon;*
       he let out the vineyard to keepers;
       each one was to bring for its fruit a thousand pieces of silver.

8:12   *My vineyard, my very own, is for myself;*
       you, O Solomon, may have the thousand,
       and the keepers of the fruit two hundred.

8:13   *O you who dwell in the gardens,*
       my companions are listening for your voice;
       let me hear it.

8:14   *Make haste, my beloved,*
       and be like a gazelle
       or a young stag
       upon the mountains of spices.

The Song of Songs in the Translation of Andrew M. Greeley

The following is Professor Andrew M. Greeley's freehand translation of the same poetry, aiming at sense rather than verbatim rendition. Greeley provides a preface essential to understanding both the Song of Songs and also his response to it.

The Egyptian love songs and the Song of Songs are first of all all songs about love. The poets reveal their views of love not by speaking about love in the abstract, but by portraying people in love, making lovers' words reveal lovers' thoughts, feelings, and deeds. The poets invite us to observe lovers, to smile at them, to empathize with them, to sympathize with them, to recall in their adolescent pains our own, to share their desires, to enjoy in fantasy their pleasures. The poets show us young lovers flush with desire and awash in waves of new and overwhelming emotions. We watch lovers sailing the Nile to a rendez-vous, walking hand in hand through gardens, lying together in garden bowers. We come upon them sitting at home aching for the one they love, standing outside the loved one's door and pouting, swimming across rivers, running frantically through the streets at night, kissing, fondling, hugging and snuggling face to face and face to breast, and – no less erotically – telling each other's praises in sensuous similes.

Michael V. Fox

How is one to understand the Song in terms of human and divine love? It is we moderns who have difficulty with this question. But the bible suggests that these loves are united and not to be separated. Israel, it is true, understood that Yahweh was beyond sex. He had no consort; and the fertility rites were not the proper mode of worship for him. Yet the union between man and woman became a primary symbol for the expression of the relationship of the Lord to His People. The covenant between God and His People is consistently portrayed as a marriage.

Roland Murphy O. Carm.

First Song

Beloved:

A captive enslaved by your amorous lips,
A prisoner of your sweet embrace,
Drawn after you in passionate chase,
Helplessly bound by your searing kiss,
Dark is my skin, I know, and slim my waist,
My breasts, dear brothers tell me, inferior.
Yet I undress swiftly when you draw near,
Of my prudish modesty you see no trace.
I am yours, my love, for what I am worth,
Play with me, I beg, however you will,
Fondle me, use me till your pleasure is filled.
I live only for your delight and mirth.

Lover:

But I am the one enraptured as slave,
Captured completely by your form and face.
Chained forever to your numinous grace,
O mistress of love whose favor I crave.
Firm and full your bosom, an exquisite gift,
Your slender legs lead to a perfumed cave.
I am, that I might draw near that sacred nave,
A meek servant to your slightest wish.

Duet:

    Lay your head against my breast,
    Sooth me with your azure eyes,
    Heal me with your gracious thighs,
    In my arms forever nest.
    You are as soft as raisin cake,
    You're as warm, dear, as new baked bread.
    You are a blossoming apple grove,
    And you a sandalwood treasure trove.
    Drink me like expensive wine!
    Consume me, I am only thine!
    Beneath this star dense sky,
    Lay quiet now on my chest.
    Then again, after a little rest,
    Drown me in your happy sighs.

My wondrous love, softly sleep
Your gift tonight I'll always keep.

Sg. 1/1 to Sg 2/7

Second Song

Beloved:

On my garden path a hint of eager feet,
At the window ardent eyes strive to see,
Then my lover's arms reach out strong for me.
My sick and defeated heart begins to beat!

Lover:

Rise up, dear one, the snow is gone.
We are drenched in lemon scented dew,
The lake again is melted blue,
See, flowers bloom and green the lawn.
Time, I insist, to play and sing and dance,
Let me see once more your laughing face
As together we run our ardent race
And, with darkness gone, we renew romance.

Beloved:

My lover left, quiet with the morning breeze,
Back to the city's busy squares and streets.
On my bed I shivered in icy air,
Unclothed, frightened, alone – what if I freeze?
All day, I pined, I missed him so,
At dusk wanton and wild, I ran to the gate
"Welcome, my darling, I could hardly wait,
I've caught you now, I'll never let you go!"

Lover:

Enough of your running, my darling, my dove,
Ah, off with your dress, and lie at my side,
My woman now I claim you, and my bride,
In triumph I possess you and seal our love!

Sg 2/8-3/5

Third Song

Beloved:

On my bed in the dark of night
I took off my gown for the one I love.
I prayed to God and the saints above
But he did not come, my life, my light.
So I sought him everywhere in town,
In alleys, streets, and decrepit bars.
Recklessly I begged the unfeeling guards,
"Tell me, my love, where is he to be found?"
I lost all I had, freedom, hope, and fame,
Those who were my friends cruelly pulled me down.
I still wait for him, cold and harshly bound,
Stripped, humiliated, and ashamed.

I dream of him:

Lover:

In the silent, windless heat of day,
Wine sparkling in our goblets, you and me,
Two alone under the eucalyptus tree,
Still your lips, listen to what I must say.
While we recline in our aromatic batch,
And my teeth your taut nipples gently bite
Let me sing, dearest, of your blazing lights:
As my fingers roam your fertile garden paths:
Your lips are chocolate, dark for a feast,
Your mouth is as sweet as honey and milk,
Your unblemished skin the finest silk,
Your clear eyes sunrise shining in the east.
Your hair is as smooth as lace,
Your complexion glows like the rising moon,
Irish linen your flesh, and roses in bloom.
An artist's miracle your lovely face.
Your ivory throat, lithe, supple and clean,
Your elegant shoulders shapely and bare,
Invite me to a bed warmed by loving care,
A house of grace where I'll be free to dream.
I take your round breasts, one prize in each hand,
Generous and rich, thick cream in my mouth –
I suckle and drain them, thirsty after drought.
Your hips sweet flowing hills round for my hand,

Your belly a peach sugared to my tongue.
Your flanks burnt cinnamon tart to my teeth
Then a mountain forest, fragrant and neat,
Whose depths I'll explore before I am done.

Beloved:

I am deprived of my sense, dear poet mine,
Swept away by the winds, the song in your voice.
Here are my poor favors, what is your choice?
I am your harvest, darling...reap me and dine!

   Sg 3/6-5/1

Fourth Song

Beloved:

My lover came to unlock the secret door –
Bathed, fragrant, and unveiled I waited on my bed –
"Unfold, O Perfect One," he gently said,
Hand in the keyhole, his forever more!
I was powerless, mere putty to shape,
He opened me up, skilled master of the game,
Filled me with his incandescent flame,
And lighted a fire I'll never escape

Then, my turn to attack, I disrobed my man.
I devoured him, uncovered, full length,
Explored, then reveled in his youthful strength,
And traced his wonders with my eager hand.
I tickled and tormented my poor darling one,
Embarrassed him, aroused him, drove him quite mad.
"Don't squirm, dearest, you're cute when you're nude;
I'll stop teasing you only when I'm done.
You are clever, good, and kind, I admit,
And also, belly, arms, and loins, rock hard,
A tree, a mountain, a fiercely loving guard,
In my body and plans I think you might fit.
Black hair, blue eyes, tawny sunrise skin,
Demanding hands, determined virile legs –
And also an appealing, trustful babe,
Savage chest outside, wounded heart within.
Lie here quietly on my garden couch,
I'll encircle you with affection and love.
My lilies and spices fit you like a glove,
It's fun to torment you with my giddy touch.

On your pleasured smile, I complacently gaze,
Oh!...Stay here, my dear, be with me all my days!"

  Sg. 5/2-6/3

Fifth Song

Lover:

There are many girls, but you're my special one,
Fierce and passionate woman, kindest friend,
Without you my hours never seem to end,
Where have you been, my sun, my moon, my dawn?
There's no escape now, I'm holding you down.
Do not pretend that you want to flee,
Tremble at my touch, you belong to me,
Be still while I slip off your frilly gown!
You were sculpted an elegant work of art,
Dark hair falling on snow white chest,
Honeydew, your high and graceful breasts,
One taste enough to break my heart.
In the curve of your wondrous thighs:
A deep valley flowing with perfumed wine
Around which wheat and blooming lilies twine
Whose sweetness invites my enchanted eyes.
I will seize the fruit, press them to my teeth.
Then, famished, impassioned, and lightly deft,
Explore the valley's tantalizing cleft
And your delicacy savor, drink, and eat!

Beloved:

I will be dry white wine to slake your thirst
And a tasty morsel to tease your mouth.
A trembling prize from the misty south,
A plundered vessel for your nightly feast,
A submissive trophy you can carry off
To a cool treasure house in your magic lands,
A most willing slave to your artful hands,
A total gift, passionate, loving, soft!

Lover:

She sleeps now, my innocent little child,
Wake her not, good winds, adore her radiant smile!

  Sg 6/4-8/4

Sixth Song

Beloved:

Let my breasts be towers for you to scale
Above my belly's captured ivory wall.
Climb them again each day, my love, my all,
As I your victory forever hail.
Let my face be branded on your heart
That you may feel my heat in every breath,
My love, implacable as death,
My passion like a wall of raging fire,
Impervious to the storm and flood
Of deadly friction and foolish strife
And the insidious anxieties of life,
A burning need forever in my blood.

Sg 8/5-8

Whatever answer one may give to the problem...one cannot be unaware of the fact that even if it is only an anthology, in the vision of the final redactor (unless he be taken for a simpleton), Canticles does not end: true love is always a quest of one person for another; it is a constant straining toward the unity of the one who is preeminently the beloved with the companion who is the unique one.
Daniel Lys
Le Plus Beau Chant de la Creation

Part One

PARASHAH ONE

Song of Songs Chapter One

1:1   *The Song of Songs, which is Solomon's.*

1:2   *O that you would kiss me with the kisses of your mouth!*
For your love is better than wine.

1:3   *Your anointing oils are fragrant,*
your name is oil poured out;
therefore the maidens love you.

1:4   *Draw me after you, let us make haste.*
The king has brought me into his chambers.
We will exult and rejoice in you;
we will extol your love more than wine;
rightly do they love you.

1:5   *I am very dark, but comely,*
O daughters of Jerusalem,
like the tents of Kedar,
like the curtains of Solomon.

1:6   *Do not gaze at me because I am swarthy,*
because the sun has scorched me.
My mother's sons were angry with me,
they made me keeper of the vineyards;
but my own vineyard I have not kept!

1:7   *Tell me, you whom my soul loves,*
where you pasture your flock,
where you make it lie down at noon;
for why should I be like one who wanders
beside the flocks of your companions?

1:8   *If you do not know,*
O fairest among women,
follow in the tracks of the flock,
and pasture your kids
beside the shepherds' tents.

1:9   *I compare you, my love,*
to a mare of Pharaoh's chariots.

1:10   *Your cheeks are comely with ornaments,*
        your neck with strings of jewels.
1:11   *We will make you ornaments of gold,*
        studded with silver.
1:12   *While the king was on his couch,*
        my nard gave forth its fragrance.
1:13   *My beloved is to me a bag of myrrh,*
        that lies between my breasts.
1:14   *My beloved is to me a cluster of*
        henna blossoms,
        in the vineyards of En-gedi.
1:15   *Behold, you are beautiful, my love;*
        behold, you are beautiful;
        your eyes are doves.
1:16   *Behold, you are beautiful, my beloved,*
        truly lovely.
        Our couch is green;
1:17   *the beams of our house are cedar,*
        our rafters are pine.

1

Song of Songs Rabbah to Song of Songs 1:1

1:1   *The Song of Songs, which is Solomon's.*

I:i

1.   A.   "The song of songs":
        B.   This is in line with that which Scripture said through Solomon: "Do you see a man who is diligent in his business? He will stand before kings, he will not stand before mean men" (Prov. 22:29).
        C.   "Do you see a man who is diligent in his business":
        D.   This refers to Joseph: "But one day, when he went into the house to do his work [and none of the men of the house was there in the house, she caught him by his garment, saying, 'Lie with me.' But he left his garment in her hand and fled and got out of the house]" (Gen. 39:10-13).
        E.   R. Judah and R. Nehemiah:
        F.   R. Judah said, "[Following Gen. R; LXXXVII:VII:] It was a festival day for the Nile. [Everybody went to see it, but he went to the household to take up his master's account books]."
        G.   R. Nehemiah said, "It was a day of theater. Everybody went to see it, but he went to the household to take up his master's account books."
2.   A.   R. Phineas says in the name of R. Samuel bar Abba, "Whoever serves his master properly goes forth to freedom.
        B.   "Whence do we learn that fact? From the case of Joseph.
        C.   "It was because he served his master properly that he went forth to freedom."
3.   A.   "He will stand before kings":
        B.   this refers to Pharaoh: "Then Pharaoh sent and called Joseph and they brought him hastily from the dungeon" (Gen. 41:14).
4.   A.   "...he will not stand before mean men":
        B.   this refers to Potiphar, whose eyes the Holy One, blessed be He, darkened [the word for 'darkened' and 'mean men' share the same consonants], and whom he castrated.

5. A.   Another interpretation of the verse, "Do you see a man who is diligent in his business" (Prov. 22:29):

    B.   this refers to our lord, Moses, in the making of the work of the tabernacle.

    C.   Therefore: "He will stand before kings":

    D.   this refers to Pharaoh: "Rise up early in the morning and stand before Pharaoh" (Ex. 8:16).

    E.   "...he will not stand before mean men":

    F.   this refers to Jethro.

    G.   Said R. Nehemiah, "[In identifying the king with Pharaoh,] you have made the holy profane.

    H.   "Rather, 'He will stand before kings': this refers to the King of kings of kings, the Holy One, blessed be He: 'And he was there with the Lord forty days' (Ex. 34:28).

    I.   "'...he will not stand before mean men': this refers to Pharaoh: 'And there was thick darkness' (Ex. 10:22)."

6. A.   Another interpretation of the verse, "Do you see a man who is diligent in his business" (Prov. 22:29):

    B.   this refers to those righteous persons who are occupied with the work of the Holy One, blessed be He.

    C.   Therefore: "He will stand before kings":

    D.   this refers to for they stand firm in the Torah: "By me kings rule" (Prov. 8:15).

    E.   "...he will not stand before mean men":

    F.   this refers to the wicked: "And their works are in the dark" (Isa. 29:15); "Let their way be dark and slippery" (Ps. 35:6).

7. A.   Another interpretation of the verse, "Do you see a man who is diligent in his business" (Prov. 22:29):

    B.   this refers to this is R. Hanina.

8. A.   They say:

    B.   One time he saw people of his village bringing whole-offerings and peace-offerings up [on a pilgrimage to the Temple].

    C.   He said, "All of them are bringing peace-offerings to Jerusalem, but I am not bringing up a thing! What shall I do?"

    D.   Forthwith he went out to the open fields of his town, the unoccupied area of his town, and there he found a stone. He went and plastered it and polished it and painted it and said, "Lo, I accept upon myself the vow to bring it up to Jerusalem."

    E.   He sought to hire day-workers, saying to them, "Will you bring this stone up to Jerusalem for me?"

    F.   They said to him, "Pay us our wage, a hundred gold pieces, and we'll be glad to carry your stone up to Jerusalem for you."

    G.   He said to them, "Where in the world will I get a hundred gold pieces, or even fifty, to give you?"

    H.   Since at the time he could not find the funds, they immediately went their way.

    I.   Immediately the Holy One, blessed be He, arranged for him for fifty angels in the form of men [to meet him]. They said to him, "My lord, give us five selas, and we shall bring your stone to Jerusalem, on condition that you help us with the work."

J.   So he put his hand to the work with them, and they found themselves standing in Jerusalem. He wanted to pay them their wage, but he could not find them.

K.   The case came to the Chamber of the Hewn Stone [where the high court was in session]. They said to him, "It appears that in the case of our lord, ministering angels have brought the stone up to Jerusalem."

L.   Immediately he gave sages that wage for which he had hired the angels.

9. A.   Another interpretation of the verse, "Do you see a man who is diligent in his business" (Prov. 22:29):

B.   this refers to Solomon son of David.

C.   "He will stand before kings."

D.   for he was diligent in building the house of the sanctuary: "So he spent seven years in building it" (1 Kgs. 6:38).

10. A.   [Supply: "So he spent seven years in building it" (1 Kgs. 6:38),] but a different verse says, "And Solomon was building his own house for thirteen years" (1 Kgs. 7:1),

B.   so the building of the house of Solomon was lovelier and more elaborate than the building of the house of the sanctuary.

C.   But this is what they said:

D.   In the building of his house he was slothful, in the building of the house of the sanctuary he was diligent and not slothful.

11. A.   Huna in the name of R. Joseph: "All help the king, all the more so do all help out on account of the glory of the King of kings of kings, the Holy One, blessed be He,

B.   "even spirits, demons, ministering angels."

12. A.   Isaac b. R. Judah b. Ezekiel said, "'I have surely built you a house of habitation' (1 Kgs. 8:13): 'I have built what is already built.'"

13. A.   R. Berekiah said, "'The house that they were building' is not what is said,

B.   "but rather, 'the house in its being built' (1 Kgs. 6:7), which is to say, it was built of itself.

C.   "'It was built of stone made ready at the quarry' (1 Kgs. 6:7):

D.   "what it says is not 'built' but 'it was built,' which is to say, the stones carried themselves and set themselves on the row."

14. A.   Said Rab, "Do not find this astonishing. What is written elsewhere? 'And a stone was brought and laid upon the mouth of the den' (Dan. 6:18).

B.   "Now are there any stones in Babylonia? [Of course not.] But from the land of Israel it flew in a brief moment and came and rested on the mouth of the pit."

15. A.   R. Huna in the name of R. Joseph said [concerning the verse, "And a stone was brought and laid upon the mouth of the den" (Dan. 6:18)], "An angel came down in the form of a lion made of stone and put itself at the mouth of the pit.

B.   "That is in line with this verse: 'My God has sent his angel and has shut the lions mouths' (Dan. 6:23).

C.   "Now do not find it astonishing. If for the honor owing to that righteous man, it is written, 'a certain stone was brought' (Dan.

6:18), for the honoring of the Holy One, blessed be He, how much the more so [will stones be provided in a magical manner]."

16. A.   [Resuming where the discussion of 8.D:] "He will stand before kings":

B.   before the kings of the Torah he will stand.

C.   "...he will not stand before mean men":

D.   this refers to a conspiracy of wicked men.

17. A.   Said R. Joshua b. Levi, "When they took a vote and decided, **Three kings and four ordinary folk have no share in the world to come [M. San. 10:1],**

B.   "they wanted to include Solomon with them.

C.   "But an echo came forth and said, 'Do not lay hands on my anointed ones' (Ps. 105:15)."

D.   Said R. Judah b. R. Simon, "And not only so, but he was given the place of honor at the head of three genealogical tables: 'And Rehoboam, son of Solomon, reigned in Judah' (1 Kgs. 14:21). [Simon, p. 4: "He was placed at the head of a genealogical tree...." Simon, p. 4, n. 11: "The mention of his name here being superfluous implies that he was a founder of a royal line.]

E.   Said R. Yudan b. R. Simon, "Not only so, but the Holy Spirit rested on him, and he said the following three books: Proverbs, the Song of Songs, and Qohelet."

While this somewhat overburdened composition hardly conforms to the required form, its basic outlines are not difficult to discern. We have an intersecting verse, Prov. 22:29, aimed at reaching the goal of Solomon, who is author of the Song of Songs, and showing him in the context of Joseph, the righteous, and Moses, four in all. The reason in both cases is the same: each one of them "stood before kings, not before mean men." The invocation of the figure of Joseph ought to carry in its wake the contrast between the impure lust of Potiphar's wife and the pure heart of Joseph, and, by extension, Solomon in the Song. But I do not see that motif present. The form is scarcely established – clause-by-clause exegesis in light of the principal's life – before it is broken with the insertion of 1.E-G, lifted whole from Gen. R. LXXXVII:VII, where it belongs. No. 2 is then parachuted down as part of the Joseph-sequence; but it does not occur in the parallel. No. 3 then resumes the broken form, and No. 4 completes it. So the first statement of the formal program is not difficult to follow. The confluence of the consonants for "mean" and "dark" accounts for the sequence of applications of the third clause to the theme of darkness.

The second exercise, with Moses, runs is laid out with little blemish in No. 5. No. 6 goes on to the righteous, and here too the sages' passage is worked out with no interpolations. No. 7, by contrast, provides an excuse to insert No. 8. Without No. 7, No. 8 of course would prove incomprehensible in this context (though entirely clear standing on its own). Finally, at No. 9, we come to Solomon. Perhaps the coming theme of the magical works performed through stones, those used in the Temple, with Daniel, and so on, persuaded the person who inserted Nos. 7-8 of the relevance of those passages; but even if they prove thematically in place, the sequence is disruptive and hardly respects the formal program that clearly has guided the framer. One may theorize, to be sure, that the breakup of the initial form – three cases, disruptive insertion, then the goal and purpose of the whole – signals the advent of the central figure in the exegesis. But that would prove a viable thesis only if we should find a fair number of others instances. It is the simple fact that the Mishnah's rhetoric allows for signals of that kind, and we cannot rule out the possibility. But in the present case it seems to me we have nothing more than a rude interpolation. But that is not the only disruptive component of Solomon's passage.

No. 10 introduces the contrast of the two verses, our prooftext at No. 9 plus a contradictory one. This yields a suitable harmonization, which sustains the supplements at Nos. 11, 12, and 13. Nos. 11 and 12 are simply free-standing sentences. No. 13, with Nos. 14, 15, in its wake, by contrast is a full-scale composition, again about miracles done with stones. Hanina's passage would have found a more comfortable home here (if anywhere). Only at No. 16 are we permitted to resume our progress through the established form. No. 17 is tacked on because of the reference of 16.D to a conspiracy of wicked men; the issue then is whether Solomon belongs with them, in line with 17.A-B. 17.E forms a bridge to the sustained discussion of Ps. 45:17. But since the exposition of that verse makes no reference to the foregoing, we should regard the rather run-on sequence before us as winding down at No. 17, and, despite the rhetorical joining language of "therefore," I treat the discussion of Ps. 45:17 as autonomous. It assuredly has no formal ties to the intersecting verse on which we have been working.

I:ii

1. A. That is in line with this verse: "Instead of your fathers shall be your sons" (Ps. 45:17).
   B. You have cases in which a righteous man fathers a righteous man, a wicked man fathers a wicked man, a righteous man fathers a wicked man, and a wicked man fathers a righteous man.
   C. And all of them derives from a verse of Scripture and also from a proverb and a popular saying.
2. A. That a righteous man fathers a righteous man can be shown in a verse of Scripture, a proverb, and a popular saying:
   B. In Scripture: "Instead of your fathers shall be your sons" (Ps. 45:17).
   C. In a proverb: "A scion proves the value of the fig tree."
3. A. That a wicked man fathers a wicked man can be shown in a verse of Scripture, a proverb, and a popular saying:

B.   In Scripture: "And behold you have risen up in your fathers' place, a brood of sinful men" (Num. 32:14).

C.   In a proverb: "As says the proverb of the ancients, Out of the wicked comes forth wickedness" (1 Sam. 24:14).

D.   In a popular saying: "What does the beetle bear? Insects worse than itself" [following Simon, p. 5].

4.   A.   That a righteous man fathers a wicked man can be shown in a verse of Scripture, a proverb, and a popular saying:

B.   In Scripture: "Let thistles grow instead of wheat" (Job 31:40).

C.   In a proverb: "They father those who are not like them, they raise those who are not similar to them."

5.   A.   That a wicked man fathers a righteous man can be shown in a verse of Scripture, a proverb, and a popular saying:

B.   In Scripture: "Instead of the thorn shall come up the cypress" (Isa. 55:13).

C.   In a proverb: "The thorn produces the rose."

6.   A.   Truly, Solomon was king, son of a king, sage son of a sage, righteous man, son of a righteous man, [Simon:] noble son of a noble.

B.   You find that everything that is written concerning this one [David] is written concerning that one [Solomon].

C.   David ruled for forty years, and this one ruled for forty years.

D.   David ruled over Israel and Judah, and his son ruled over Israel and Judah.

E.   His father built the foundations and he built the main structure [of the Temple].

F.   His father ruled from one end of the world to the other, and this one ruled from one end of the world to the other.

G.   David wrote books, and Solomon wrote books.

H.   David said songs, and Solomon said songs.

I.   David spoke about the vanity of things, and Solomon spoke about the vanity of things.

J.   David said important statements, and Solomon said important statements.

K.   David said proverbs, and Solomon said proverbs.

L.   David praised [God] with a passage starting with "then," and Solomon praised [God] with a passage starting with "then."

M.   David built an altar, and Solomon built an altar.

N.   David made an offering, and Solomon made an offering.

O.   David brought up the ark, and Solomon brought up the ark.

P.   David ruled for forty years: "And the days that David ruled over Israel were forty years" (1 Kgs. 2:11); and this one ruled for forty years: "And Solomon reigned in Jerusalem over all Israel forty years" (2 Chr. 9:30).

Q.   David ruled over Israel and Judah, and his son ruled over Israel and Judah: "The Lord, the God of Israel, chose me out of all the house of my father to be king over Israel for ever, for he has chosen Judah to be prince" (1 Chr. 28:4); "Judah and Israel were many" (1 Kgs. 4:20).

R.   David [his father] built the foundations and Solomon built the main structure [of the Temple]: "The David the king stood up

	upon his feet and said...I had made ready for the building" (1 Chr. 28:2); "I have surely built you a house of habitation" (1 Kgs. 8:13).
S.	[Omitted: His father ruled from one end of the world to the other, and this one ruled from one end of the world to the other.]
T.	David wrote books, for the Psalms bear his name, and Solomon wrote books, specifically, Proverbs, Qohelet, and the Song of Songs.
U.	David spoke about the vanity of things, and Solomon spoke about the vanity of things: "Surely every man at his best estate is altogether vanity" (Ps. 39:6); "Vanity of vanities, says Qoheleth, vanity of vanities, all is vanity" (Qoh. 1:2).
V.	David said important statements, and Solomon said important statements: "Now these are the last words of David" (2 Sam. 23:1); "The words of Qoheleth, son of David, king in Jerusalem" (Qoh. 1:1).
W.	David said proverbs, and Solomon said proverbs: "As says the proverb of the ancients, out of the wicked comes forth wickedness" (1 Sam. 24:14); "The proverbs of Solomon, son of David, king of Israel" (Prov. 1:1).
X.	David praised [God] with a passage starting with "then," and Solomon praised [God] with a passage starting with "then": "Then was our mouth filled with laughter and our tongue with singing, then they said among the nations" (Ps. 126:2); "Then said Solomon, the Lord has said" (1 Kgs. 8:12).
Y.	David brought up the ark, and Solomon brought up the ark: "So David and the elders of Israel...went to bring up the ark" (1 Chr. 15:25); "Then Solomon assembled the elders of Israel to bring up the ark" (1 Kgs. 8:1).
Z.	David said songs, and Solomon said songs: "And David spoke unto the Lord the words of this song" (2 Sam. 22:1); "The Song of Songs which is Solomon's" (Song 1:1).

7.	A.	R. Simon in the name of R. Jonathan of Bet Gubrin in the name of R. Joshua b. Levi said, "Since you are comparing him [to his father], compare him in every aspect.
	B.	"Just as his father was forgiven for all his transgressions, 'The Lord has put away your sin, you will not die' (2 Sam. 12;13),
	C.	"so he too was treated in the same way.
	D.	"And not only so, but the Holy Spirit rested on him, and Solomon spoke the books of Proverbs, Qohelet, and the Song of Songs."

The connector, I:ii.1.A, serves only a redactional purpose, since this entire, magnificent composition commences at B and fully exposes its thought in the amplification of Nos. 2-5. We note that we are not given all that is promised, there lacking a number of popular sayings. But all of this then serves as prologue to No. 6, and that sets forth the close parallels in the lives and careers of David and Solomon, the point of the whole. The rather prolix exposition of this point sets forth a variety of points of comparison, and these thereafter are illustrated by verses of Scripture. In the text the order is not precise, and I have reordered matters. But the goal is to end with the three books written by Solomon, and that is the main point. The composition of course is autonomous of its setting, but it serves as did the one before to establish the authorship of all that follows, and to make the point that this book is of the same standing as Psalms, which David wrote, and the more readily accepted books of Proverbs and Qohelet. The entire composition, therefore, is both free-standing and also wholly at home in the larger document in which it appears. Not only so, but since the main point is to establish the legitimacy of Solomon's authorship by appeal to David, and the comparability of Song of Songs and Psalms, we must say that the entire, sustained and beautifully composed essay has served the compilers' program. This is a kind of writing, fully exposed and redactionally cogent to the documentary setting, to which we simply cannot point in the earlier Midrash compilations.

I:iii
1. A.   Another interpretation of "The Song of Songs":
   B.   This is in line with the following verse of Scripture: "The heart of the wise teaches his mouth [and adds learning to his lips]" (Prov. 16:23).
   C.   The heart of the wise man is full of wisdom, so who guides him, and who makes his mouth wise for him? [Simon, p. 7: "who endows him with the power to make intelligent and orderly use of his wisdom?"]
   D.   "His mouth": it is his mouth that makes him wise, his mouth that teaches him [Simon: what he is].
2. A.   "...and adds learning to his lips":
   B.   When he brings forth words of Torah from his heart, [by that very act] he adds to the lessons learned from the Torah.
   C.   They made a comparison: to what is this matter to be compared?
   D.   To a jar full of precious stones and pearls, tightly sealed, set in a corner, concerning the contents of which no one is aware.
   E.   Someone came along and emptied it. Then everybody knew what is in it.
   F.   So the heart of Solomon was full of wisdom, but no one knew what was in it.
   G.   When the Holy Spirit rested on him, so he set forth three books, everybody knew his wisdom.
3. A.   "...and adds learning to his lips":
   B.   The learning that he added to the words of Torah exalted him:
   C.   "And I applied my heart to seek and to explore by wisdom" (Qoh. 1:13).
4. A.   [Supply: "And I applied my heart to seek and to explore by wisdom" (Qoh. 1:13):]
   B.   What is the meaning of the clause, "to explore by wisdom"?
   C.   He became an explorer of wisdom: "And they explored the land" (Num. 13:21).
   D.   If there was someone who read Scripture well, he went to him.
   E.   If there was someone who repeated Mishnah-sayings well, he went to him,

F. for it is said, "and to explore by wisdom" (Qoh. 1:13).

5. A. Another interpretation of the phrase, "And I applied my heart to seek and to explore by wisdom" (Qoh. 1:13):

B. The letters in the word "to explore" may yield the word "to leave over."

C. When a poet is making an acrostic poem, sometimes he finishes [the alphabet], and sometimes he does not.

D. [Simon, p. 8:] But Solomon made alphabetical poems with five extra letters in addition: "And his poem was a thousand and five" (1 Kgs. 5:12), meaning, "what was left over from the alphabet was five."

6. A. And it was not only words of Torah alone that he explored, but everything that was done under the sun,

B. for example, how to sweeten mustard or lupines.

C. Said to him the Holy One, blessed be He, "After words of Torah you have ventured, by your life, I will not withhold your reward. Lo, I shall bring to rest on you the Holy Spirit."

D. Forthwith the Holy Spirit rested on him, and he recited these three books: Proverbs, Qohelet, and Song of Songs.

The exposition of a fresh intersecting verse, Prov. 16:23, does not lead us to our goal, which is the same as before. That goal is attained only through a second verse, which is brought into the composition to serve the interests of the first. It is only at 3.C that the principal verse is introduced. And yet, we see, the movement from there to the end is inexorable and smooth. So what we have is a variation and improvement of the intersecting verse/base verse construction; now the intersecting verse yields yet another verse, and only by indirection, producing a vast expansion in the range of available themes and provocations, do we move to our desired goal. It is like the move, so to speak, from baroque to rococo – but the aesthetic result is one of improvement and enrichment, not excess.

I:iv

1. A. Another interpretation of "The Song of Songs":

B. This is in line with the following verse of Scripture: "And more so because Qohelet was wise; [he also taught the people knowledge, yes, he pondered and sought out and set in order many proverbs]" (Qoh. 12:9):

C. If any other person had said them, you would have had to pay attention and listen to these things. All the more so, since Solomon said them.

D. If he had made them up from his own mind, you you would have had to pay attention and listen to these things. All the more so, since Solomon said them through the Holy Spirit.

2. A. "And more so because Qohelet was wise; he also taught the people knowledge, yes, he pondered and sought out and set in order many proverbs" (Qoh. 12:9):

B.   "He pondered" words of the Torah, and "he sought out" words of the Torah.

C.   He made "handles" for the Torah. [This is spelled out at 4.A-C below.]

D.   For you find that before Solomon came along, there was no [Simon:] parable [Hebrew: *dugma*, e.g., paradigm].

3.   A.   R. Nahman said two things [in this connection].

B.   R. Nahman said, "[The matter may be compared] to the case of a huge palace that had many doors, so whoever came in would wander from the path to the entry.

C.   "A smart fellow came along and took a skein of string and hung the string on the way to the entry, so everybody came and went following the path laid out by the skein.

D.   "So too, until Solomon came along, no person could comprehend the words of the Torah. But when Solomon came along, everyone began to make sense of the Torah."

E.   R. Nahman said the matter in yet another way: "[The matter may be compared] to the case of a reed marsh that no one could enter. A smart fellow came along and took a scythe and cut the reeds, so everybody began to go in and come out by chopping down the reeds.

F.   "So was Solomon."

4.   A.   Said R. Yosé, "[The matter may be compared] to the case of a basket full of produce but lacking a handle so no one could lift it up.

B.   "A smart fellow came along and made handles for it, so people began to carry it about holding on to the handles.

C.   "So too, until Solomon came along, no person could comprehend the words of the Torah. But when Solomon came along, everyone began to make sense of the Torah."

5.   A.   Said R. Shila, "[The matter may be compared] to the case of a big jug full of boiling water but lacking a handle so no one could lift it up.

B.   "A smart fellow came along and made handles for it, so people began to carry it about holding on to the handles.

C.   [Supply: "So too, until Solomon came along, no person could comprehend the words of the Torah. But when Solomon came along, everyone began to make sense of the Torah."]

6.   A.   Said R. Hanina, "[The matter may be compared] to the case of a deep well full of water, and the water was cold, sweet, and good, but no one could drink from it.

B.   "A smart fellow came along and provided a rope joined with another rope, a cord joined with another cord, sufficiently long so people could draw water from the well and drink it, and then everybody began to draw and drink.

C.   "So from one thing to the next, from one proverb to the next, Solomon penetrated into the secret of the Torah.

D.   "For it is written, 'The proverbs of Solomon, son of David, king of Israel, to know wisdom and instruction' (Prov. 1:1).

E.   "By means of the proverbs of Solomon, he [Simon:] mastered the words of the Torah."

7.   A.   And rabbis say, "Let a parable not be despised in your view, for it is through the parable that a person can master the words of the Torah.

     B.   "The matter me be compared to the case of a king who lost gold in his house or pearls. Is it not through a wick that is worth a penny that he finds it again?

     C.   "So let a parable not be despised in your view, for it is through the parable that a person can master the words of the Torah.

     D.   "You may know that that is so, for lo, Solomon through parables mastered the smallest details of the Torah."

8.   A.   [Supply: "And more so because Qohelet was wise; he also taught the people knowledge, yes, he pondered and sought out and set in order many proverbs]" (Qoh. 12:9):] Said R. Yudan, "This serves to teach you that whoever speaks words of the Torah in public acquires such merit that the Holy Spirit comes to rest upon him.

     B.   "And from whom do you learn that fact? From the case of Solomon.

     C.   "For it is because he spoke words of the Torah in public, he acquired such merit that the Holy Spirit came to rest upon him.

     D.   "So he wrote three books: Proverbs, Qohelet, and the Song of Songs."

We have a variety of themes rather skillfully blended into a single proposition, which comes at the end. But the exposition of the intersecting verse focuses upon the power of the parable or proverb (the word is the same, though clearly it refers to different things in different contexts). Nos. 1, 2 focus upon the opening clause, "because Qohelet was wise," and give that as a reason for paying attention to what he said. The interest in due course is in the demonstration that the Song of Songs, as much as Proverbs and Qohelet, is said under the power of the Holy Spirit. That will be repeated, but it is not the focus of the exposition. 2.C's reference to "handles for the Torah" is expounded both as a particular metaphor and also as a general proposition expressed at 2.D. It seems to me the several following parables really do serve to spell out and amplify No. 2. Nos. 3-6 fit in beautifully, and here we have no reason to doubt that the several cases do serve the general point – a much finer piece of compilation than anything to which I can point in Esther Rabbah or, all the more so, Lamentations Rabbah.

As a rough generalization, I should say that the refinement of Leviticus Rabbah is to the unpolished quality of its companion, Genesis Rabbah, as the refinement of Song Rabbah is to the unpolished quality of its companion, Lamentations Rabbah. But that is just a preliminary observation. No. 7 draws to a close the exposition begun at No. 2, and that fact is underlined by the fresh initiative of No. 8, which draws attention back to the intersecting verse in a new way and leads us directly to the desired goal. So we have two expositions of the

intersecting verse, closely tied to one another, and, of course, in the sole
possible order, given the goal of the compilers – a masterpiece of
compilation again. We are in the hands of a great authorship.

I:v
1.   A.   R. Phineas b. Yair commenced by citing this verse: "'If you seek it
              like silver [and search for it as for hidden treasures, then you will
              understand the fear of the Lord and find the knowledge of God]'
              (Prov. 2:4-5):
      B.   "If you seek words of the Torah like hidden treasures, the Holy
              One, blessed be He, will not withhold your reward.
      C.   "The matter may be compared to the case of a person, who, if he
              should lose a penny or a pin in his house, will light any number of
              candles, any number of wicks, until he finds them.
      D.   "Now the matter yields an argument *a fortiori:*
      E.   "If to find these, which are useful only in the here and now of this
              world, a person will light any number of candles, any number of
              wicks, until he finds them, as to words of Torah, which concern the
              life of the world to come as much as this world, do you not have to
              search for them like treasures?
      F.   "Thus: 'If you seek it like silver [and search for it as for hidden
              treasures, then you will understand the fear of the Lord and find
              the knowledge of God]' (Prov. 2:4-5)."
2.   A.   Said R. Eleazar, "In all my days nobody ever got to the
              schoolhouse before me, and I never left anyone there when I went
              out.
      B.   "One time, however, I got up early and found manure-carriers
              and straw-carriers out already, and I recited this verse: 'If you seek
              it like silver [and search for it as for hidden treasures, then you will
              understand the fear of the Lord and find the knowledge of God]'
              (Prov. 2:4-5).
      C.   "Yet we for our part [Simon:] do not seek it even like manure and
              straw. [Simon, p. 11, n. 2: We do not rise so early to seek it as the
              farm laborers do to seek manure and straw.]"
3.   A.   In this connection R. Phineas b. Yair would say, "Promptness leads
              to [hygienic] cleanliness, cleanliness to [cultic] cleanness,
              cleanness to holiness, holiness to humility, humility to fear of sin,
              fear of sin to true piety, true piety to the Holy Spirit, the Holy Spirit
              to the resurrection of the dead, the resurrection of the dead to
              Elijah the prophet [bringing the Day of Judgment]."
      B.   "Promptness leads to [hygienic] cleanliness": "And when he made
              an end of atoning for the holy place" (Lev. 16:20).
      C.   "...cleanliness to [cultic] cleanness": "And the priest shall make
              atonement for her, and she shall be clean" (Lev. 12:8).
      D.   "...cleanness to holiness": "And he shall purify it and make it holy"
              (Lev. 16:9).
      E.   "...holiness to humility": "For thus says the High and Lofty One,
              who inhabits eternity, whose name is holy, 'I dwell in the high and
              holy place, with the one who is of a contrite and humble spirit'
              (Isa. 57:15).

	F.	"...humility to fear of sin": "The reward of humility is the fear of the Lord" (Prov. 22:4).
	G.	"...fear of sin to true piety": "Then you spoke in a vision to your saints" (Ps. 89:20).
	H.	"...true piety to the Holy Spirit": "Then you spoke in a vision to your saints" (Ps. 89:20).
	I.	"...the Holy Spirit to the resurrection of the dead": "And I will put my spirit in you and you shall live" (Ez. 37:14).
	J.	"...the resurrection of the dead to Elijah the prophet of blessed memory": "Behold I will send you Elijah the prophet" (Mal. 3:23).
4.	A.	Said R. Mattena, "That which wisdom made a crown for her head, humility put on as a shoe for her foot.
	B.	"That which wisdom made a crown for her head: 'the fear of the Lord is the beginning of wisdom' (Ps. 111:10),
	C.	"humility put on as a shoe for her foot: 'The fear of the Lord is the heel of humility' (Prov. 22:4)."
5.	A.	The resurrection of the dead will come about through the prophet Elijah of blessed memory:
	B.	"then you will understand the fear of the Lord and find the knowledge of God"(Prov. 2:5) –
	C.	this refers to the Holy Spirit.
6.	A.	R. Simon in the name of R. Simeon b. Halafta: "The matter may be compared to a councillor who was a big man in the court of a king.
	B.	"The king said to him, 'Ask what I should give to you.'
	C.	"Thought the councillor, 'If I ask for silver and gold, he will give it to me; precious stones and pearls he will give to me.'
	D.	"He thought, 'Lo, I shall ask for the daughter of the king, and everything else will come along too.'
	E.	"So: 'In Gibeon the Lord appeared to Solomon in a dream by night, and God said, Ask what I shall give you' (1 Kgs. 3:5).
	F.	"Thought Solomon, 'If I ask for silver and gold, precious stones and pearls he will give them to me. Lo, I shall ask for wisdom, and everything else will come along too.'
	G.	"That is in line with this verse: 'Give your servant therefore an understanding heart' (1 Kgs. 3:9).
	H.	"Said to him the Holy One, blessed be He, 'Solomon, wisdom is what you have asked for yourself, and you did not ask for wealth and property and the lives of your enemies. By your life, wisdom and knowledge are given to you, and thereby I will give you also riches and possessions.'
7.	A.	"Forthwith: 'Solomon woke up and lo, it was a dream' (1 Kgs. 3:15)."
	B.	Said R. Isaac, "The dream stood solidly: if an ass brayed, he knew why it brayed, if a bird chirped, he knew why it chirped."
8.	A.	Forthwith: "He came to Jerusalem and stood before the ark of the covenant of the Lord and offered up whole-offerings, peace-offerings, and made a feast for all his servants" (1 Kgs. 3:15):
	B.	Said R. Eleazar, "On this basis we learn that people are to make a banquet at the conclusion of a cycle of the Torah."
9.	A.	[Supply: "And more so because Qohelet was wise; he also taught the people knowledge, yes, he pondered and sought out and set in

order many proverbs]" (Qoh. 12:9):] Said R. Yudan, "This serves to teach you that whoever speaks words of the Torah in public acquires such merit that the Holy Spirit comes to rest upon him.

B.   "And from whom do you learn that fact? From the case of Solomon.

C.   "For it is because he spoke words of the Torah in public, he acquired such merit that the Holy Spirit came to rest upon him.

D.   "So he wrote three books: Proverbs, Qohelet, and the Song of Songs."

The basic theme remains the importance of Torah-study, and now the conventional conclusion really is out of place, since it has slight bearing on what has gone before. The issue here is not teaching the Torah publicly but rather the importance of studying the Torah, valuing Torah-study at least as much as one values one's own possession. That is the point of No. 1. No. 2 works over the same intersecting verse, which is well chosen to convey the desired proposition. The Hebrew of 2.C is not adequately translated by Simon, and I could not improve on his rendering. Nor can I account in any way for the intrusion of the vast exposition of No. 3, except because of the appearance of Phineas b. Yair's name at No. 1. If that is the case, and we have ample precedent, then the initial principle of conglomeration is the name of an authority, and once materials in a given name have been compiled, then they stuck together, even while the whole has been inserted into a compilation organized around a different principle of conglomeration, namely, amplification of a given verse of Scripture to make a given point. That is the only way I can explain how No. 3 has found a suitable place here, in the mind of someone who joined Nos. 1-2 to No. 3. No. 4 is intruded, and No. 5 amplifies the conclusion of No. 3.

Nos. 6-8 serve 1 Kgs. 3:5f., and I assume they are intruded as an amplification of the general theme of the commencement verse, "If you seek it like silver and search for it as for hidden treasures, then you will understand the fear of the Lord and find the knowledge of God" (Prov. 2:4-5). But now the imputed sense is, if you get Torah, you'll get silver and gold too, which is a nice thought. I cannot imagine a less appropriate finish than No. 9, moved from where it fit to where it does not fit. But the repetition of a single, fixed conclusion in the *petihtaot* of Lamentations Rabbah, whether the conclusion relates or does not relate to the prior discourse, is commonplace.

I:vi

1.   A.   Another interpretation of "The Song of Songs":

     B.   R. Aibu and R. Judah:

     C.   R. Aibu said, "'Song' – lo, one. 'Songs' – two. Lo, there are three in all."

D. R. Judah bar Simon said, "'Song of Songs' all together adds up to one."

E. Then as to the other two songs, how do you deal with them?

F. "A song of ascent of Solomon" (Ps. 127) is one, and "A psalm, a song at the dedication of the house of David" (Ps. 30) is the other.

G. People suppose that David said them.

H. But you assign them to David [in the same way in which] it is said, "Like the tower of David is your neck" (Song 4:4).

I. In the case of "Song of Songs" [better: Ps. 30] too, Solomon said it but assigned it to David.

2. A. When you find occasion, you may say that all of the events affecting that man came in groups of threes.

B. Solomon ascended to the throne in three stages.

C. Of the first stage it is written, "For he had dominion over all the region on this side of the river" (1 Kgs. 5:4).

D. Of the second stage: "And Solomon ruled" (1 Kgs. 5:1).

E. Of the third stage: "Then Solomon sat on the throne of the Lord as king" (1 Chr. 29:23).

3. A. [As to the verse, "Then Solomon sat on the throne of the Lord as king" (1 Chr. 29:23):] said R. Isaac, "Now is it really possible for someone to sit on the throne of the Lord,

B. "of whom it is written: 'For the Lord your God is a devouring fire' (Dt. 4:24); 'A fiery stream issued and came forth' (Dan. 7:10); 'his throne was fiery flames' (Dan. 7:9)?

C. "Yet you say, "Then Solomon sat on the throne of the Lord as king" (1 Chr. 29:23)!

D. "But [the statement serves to validate the following analogy:] just as the throne of the Holy One, blessed be He, rules from one end of the world to the other, so the throne of Solomon rules from one end of the earth to the other.

E. "Just as the throne of the Lord reaches judgment without witnesses and prior admonition, so the throne of Solomon reaches judgment without witnesses and prior admonition.

F. "And what case was that? It was the case involving the two whores: 'Then came there two women' (1 Kgs. 3:16)."

4. A. [Supply: "Then came there two women" (1 Kgs. 3:16):] who were they?

B. Rab said, "They were spirits."

C. Rabbis said, "They were co-wives of a deceased childless brother-in-law."

D. R. Simon in the name of R. Joshua b. Levi said, "They were really whores."

5. A. [Resuming 3.F:] "And he produced a judgment concerning them without witnesses and prior admonition."

6. A. [Resuming 2.E:] Solomon went down by three stages.

B. The first descent was that, after he had been a great king, ruling from one end of the world to another, his dominion was reduced, and he ruled as king only over Israel: "The Proverbs of Solomon, son of David, king of Israel" (Prov. 1:1).

C.   The second descent was that, after he had been king over Israel, his dominion was reduced, and he was king only over Jerusalem: "I Qohelet have been king over Israel in Jerusalem" (Qoh. 1:12).

D.   The third descent was that, after he had been king over Jerusalem, his dominion was reduced, and he was king only over his own house: "Behold it is the litter of Solomon! About it are sixty mighty men of the might men of Israel, all girt with swords and expert in war, each with his sword at his thigh, against alarms by night" (Song 3:7-8).

E.   But even over his own bed he did not really rule, for he was afraid of spirits.

7. A.   He saw three ages [Simon: "he lived three lives"].

B.   R. Yudan and R. Hunia:

C.   R. Yudan said, "He was king, a commoner, then king; a sage, a fool, and then a sage; rich, poor, then rich.

D.   "What verse of Scripture suggests so? 'All things I have seen in the days of my vanity' (Qoh. 7:15).

E.   "Someone does not rehearse his sufferings unless he is again at ease."

F.   R. Hunia said, "He was commoner, king, and commoner; fool, sage, and fool; poor, rich, then poor.

G.   "What verse of Scripture suggests so? 'I Qohelet have been king over Israel' (Qoh. 1:12).

H.   "'I was' – 'I was when I was, but now I am not any more.'"

8. A.   He committed three transgressions.

B.   He accumulated too many horses, he accumulated too many wives, he accumulated too much silver and gold: "And the king made silver in Jerusalem as stones" (2 Chr. 9:27).

9. A.   [With reference to the verse, "And the king made silver in Jerusalem as stones" (2 Chr. 9:27):] And were they not stolen?

B.   Said R. Yosé b. R. Hanina, "They were stones of ten cubits and stones of eight cubits."

C.   R. Simeon b. Yohai repeated on Tannaite authority: "Even the weights in the time of Solomon were made of gold: 'Silver was thought worthless in the time of Solomon' (1 Kgs. 10:21)."

10. A.   [Resuming 8.B:] He accumulated too many wives: "Now king Solomon loved many foreign women, besides the daughter of Pharaoh...of the nations concerning which the Lord said to the children of Israel, you shall not go among them, nor shall they come among you...Solomon did cleave to them in love" (1 Kgs. 11:1-2).

B.   R. Joshua b. Levi said, "It was on the count of 'you shall not marry them' (Dt. 7:3)."

C.   R. Simeon b. Yohai says, "'In love,' meaning, it was actually [Simon:] harlot-love."

D.   R. Eliezer, son of R. Yosé the Galilean, says, "It is written, 'Nevertheless even him did the foreign women cause to sin' (Neh. 13:26).

E.   "This teaches that he would have sexual relations with them when they were menstruating, but they did not inform him."

F.   R. Yosé b. Halapta says, "'In love' meaning, to make them beloved, that is, to draw them near, to convert them and to bring them under the wings of the Presence of God."

G.   It turns out that R. Joshua b. Levi, R. Simeon b. Yohai, and R. Eliezer, son of R. Yosé the Galilean, held one position, while R. Yosé b. Halapta differs with all three of them.

11. A.   Three adversaries fought against him:

B.   "And the Lord raised up an adversary to Solomon, Hadad the Edomite" (1 Kgs. 11:14);

C.   "And God raised up another adversary to him, Rezon, son of Eliada" (1 Kgs. 11:23).

D.   "And he was an adversary to Israel all the days of Solomon" (1 Kgs. 11:23).

12. A.   [Resuming 8.B:] He accumulated too many horses:

B.   "And a chariot came up and went out of Egypt for six hundred shekels of silver, and a horse for a hundred and fifty" (1 Kgs. 10:29).

13. A.   He said three sets of proverbs:

B.   "The proverbs of Solomon, son of David, king of Israel" (Prov. 1:1);

C.   "the proverbs of Solomon: a wise son makes a happy father" (Prov. 10:1);

D.   "These also are proverbs of Solomon, which the staff of Hezekiah, king of Judah, copied out" ()Prov. 25:1).

14. A.   He said three "vanities":

B.   "Vanity of vanities, says Qohelet, all is vanity" (Qoh. 1:1).

C.   "Vanity" – one; "vanities" – two; lo, three in all.

15. A.   He said three songs:

B.   "Song" – one; "Songs" – two; lo, three in all.

16. A.   He was called by three names: Yedidiah [2 Sam. 12:25], Solomon, and Qohelet.

B.   R. Joshua b. Levi said, "These are three; then Agur, Jakeh, Lemuel, and Ithiel – seven in all."

C.   Said R. Samuel b. R. Nahman, "The main names that belong to him are Yedidiah, Solomon, and Qohelet."

D.   But R. Samuel b. R. Nahman concedes that the four in addition applied as well and he was called by those names too.

E.   So they require explanation.

F.   Agur: he gathered words of Torah [and the word for gather uses the same consonants as the name].

G.   Jakeh: [Simon, p. 17:] the son who vomited it out for a time [and the words for vomit and the name use the same consonants], like a dish that was filled and then emptied. So too, Solomon studied Torah for a time and then forgot it.

H.   Lemuel: for he spoke with God with all his heart. He said, "I can accumulate [many women] and not sin."

I.   Ithiel: "God is with me, and I can prevail," [for] the name "Ithiel" divided into its two clauses reads, "with me is God," so I can prevail.

17. A.   He wrote three books: Proverbs, Qohelet, and Song of Songs.

B.   Which of them did he write first of all?

C.   R. Hiyya the Elder and R. Jonathan:

D. R. Hiyya the Elder said, "He wrote Proverbs first, then Song of Songs, and finally Qohelet."

E. He brings evidence for that position from the following verse of Scripture: "And he spoke three thousand proverbs" (1 Kgs. 5:12) – the book of Proverbs; 'and his songs were a thousand and five' (1 Kgs. 5:12) – that is the Song of songs. And Qohelet he wrote later on."

F. There is a statement on Tannaite authority attributed to R. Hiyya the Elder that differs from this view. The statement maintains that all three of them he wrote at the same time, while this statement takes the view that he wrote each one by itself.

G. R. Hiyya the Elder repeated on Tannaite authority, "Only in the old age of Solomon did the Holy Spirit rest on him, and he said three books: Proverbs, Qohelet, and the Song of Songs."

H. And R. Jonathan said, "He wrote Song of Songs first, then Proverbs, finally Qohelet."

I. R. Jonathan brings evidence for that position from the natural course of life: "When a man is young, he composes songs; when he grows up, he speaks in proverbs; when he gets old, he speaks of vanities."

J. R. Yannai, father in law of R. Ammi, said, "All concur that he wrote Qohelet last of all."

18. A. R. Eliezer b. R. Abinah in the name of R. Aha, and Rabbis:

B. R. Eliezer b. R. Abinah in the name of R. Aha said, "'And he spoke three thousand proverbs' (1 Kgs. 5:12) with a proverb for each one; 'And his songs were a thousand and five' (1 Kgs. 5:12) with a thousand and five [Simon:] reasons for each statement."

C. Rabbis said, "'And he spoke three thousand proverbs' (1 Kgs. 5:12) on each verse; 'And his songs were a thousand and five' (1 Kgs. 5:12) a thousand and five reasons for each proverb.

D. "What is written is not, 'and his proverbs were,' but only, 'and his songs were,' and 'the songs of the proverb' bears the sense of 'the reason for each thing.'"

19. A. [With reference to the verse, "And he spoke three thousand proverbs. And his songs were a thousand and five" (1 Kgs. 5:12)], said R. Samuel b. R. Nahman, "We have reviewed the entire book of Proverbs, and we find written in it only nine hundred fifteen verses,

B. "and yet you say, 'And he spoke three thousand proverbs'?

C. "But you have no verse on which there are not two or three meanings [or applications];

D. "for example: 'as an earring of gold and an ornament of fine gold' (Prov. 25:12); 'as a ring of gold in a swine's snout, so is a fair woman that turns aside from discretion' (Prov. 11:22); 'Glorify not yourself in the presence of the king, and do not stand in the place of great men' (Prov. 25:6).

E. "And it is not necessary to say, do not sit.

F. "'Do not sit' – and it is not necessary to say, do not speak. [Here is an instance in which a single statement bears three meanings.]"

20. A. We have learned in the Mishnah: [All sacred scriptures impart uncleanness to hands. The Song of Songs and Qohelet impart

uncleanness to hands. R. Judah says, "The Song of Songs imparts uncleanness to hands, but as to Qohelet there is dispute." R. Yosé says, "Qohelet does not impart uncleanness to hands, but as to Song of Songs there is dispute." Rabbi Simeon says, "Qohelet is among the lenient rulings of the House of Shammai and strict rulings of the House of Hillel." Said R. Simeon b. Azzai, "I have a tradition from the testimony of the seventy-two elders, on the day on which they seated R. Eleazar b. Azariah in the session, that the Song of Songs and Qohelet do impart uncleanness to hands."].

B.   Said R. Aqiba, "Heaven forbid! No Israelite man ever disputed concerning Song of Songs that it imparts uncleanness to hands. For the entire age is not so worthy as the day on which the Song of Songs was given to Israel For all the scriptures are holy, but the Song of Songs is holiest of all. And if they disputed, they disputed only concerning Qohelet."

C.   Said R. Yohanan b. Joshua the son of R. Aqiba's father-in-law, according to the words of Ben Azzai, "Indeed did they dispute, and indeed did they come to a decision" [M. Yadayim 3:5G-S].

21. A.   R. Eleazar b. Azariah offered a parable: "The matter may be compared to the case of a man who took a seah of wheat to a baker, saying to him, 'Make for me from it flour and bake one cake of the best quality.'

B.   "So all of the wisdom of Solomon produced for Israel as fine flour only the Song of Songs.

This enormous composition pursues the general theme of the base verse, "song of songs." Since we ask how many are involved and maintain that there are three, we proceed to the proposition of 2.A: the events in Solomon's life are in sets of three. Everything from that point to the end, except for the final entries, is spun out of that allegation, amplifies what is at issue, or contains secondary or tertiary developments of primary materials. These are signified throughout. Where we clearly have an exegesis of a prooftext that is then treated in its own right, I supply it in square brackets; this helps us to see the units of which the whole is composed. The real goal, of course, emerges only at No. 17, which is our recurrent leitmotif. I cannot account for the interpolation of No. 20; it scarcely belongs in context. But it surely affirms our basic proposition about the Song of Songs as holy, and the passage serves as well as any other to advance the interests of the compilers.

I:vii
1. A.   "The Song of Songs":
    B.   the best of songs, the most excellent of songs, the finest of songs.
    C.   "Let us recite songs and praise the One who has made us a a theme of song in the world: 'And they shall shout aloud the songs of the Temple' (Amos 8:3), that is, praise of the Temple."
2. A.   Another interpretation of "The Song of Songs":
    B.   the best of songs, the most excellent of songs, the finest of songs.

C.   "Let us recite songs and praise the One who has made us a remnant for the world: 'The Lord alone shall lead him [Simon: in solitude]' (Dt. 32:12)."

3. A.   R. Yohanan in the name of R. Aha in the name of R. Simeon b. Abba: "Let us recite songs and praise for the One who will one day cause the Holy Spirit to come to rest upon us.

B.   "Let us say before him many songs."

4. A.   In all other songs, either He praises them, or they praise him.

B.   In the Song of Moses, they praise him, saying, "This is my God and I will glorify him" (Ex. 15:2).

C.   In the Song of Moses, he praises them: "He made him ride on the high places of the earth" (Dt. 32:13).

D.   Here, they praise him and he praises them.

E   He praises them: "Behold, you are beautiful, my love; behold, you are beautiful; your eyes are doves."

F.   They praise him: "Behold, you are beautiful, my beloved, truly lovely" (Song 1:15-16).

5. A.   R. Simeon in the name of R. Hanin of Sepphoris said, "['The Song of Songs'] means a double song."

B.   R. Simon said, "Doubled and redoubled."

6. A.   R. Levi said, "[The numerical value of the letters in the word for song] corresponds to the lifespan of the patriarchs and the Ten Commandments.

B.   "The numerical value of those letters is five hundred ten. [Abraham lived 175 years, Isaac 180, Jacob, 147, a total of 502, plus 10 for the Ten Commandments].

C.   "Now should you object that there are two extra, deduct the years of famine [one in Abraham's, one in Isaac's lifetime], since these do not count."

7. A.   Another interpretation [of "The Song of Songs, which is Solomon's]":

B.   R. Yudan and R. Levi in the name of R. Yohanan: "In every passage in this scroll in which you find the words, 'King Solomon,' the intent is actually King Solomon.

C.   "And whenever the text says, 'the king,' it means the Holy One, blessed be He."

D.   And rabbis say, "Wherever you find 'King Solomon,' the reference is to the King who is the master of peace. When it speaks of 'the king' it refers to the Community of Israel."

The concluding treatment of the base verse has two elements. First, at Nos. 1, 2, 3, 4, 5 we deal with the sense of the words, "song of Songs," taken to mean the superlative. No. 6 then adds a philological point. No. 7 sets the hermeneutic issue for all that follows. And so concludes the treatment of Song 1:1, which is not a *petihta* like the *petihtaot* that commence Esther Rabbah, Ruth Rabbah, and Lamentations Rabbah, but is also not utterly outside of their formal framework. It is something new, connected to something familiar.

2

Song of Songs Rabbah to Song of Songs 1:2

1:2   *O that you would kiss me with the kisses of your mouth!*
       For your love is better than wine.

II:I
1. A.   "O that you would kiss me with the kisses of your mouth! [For your love is better than wine]":
   B.   In what connection was this statement made?
   C.   R. Hinena b. R. Pappa said, "It was stated at the sea: '[I compare you, my love,] to a mare of Pharaoh's chariots' (Song 1:9)."
   D.   R. Yuda b. R. Simon said, "It was stated at Sinai: 'The Song of Songs' (Song 1:1) – the song that was song by the singers: 'The singers go before, the minstrels follow after' (Ps. 68:26)."
2. A.   It was taught on Tannaite authority in the name of R. Nathan, "The Holy One, blessed be He, in the glory of his greatness said it: 'The Song of Songs that is Solomon's' (Song 1:1),
   B.   "[meaning,] that belongs to the King to whom peace belongs."
3. A.   Rabban Gamaliel says, "The ministering angels said it: 'the Song of Songs' (Song 1:1) –
   B.   "the song that the princes on high said."
4. A.   R. Yohanan said, "It was said at Sinai: 'O that you would kiss me with the kisses of your mouth!' (Song 1:2)."
5. A.   R. Meir says, "It was said in connection with the tent of meeting."
   B.   And he brings evidence from the following verse: "Awake, O north wind, and come, O south wind! Blow upon my garden, let its fragrance be wafted abroad. Let my beloved come to his garden, and eat its choicest fruits" (Song 4:16).
   C.   "Awake, O north wind": this refers to the burnt-offerings, which were slaughtered at the north side of the altar.
   D.   "...and come, O south wind": this refers to the peace-offerings, which were slaughtered at the south side of the altar.
   E.   "Blow upon my garden": this refers to the tent of meeting.
   F.   "...let its fragrance be wafted abroad": this refers to the incense-offering.

57

G.   "Let my beloved come to his garden": this refers to the Presence of God.

H.   "...and eat its choicest fruits": this refers to the offerings.

6. A.   Rabbis say, "It was said in connection with the house of the ages [the Temple itself]."

B.   And they bring evidence from the same verse: "Awake, O north wind, and come, O south wind! Blow upon my garden, let its fragrance be wafted abroad. Let my beloved come to his garden, and eat its choicest fruits" (Song 4:16).

C.   "Awake, O north wind": this refers to the burnt-offerings, which were slaughtered at the north side of the altar.

D.   "and come, O south wind": this refers to the peace-offerings, which were slaughtered at the south side of the altar.

E.   "Blow upon my garden": this refers to the house of the ages.

F.   "...let its fragrance be wafted abroad": this refers to the incense-offering.

G.   "Let my beloved come to his garden": this refers to the Presence of God.

H.   "...and eat its choicest fruits": this refers to the offerings.

I.   The Rabbis furthermore maintain that all the other verses also refer to the house of the ages.

J.   Said R. Aha, "The verse that refers to the Temple is the following: 'King Solomon made himself a palanquin, from the wood of Lebanon. He made its posts of silver, its back of gold, its seat of purple; it was lovingly wrought within by the daughters of Jerusalem'(Song 3:9-10)."

K.   Rabbis treat these as the intersecting verses for the verse, 'And it came to pass on the day that Moses had made an end of setting up the tabernacle' (Num. 7:1)."

7. A.   In the opinion of R. Hinena [1.C], who said that the verse was stated on the occasion of the Sea, [the sense of the verse, "O that you would kiss me with the kisses of your mouth"] is, "may he bring to rest upon us the Holy Spirit, so that we may say before him many songs."

B.   In the opinion of Rabban Gamaliel, who said that the verse was stated by the ministering angels, [the sense of the verse, "O that you would kiss me with the kisses of your mouth"] is, "may he give us the kisses that he gave to his sons."

C.   In the opinion of R. Meir, who said that the verse was stated in connection with the tent of meeting, [the sense of the verse, "O that you would kiss me with the kisses of your mouth"] is, "May he send fire down to us and so accept his offerings."

D.   In the opinion of R. Yohanan, who said that the verse was stated in connection with Sinai, [the sense of the verse, "O that you would kiss me with the kisses of your mouth"] is, "May he cause kisses to issue for us from his mouth.

E.   "That is why it is written, 'O that you would kiss me with the kisses of your mouth.'"

No. 7 once again shows us that our compilers are first-class editors, since they have assembled quite disparate materials and drawn them together into a cogent statement. But the subject is not our base verse, and hence the compilers cannot have had in mind the need of a commentary of a verse-by-verse principle of conglomeration and organization. The passage as a whole refers in much more general terms to the Song of Songs, and hardly to Song 1:2 in particular. That is shown by the simple fact that various opinions invoke other verses than the one to which the whole is ultimately assigned. No. 1 serves Song 1:1, and so does No. 2. Indeed, No. 2 could have been placed in the prior assembly without any damage to its use and meaning. The same is to be said for No. 3. In fact, only Yohanan requires the verse to stand where it now does. No. 5 and No. 6 of course invoke Song 4:16 and do a fine job of reading that verse in light of the tent of meeting in the wilderness or the Temple in Jerusalem. Song 3:9-10 serves as an appropriate locus as well. Then the conclusion draws a variety of senses for Song 1:2 alone, and that conclusion points to the compilers of the whole for its authorship. This is once more highly sophisticated work of compilation, involving rich editorial intervention indeed.

II.ii

1. A. Another interpretation of the verse, "O that you would kiss me with the kisses of your mouth":
   B. Said R. Yohanan, "An angel would carry forth the Word [the Ten Commandments] from before the Holy One, blessed be He, word by word, going about to every Israelite and saying to him, 'Do you accept upon yourself the authority of this Word? There are so and so many rules that pertain to it, so and so many penalties that pertain to it, so and so many decrees that pertain to it, and so are the religious duties, the lenient aspects, the stringent aspects, that apply to it. There also is a reward that accrues in connection with it.'
   C. "And the Israelite would say, 'Yes.'
   D. "And the other would go and say to him again, 'Do you accept the divinity of the Holy One, blessed be He?'
   E. "And the Israelite would say, 'Yes, yes.'
   F. "Then he would kiss him on his mouth.
   G. "That is in line with this verse: 'To you it has been shown, that you might know' (Dt. 4:25) – that is, by an angel."
   H. Rabbis say, "It was the Word itself that made the rounds of the Israelites one by one, saying to each one, 'Do you accept me upon yourself? There are so and so many rules that pertain to me, so and so many penalties that pertain to me, so and so many decrees that pertain to me, and so are the religious duties, the lenient aspects, the stringent aspects, that apply to me. There also is a reward that accrues in connection with me.'
   I. "And the Israelite would say, 'Yes.' [Delete the words that can be translated, 'for Adqulain son of Hadimah'].
   J. "So he taught him the Torah.

K.   "That is in line with this verse: 'Lest you forget the things your eyes saw' (Dt. 4:9) – how the Word spoke with you."

2. A.   Another explanation of the phrase, "Lest you forget the things your eyes saw" (Dt. 4:9):

B.   The Israelites heard two acts of speech from the mouth of the Holy One, blessed be He.

3. A.   [Reverting to No. 1:] R. Joshua b. Levi said, "The scriptural foundation for the position of rabbis is that after all the commandments, it then is written, 'You speak with us, and we will hear' (Ex. 20:16)."

B.   How does R. Joshua b. Levi explain this verse?

C.   He rejects the view that temporal order does not pertain to the Torah.

D.   Or perhaps the statement, "You speak with us and we will hear" applies only after every two or three of the Ten Commandments.

4. A.   R. Azariah and R. Judah b. R. Simon in the name of R. Joshua b. Levi took his position. They said, "It is written, 'Moses commanded us the Torah' (Dt. 33:4).

B.   "In the entire Torah there are six hundred thirteen commandments. The numerical value of the letters in the word 'Torah' is only six hundred eleven. These are the ones that Moses spoke to us.

C.   "But 'I [am the Lord your God]' and 'You will not have [other gods besides me]' (Ex. 20:1-2) we have heard not from the mouth of Moses but from the Mouth of the Holy One, blessed be He.

D.   "That is in line with this verse: 'O that you would kiss me with the kisses of your mouth.'"

5. A.   How did the Word issue forth from the mouth of the Holy One, blessed be He?

B.   R. Simeon b. Yohai and Rabbis:

C.   R. Simeon b. Yohai says, "It teaches that the Word came forth from the right hand of the Holy One, blessed be He, to the left hand of the Israelites. It then made the round and circumambulated the camp of Israel, a journey of eighteen miles by eighteen miles, and then went and returned from the right hand of Israel to the left hand of the Holy One, blessed be He.

D.   "The Holy One, blessed be He, received it in his right hand and incised it on the tablets, and the sound went from one end of the world to the other: 'The voice of the Lord hews out flames of fire' (Ps. 29:7)."

E.   Rabbis say, "But is it there a consideration of 'left' above? And is it not written, 'Your right hand, O Lord, is glorious in power, your right hand, O Lord' (Ex. 15:6)?

F.   "But the Word came forth from the mouth of the Holy One, blessed be He, from his right hand to the right hand of Israel. It then made the round and circumambulated the camp of Israel, a journey of eighteen miles by eighteen miles, and then went and returned from the right hand of Israel to the right hand of the Holy One, blessed be He.

G.   "The Holy One, blessed be He, received it in his right hand and incised it on the tablets, and the sound went from one end of the world to the other: 'The voice of the Lord hews out flames of fire' (Ps. 29:7)."

6. A.   Said R. Berekhiah, "R. Helbo repeated to me the tradition that the Word itself was inscribed on its own, and when it was inscribed, and the sound went from one end of the world to the other: 'The voice of the Lord hews out flames of fire' (Ps. 29:7).

B.   "I said to R. Helbo, 'And lo, it is written, "written with the finger of God" (Ex. 31:18).'

C.   "He said to me, 'Strangler! Are you thinking of strangling me?'

D.   "I said to him, 'And what is the sense of this verse: "tables of stone, written with the finger of God" (Ex. 31:18)?'

E.   "He said to me, 'It is like a disciple who is writing, with the master's hand guiding his hand.'"

7. A.   R. Joshua b. Levi and Rabbis:

B.   R. Joshua b. Levi says, "Two Words [two of the Ten Commandments] did the Israelites hear from the mouth of the Holy One, blessed be He: 'I' and 'you will not have other gods, besides me' (Ex. 20:1-2), as it is said, 'O that you would kiss me with kisses of your mouth,' some, but not all of the kisses [commandments]."

C.   Rabbis say, "All of the Words did the Israelites hear from the mouth of the Holy One, blessed be He."

D.   R. Joshua of Sikhnin in the name of R. Levi: "The scriptural basis for the position of sages is the following verse of Scripture: 'And they said to Moses, Speak with us, and we will hear' (Ex. 20:16)."

E.   How does R. Joshua b. Levi interpret the verse?

F.   He differs, for considerations of temporal order do not apply in the Torah.

G.   Or perhaps the statement, "You speak with us and we will hear" applies only after every two or three of the Ten Commandments.

8. A.   R. Azariah and R. Judah b. R. Simon in the name of R. Joshua b. Levi took his position. They said, "It is written, 'Moses commanded us the Torah' (Dt. 33:4).

B.   "In the entire Torah there are six hundred thirteen commandments. The numerical value of the letters in the word 'Torah' is only six hundred eleven. These are the ones that Moses spoke to us.

C.   "But 'I [am the Lord your God]' and 'You will not have [other gods besides me]' (Ex. 20:1-2) we have heard not from the mouth of Moses but from the Mouth of the Holy One, blessed be He.

D.   "That is in line with this verse: 'O that you would kiss me with the kisses of your mouth.'"

9. A.   R. Yohanan interpreted the verse ["O that you would kiss me with the kisses of your mouth"] to speak of the Israelites when they went up to Mount Sinai:

B.   "The matter may be compared to the case of a king who wanted to marry a woman, daughter of good parents and noble family. He sent to her a messenger to speak with her. She said, 'I am not worthy to be his serving girl. But I want to hear it from his own mouth.'

C. "When that messenger got back to the king, [Simon:] his face was full of smiles, but what he said was not grasped by the king.

D. "The king, who was astute, said, 'This one is full of smiles. It would appear that she has agreed. But what he says is not to be understood by me. It appears that she has said, 'I want to hear it from his own mouth.'

E. "So the Israelites are the daughter of good parents. The messenger is Moses. The king is the Holy One, blessed be He.

F. "At that time: 'And Moses reported the words of the people to the Lord' (Ex. 19:8).

G. "Then why say, 'And Moses told the words of the people to the Lord' (Ex. 19:9)?

H. "Since it says, 'Lo, I come to you in a thick cloud, so that the people may hear when I speak to you, and may also believe you forever' (Ex. 19:9), therefore, 'And Moses told the words of the people to the Lord' (Ex. 19:9).

I. "He said to him, 'This is what they have asked for.'

J. "He said to him, 'They tell a child what he wants to hear.'"

10. A. R. Phineas in the name of R. Levi said, "There is a proverb that people say: 'One who has been bitten by a snake is afraid even of a rope.'

B. "So said Moses, 'Yesterday, when I said, 'But behold, they will not believe me' (Ex. 4:1), I got what was coming to me on their account. [He was struck by leprosy (Simon, p. 25, n. 3).] Now what am I going to do for them?'

11. A. It was taught on Tannaite authority by R. Simeon b. Yohai, "This is what they asked.

B. "They said, 'We want to see the glory of our King.'"

12. A. R. Phineas in the name of R. Levi: "It was perfectly obvious before the Holy One, blessed be He, that the Israelites were going to exchange his glory for another: 'They exchanged their glory for the likeness of an ox that eats grass' (Ps. 106:20).

B. "Therefore, [Simon, p. 25: he left them no excuse for saying] so that they might not say, 'If he had shown us his glory and greatness, we should certainly have believed in him, but not that his glory and greatness has not been shown to us, we do not believe in him.'

C. "This confirms the following: 'And enter not into judgment with your servant' (Ps. 143:2)."

13. A. R. Yudan in the name of R. Judah b. R. Simon, R. Judah, and R. Nehemiah:

B. R. Judah says, "When the Israelites heard, 'I am the Lord your God' (Ex. 20:1), the study of the Torah was fixed in their hearts, and they would study and not forget.

C. "They came to Moses saying, 'Our lord, Moses, you serve as intermediary, the messenger between us [and God]: "You speak with us, and we will hear" (Ex. 20:16), "...now therefore why should we die" (Dt. 5:22). Who gains if we perish?'

D. "Then they would study and forget what they have learned.

E. "They said, 'Just as Moses is mortal and passes on, so his learning passes away.'

F.   "Then they came again to Moses, saying to him, 'Our lord, Moses, would that he would reveal it to us a second time.' 'O that you would kiss me with the kisses of your mouth!' Would that the learning of Torah would be set in our hearts as it was before.'

G.   "He said to them, 'That cannot be now, but it will be in the age to come.'

H.   "For it is said, 'I will put my Torah in their inner part, and on their heart I shall write it' (Jer. 31:33)."

I.   R. Nehemiah said, "R. Nehemiah said, "When the Israelites heard the word, 'You will not have other gods besides me,' the impulse to do evil was uprooted from their hearts.

J.   "They came to Moses and said to him, 'Our lord, Moses, you serve as intermediary, the messenger between us [and God]: "You speak with us, and we will hear" (Ex. 20:16), "...now therefore why should we die" (Dt. 5:22). Who gains if we perish?'

K.   "Forthwith the impulse to do evil came back.

L.   "Then they came again to Moses, saying to him, 'Our lord, Moses, would that he would reveal it to us a second time.' 'O that you would kiss me with the kisses of your mouth!'

M.   "He said to them, 'That cannot be now, but it will be in the age to come.'

N.   "For it is said, 'And I will take away the stony heart out of your flesh' (Ez. 36:26).'"

14. A   R. Azariah, and some say R. Eliezer and R. Yosé b. R. Hanina and rabbis:

B.   R. Eliezer says, "The matter may be compared to the case of a king who had a wine cellar.

C.   "The first guest came to him first, and he mixed a cup for him and gave it to him.

D.   "A second came and he mixed a cup for him and gave it to him.

E.   "When the son of the king came, he gave him the whole cellar.

F.   "So the First Man was commanded in respect to seven commandments.

G.   "That is in line with this verse: 'And the Lord God commanded the man, saying, You may freely eat of every tree of the garden, [but of the tree of the knowledge of good and evil you shall not eat, for in the day that you eat of it you shall die]' (Gen. 2:16)."

15. A   ["And the Lord God commanded the man, saying, 'You may freely eat of every tree of the garden, [but of the tree of the knowledge of good and evil you shall not eat, for in the day that you eat of it you shall die]'" (Gen. 2:16).]

B.   [Gen. R. XVI:VI.1B adds:] R. Levi said, "He made him responsible to keep six commandments.

C.   "He commanded him against idolatry, in line with this verse: 'Because he willingly walked after idols' (Hos. 5:11).

D.   "'The Lord' indicates a commandment against blasphemy, in line with this verse: 'And he who blasphemes the name of the Lord' (Lev. 24:16).

E.   "'God' indicates a commandment concerning setting up courts [and a judiciary]: 'You shall not revile the judges' [in the verse at hand, 'God'] (Ex. 22:27).

F.   "'...the man' refers to the prohibition of murder: 'Whoever sheds man's blood' (Gen. 9:6).

G.   "'...saying' refers to the prohibition of fornication: 'Saying, "If a man put away his wife"' (Jer. 3:1).

H.   "'Of every tree you may eat' (Gen. 2:16) indicates that he commanded him concerning theft. [There are things one may take, and there are things one may not take.]"

16. A.   [Continuing Eliezer's statement, 14:G:] "As to Noah, a further commandment was assigned to him, not eating a limb cut from a living animal: 'Only flesh with the life thereof which is the blood thereof' (Gen. 9:4).

B.   "As to Abraham, a further commandment was assigned to him, circumcision.

C.   "Isaac devoted the eighth day to that rite.

D.   "As to Jacob, a further commandment was assigned to him, the prohibition of the sinew of the thigh-vein: 'Therefore the children of Israel do not eat the sinew of the thigh-vein' (Gen. 32:33).

E.   "As to Judah, a further commandment was assigned to him, levirate marriage: 'And Judah said to Onan, Go into your brother's wife and perform the duty of a husband's brother for her' (Gen. 38:8).

F.   "The Israelites, by contrast, made their own all of the religious duties, positive and negative alike."

17. A.   R. Yosé b. R. Hanina and rabbis say, "The matter may be compared to the case of a king who was divvying up rations to his legions through his generals, officers, and commanders.

B.   "But when the turn of his son came, he gave him his rations with his own hand."

18. A.   R. Isaac says, "The matter may be compared to a king who was eating sweetmeats,

B.   "And when the turn of his son came, he gave him his rations with his own hand."

19. A.   Rabbis say, "The matter may be compared to the case of a king who was eating meat.

B.   "And when the turn of his son came, he gave him his rations with his own hand."

C.   And some say, "He took it out of his mouth and gave it to him: 'For the Lord gives wisdom, out of his mouth comes knowledge and discernment' (Prov. 2:6)."

20. A.   R. Abbahu, and some say the following in the name of R. Judah, and R. Nehemiah:

B.   R. Nehemiah said, "[The matter of 'O that you would kiss me with the kisses of your mouth!' may be compared to] two colleagues who were occupied with teachings of the law. This one states a general principle of law, and that one states a general principle of law.

C.   "Said the Holy One, blessed be He, 'Their source is through my power.' [Simon, p. 28: 'Their source comes from me.']

D.   R. Judah said, "Even as to the breath that comes forth from one's mouth, as you say, 'But Job does open his mouth with a breath'

		(Job 35:16), said the Holy One, blessed be He, 'Their source is through my power.' [Simon, p. 28: 'Their source comes from me.']
	E.	Rabbis say, "The souls of these are going to be taken with a kiss."
21.	A.	Said R. Azariah, "We find that the soul of Aaron was taken away only with a kiss: 'And Aaron the priest went up to Mount Hor at the mouth of the Lord and died there' (Num. 33:38).
	B.	"How do we know the same in the case of the soul of Moses? 'So Moses the servant of the Lord died there...according to the mouth of the Lord' (Dt. 34:5).
	C.	"How do we know the same in the case of the soul of Miriam? 'And Miriam died there' (Num. 30:1). And just as 'there' in the former passage means, 'by the mouth of the Lord,' so here too the fact is the same.
	D.	"But it would have been inappropriate to say it explicitly.
	E.	"How do we know the same in the case of the soul of all the righteous? 'O that you would kiss me with the kisses of your mouth!'
	F.	"[The sense is,] 'If you have occupied yourself with teachings of the Torah, so that your lips are [Simon, p. 28:] well armed with them, then, at the end, everyone will kiss you on your mouth.'"

The whole point of including II:ii.1.B through 4 is at 4.D. Without that reversion to the base verse, we must be mystified by the inclusion of the entire composition at this particular point, since it has no bearing upon the base verse at all. Yohanan's and sages' disagreement concerns whether an angel carried the Ten Commandments, or whether the Word – the Ten Commandments – went on its own. If we had to choose a base verse for the present composition, absent our base verse of course, it would obviously have to be Dt. 4:25/Dt. 4:9. The interpolation of No. 2 may be ignored, and No. 3 expands on No. 1. No. 4 then is continuous with No. 3 and serves very well. So the whole has been composed in connection with the requirements of Dt. 4:9, 25, and then the revisions for insertion here are minimal. But that has not prevented the framers from adding on the immense secondary exposition of just how the Ten Commandments came out of God's mouth, Nos. 5ff. The reason is not farfetched, however, since the base verse and the theme of the passage at hand surely justify raising such a secondary question of amplification. That is, if we read God's kisses as a reference to the Ten Commandments, then we are going to ask how the "kisses" came out of God's mouth. That accounts for the continuation at No. 7, with No. 8 tacked on as before. Nos. 9, 10, 11, 12, 13, then carry forward the theme of the revelation at Sinai, introduced as it is by the verse at hand. No. 13 happens to appeal to our base verse, but that is in the context of an on-going exposition, and the composition, which is first-class, cannot be credited to the ultimate redactors of our document merely because our base verse makes its appearance. The story can have worked very well without Song 1:2, and it is at least plausible that the base verse was inserted later on; it certainly does not flow within F, where it first occurs. No. 14-15 is thrown in to illustrate the greater intimacy implied in the words "his mouth," so Simon, p. 27, n. 4. While No. 15 continues the exposition of Gen. 2:16 which is integral to No. 14, it is in fact a free-standing composition, which is why I present it separately. But that requires duplicating Gen. 2:16 for clarity. Then No. 14 continues at No. 16, 17, 18, 19. I treat as distinct entries what is assigned to the others listed at 14.A. The point of No. 20 has no bearing on the foregoing, but it does address our base verse, now with a quite different focus. The point emerges only at No. 21's expansion of 20.E's point.

II:iii
1.   A.   Another explanation of the verse, "O that you would kiss me with the kisses of your mouth! [For your love is better than wine]":
     B.   "Let him arm me, purify me, make me cleave to him."
     C.   "Let him arm me": "They were armed with bows and could use both the right hand and the left" (1 Chr. 12:2).
2.   A.   Said R. Simeon b. R. Nahman, "The words of Torah are to be compared to weapons.
     B.   "Just as weapons protect their owners in wartime, so words of Torah protect those who works sufficiently hard at learning them."
     C.   R. Hana b. R. Aha brings proof from the following verse for the same proposition: "'Let the high praises of God be in their mouth and a double-edged sword in their hand' (Ps. 149:6):
     D.   "Just as a sword consumes on both its edges, so the Torah gives life in this world and life in the world to come."
3.   A.   R. Judah, R. Nehemiah, and rabbis:
     B.   R. Judah says, "The Torah, which was said with one mouth, was said with many mouths."
     C.   R. Nehemiah said, "Two Torahs were stated, one by mouth, one in writing."
     D.   Rabbis say, "It is because they make a decree on creatures above and they do it, on creatures below and they do it." [Simon, p. 29: "[The Torah is said to have many mouths] because its students impose their will on the beings of the upper world and on the beings of the lower world."]
     E.   R. Joshua of Sikhnin in the name of R. Levi said, "The scriptural verse that supports the position of rabbis is as follows: 'For they were princes of holiness and princes of God' (1 Chr. 24:5).
     F.   "'...princes of holiness': these are the ministering angels, thus: 'Therefore I have profaned the princes of the sanctuary' (Isa. 43:28).
     G.   "'...and princes of God': this refers to Israel, thus, 'I said, "You are godlike beings"' (Ps. 82:6).
     H.   "'...they make a decree on creatures above and they do it, on creatures below and they do it': for they carry out their deeds in a state of cultic cleanness."

The basic point here concerns the meanings to be imputed to the letters that spell out "kiss," and, as we know from the foregoing, among the available meanings is "arm." That accounts for the sense important at No. 1, which then accounts for the addition of No. 2. No. 3 then works on the notion of the Torah have many mouths, provoked by the introduction of the Torah as a double-edged sword.

II:iv
1.   A.   Another explanation of the verse, "O that you would kiss me with the kisses of your mouth! [For your love is better than wine]":
     B.   "Let him purify me, make me cleave to him, let him kiss me."
     C.   "Let him purify me": like a man who joins together ["kisses"] the water in two cisterns to one another and makes them cleave together [and so forms of them a valid immersion-pool].
     D.   That is in line with the usage in the following verse: "Like the joining of cisterns he joins it" (Isa. 33:4).

We now work on the sense of the consonants used for "kiss" that yield "run," "join." That accounts for No. 1, who runs water from cistern to cistern and so forms of the two a valid immersion-pool for purifying unclean objects.

II:v
1.   A.   Another explanation of the verse, "O that you would kiss me with the kisses of your mouth":
     B.   "Let him kiss me, let him make me cleave to him."
     C.   That is in line with the usage in this verse: "The noise of the wings of the living creatures as they touched one another" (Ez. 3:13).
2.   A.   Another explanation of the verse, "O that you would kiss me [with the kisses of your mouth]":
     B.   Let him make for me the sound of kissing with his mouth.

The interest now is in the sense of the consonants used for "cleave," shown in 1.C for B. No. 2 works on the simple sense of "kiss" that the same consonants produce.

II:vi
1.   A.   "For your love is better than wine": There we have learned in the Mishnah [following the version in the Mishnah, which differs slightly from the version before us:] Said R. Judah, "R. Ishmael asked R. Joshua as they were going along the road.
     B.   "He said to him, 'On what account did they prohibit cheese made by gentiles?'
     C.   "He said to him, 'Because they curdle it with rennet from carrion.'
     D.   "He said to him, 'And is not the rennet from a whole-offering subject to a more stringent rule than rennet from carrion, and yet they have said, 'A priest who is not squeamish sucks it out raw?' [That is not deemed an act of sacrilege, even though the priests have no right to any part of a whole-offering; hence the rennet is

deemed null. Why then take account of rennet in the present circumstance, which is, after all, of considerably less weight than the sin of sacrilege?]"

E.   For R. Simeon b. Laqish said, "They treated it as one who drinks from a dirty cup. While, on the one side, one may derive no benefit from such a cup that belongs to the cult, yet one also is not liable for having violated the rule against sacrilege in making use of that cup."

F.   [Lacking in Song:] (But they did not concur with him and ruled, "It is not available for [the priests'] benefit, while it also is not subject to the laws of sacrilege.")

G.   [Lacking in Song:] [Judah resumes his narrative:] "He went and said to him, 'Because they curdle it with rennet of calves sacrificed to idols.'"

H.   [Lacking in Song:] "He said to him, 'If so, then why have they not also extended the prohibition affecting it to the matter of deriving benefit from it?'

I.   "He moved him on to another subject.

J.   "He said to him, 'Ishmael, my brother, how do you read the verse: "For your [masculine] love is better than wine," or, "Your [feminine] love is better than wine" (Song 1:2)?'

K.   "He said to him, '"For your [feminine] love is better than wine."'

L.   "He said to him, 'The matter is not so. For its neighbor teaches concerning it, "Your [masculine] ointments have a goodly fragrance"' (Song 1:3)" [M. Abodah Zarah 2:5A-K].

M.   But why did he not tell him the reason [H, instead of just changing the subject, I]?

N.   Said R. Jonathan, "It is because it was only recently that they had made the ruling, and R. Ishmael was junior."

2. A.   R. Simeon b. Halafta and R. Haggai in the name of R. Samuel b. R. Nahman: "It is written, 'The lambs will be for your clothing' (Prov. 27:26).

B.   "What is actually written may be read 'hidden,' yielding the meaning, 'when your disciples are junior, you should head from them words of Torah. When they grow up and become disciples of sages, you may reveal to them the secrets of the Torah.'"

3. A.   R. Simeon b. Yohai taught on Tannaite authority: "'Now these are the ordinances which you shall set before them' (Ex. 21:1).

B.   "[Since the consonants in 'set' may yield 'treasure,' we interpret in this way:] just as a treasure is not shown to any one who comes along, so is the case with teachings of the Torah."

4. A.   R. Huna raised the question, and R. Hama b. Uqba presented the same as an objection [to 1.M's response to 1.H:] "If his intention was only to put him off, he should have put him off with one of the five equivalent points of unclarity in the Torah, which are [Simon, p. 31:] 'uplifting, cursed, tomorrow, almond-shaped, and arise.'

B.   "['Uplifting':] do we read 'If you do well, will it not be lifted up? (Gen. 4:7), or 'It is incurring sin if you do not do well' (Gen. 4:7)?" [That is another example of a point of unclarity in Scripture. He did not have to choose the one he chose. The others are not specified here.]"

C.   Said R. Tanhuma, "I have another [a sixth]: 'The sons of Jacob came in from the field when they heard it' (Gen. 34:7), or, 'When they heard it, the men were grieved' (Gen. 34:7-8) [so where is the break between the two sentences?]"

5.   A.   Said R. Isaac, "It is written, 'And me did the Lord command' (Dt. 4:14):

B.   "'There are matters that he said to me, all by myself, and there are matters that he said to me to say to his children.'"

6.   A.   [Following Simon, p. 31, n. 2, the point of reference in what follows is our base verse, "O that you would kiss me with the kisses of your mouth! For your love is better than wine]": Said R. Ila, "There are matters about which one's [Simon:] lips are sealed. [Simon, p. 31, n. 2: It was for this reason that he put him off with the verse, because 'let him kiss me' may also mean, 'let him seal my lips,' and thus he hinted by this quotation that not everything is to be explained.]

B.   "How so? One verse of Scripture says, 'Your word have I laid up in my heart, that I might not sin against you' (Ps. 119:11), while another verse says, 'With my lips have I told all the ordinances of your mouth' (Ps. 119:13). How hold the two together?

C.   "So long as Ira the Jairite was the master of David, he observed the verse, 'Your word have I laid up in my heart, that I might not sin against you' (Ps. 119:11), but after he died, then he followed this verse: 'With my lips have I told all the ordinances of your mouth' (Ps. 119:13)."

Here is a classic case of parachuting a complete composition that in no way serves the interests of a sustained reading of a base-document. The only reason that this entire *talmud* has been inserted here – by *talmud* I mean a sustained discussion with its own dialectic and dynamic – is that our base verse forms part of the whole. But nothing that is said about our base verse fits together with any of the prevailing points of interest, let alone important propositions. But it is perfectly routine for framers of documents of the present type to collect everything they can in which the base verses appear, even though what they gather has been made up for purposes quite different from the ones that define the document under aggregation. We now move on to a separate theme, comparing "love" to words of Torah, with the sense of "love" as "loved ones," hence, "words of Torah.

II:vii
1.   A.   "For your love is better than wine":
B.   Words of Torah complement one another, friends of one another, close to one another,
C.   in line with the usage [of the consonants that are translated "love"] in the following verse: "or his uncle or his uncle's son" (Lev. 25:49).
2.   A.   [Supply: water removes uncleanness, when the water is of the correct classification:] "But a fountain or cistern wherein is a gathering of water" (Lev. 11:36).

B.   Water imparts susceptibility to uncleanness: "If water be put on seed" (Lev. 11:38). [The point of the juxtaposition is that while water can remove uncleanness, water can also impart susceptibility to uncleanness. The relationship of the two verses shows how words of Torah "complement one another, friends of one another, close to one another."]

3. A.   Simeon b. R. Abba in the name of R. Yohanan: "Words of scribes are as precious as words of the Torah.

    B.   "What is the scriptural basis for that view? [Following Simon:] 'And the roof of your mouth like the best wine' [Simon, p. 32, n. 3: The roof of the mouth is taken as a symbol of the Oral Torah and wine as a symbol of the written Torah.]"

    C.   Colleagues in the name of R. Yohanan: "Words of scribes are more precious than words of Torah: 'For your love is better than wine' (Song 1:2).

    D.   "If one says, 'there is no requirement as to phylacteries,' so as to violate the requirements of the explicit words of the torah, he is exempt from liability.

    E.   "If he says, 'There is a requirement that the phylacteries contain five [not four] compartments,' intending thereby to add to the requirements of the teachings of the scribes, by contrast, he is liable to a penalty."

4. A.   R. Abba b. R. Kahana in the name of R. Judah b. Pazzi derived the same lesson from the following:

    B.   Said R. Tarfon, "I was coming along the road [in the evening] and reclined to recite the Shema as required by the House of Shammai. And [in doing so] I placed myself in danger of [being attacked by] bandits." [They said to him, "You are yourself responsible [for what might have befallen you], for you violated the words of the House of Hillel."] [M. Berakhot 1:3G-H].

    C.   You see that had he not recited the Shema at all, he would have violated a positive commandment alone. Now that he has recited the Shema, he has become liable for his life.

    D.   That proves that Words of scribes are more precious than words of Torah.

5. A.   R. Hanina b. R. Aha in the name of R. Tanhum b. R. Aha said, "They are subject to more stringent penalties than the words of the Torah and of the prophets.

    B.   "It is written, 'Do not preach, they preach' (Mic. 2:6). [Simon, p. 32, n. 9: implying that prophecy can be interrupted, but not so the teaching of the sages.]

    C.   "[The relationship of teachings of scribes and prophets] yields the following simile: the matter may be compared to the case of a king who sent his agents to a town. Concerning one of them he wrote, 'If he shows you my seal and signature, believe him, and if not, do not believe him,' and concerning the other of them he wrote, 'Even if he does not show you my seal and signature, believe him.'

    D.   "So in connection with teachings of prophecy: 'If there arise in your midst a prophet...and he gives you a sign' (Dt. 13:2).

E.   "But as to words of scribes: 'According to the Torah that they will teach you' (Dt. 17:11).

F.   "What is written is not, 'according to the Torah that the Torah will teach you,' but 'according to the Torah that they will teach you.'

G.   "What is written is not, 'according to the judgment that it will tell you,' but, '...that they shall tell you.'

H.   "Further: 'You shall not turn aside from the sentence that they shall declare to you to either the right hand or to the left' (Dt. 17:11):

I.   "If they tell you that the right hand is right and the left hand is left, obey; and even if they tell you that the right hand is left and the left hand is right!"

The point of Nos. 1, 2 is clear; No. 2 illustrates No. 1. The word for "love" is now under examination. A play on the word for "love" yields "roof of your mouth," and the entirety of what follows is tacked on for that reason. The point now is to compare the Oral Torah with the written, and that forthwith yields the comparison of teachings of scribes ("sages" in Simon's translation) and teachings of the Written Torah. We start with the claim that the two are equal, No. 3, and move on for the rest to the allegation that teachings of scribes or of the Oral Torah are more to be valued and are subject to more severe penalties.

II:viii

1.   A.   Another explanation of the verse, "For your love is better than wine":

     B.   Words of the Torah are compared to water, wine, oil, honey, and milk.

2.   A.   To water: "Ho, everyone who thirsts come for water" (Isa. 55:1).

     B.   Just as water is from one end of the world to the other, "To him who spread forth the earth above the waters" (Ps. 136:6), so the Torah is from one end of the world to the other, "The measure thereof is longer than the earth" (Job 11:9).

     C.   Just as water is life for the world, "A fountain of gardens, a well of living waters" (Song 4:15), so the Torah is life for the world, "For they are life to those who find them and health for all their flesh" (Prov. 4:22); "Come, buy and eat" (Isa. 55:1).

     D.   Just as water is from heaven, "At the sound of his giving a multitude of waters in the heavens" (Jer. 10:13), so the Torah is from heaven, "I have talked with you from heaven" (Ex. 20:19).

     E.   Just as water [when it rains] is with loud thunder, "The voice of the Lord is upon the water" (Ps. 29:3), so the Torah is with loud thunder, "And it came to pass on the third day, when it was morning, that there were thunderings and lightnings" (Ex. 19:16).

     F.   Just as water restores the soul, "But God cleaves the hollow place which was in Levi and water came out, and when he had drunk, he revived" (Judges 15:19), so the Torah [restores the soul], "The Torah of the Lord is perfect, restoring the soul" (Ps. 19:8).

G.   Just as water purifies a person from uncleanness, "And I will sprinkle clean water upon you, and you will be clean" (Ez. 36:25), so the Torah cleans a person of uncleanness, "The words of the Lord are pure" (Ps. 12:7).

H.   Just as water cleans the body, "He shall bathe himself in water" (Lev. 17:15), so the Torah cleans the body, "Your word is purifying to the uttermost" (Ps. 119:140).

I.   Just as water covers over the nakedness of the sea, "As the waters cover the sea" (Isa. 11:9), so the Torah covers the nakedness of Israel, "Love covers all transgressions" (Prov. 10:12).

J.   Just as water comes down in drops but turns into rivers, so the Torah – a person learns two laws today, two tomorrow, until he becomes an overflowing river.

K.   Just as water, if one is not thirsty, has no sweetness in it, so the Torah, if one does not labor at it, has no sweetness in it.

L.   Just as water leaves the height and flows to a low place, so the Torah leaves one who is arrogant on account of [his knowledge of] it and cleaves to one who is humble on account of [his knowledge of] it.

M.   Just as water does not keep well in utensils of silver and gold but only in the most humble of utensils, so the Torah does not stay well except in the one who treats himself as a clay pot.

N.   Just as with water, a great man is not ashamed to say to an unimportant person, "Give me a drink of water," so as to words of Torah, the great man is not ashamed to say to an unimportant person, "Teach me a chapter," or "a verse," or even "a single letter."

O.   Just as with water, when one does not know how to swim in it, in the end he will be swallowed up, so words of Torah, if one does not know how to swim in them and to give instruction in accord with them, in the end he will be swallowed up.

P.   Said R. Hanina of Caesarea, "Just as water is drawn not only for gardens and orchards, but also for baths and privies, shall I say that that is so also for words of the Torah?

Q.   "Scripture says, 'For the ways of the Lord are right' (Hos. 14:10)."

R.   Said R. Hama b. Uqba, "Just as water makes plants grow, so words of the Torah make everyone who works in them sufficiently grow.

S.   Then [may one say,] just as water becomes rancid and smelly in a vessel, so words of the Torah are the same way? Scripture says that the Torah is like wine. Just as with wine, so long as it ages in the bottle, it improves, so words of the Torah, so long as they age in the body of a person, they improve in stature.

T.   Then [may one say,] just as water is not to be discerned in the body, so is the case with words of the Torah? Scripture says that the Torah is like wine. Just as with wine. its presence is discerned when it is in the body, so words of the Torah are discerned when they are in the body.

U.   [For] people hint and point with the finger, saying, "This is a disciple of a sage."

V.   Then [may one say,] just as water does not make one happy, so is the case with words of the Torah? Scripture says that the Torah is like wine. Just as wine "makes the heart of man glad" (Ps. 104:15), so words of the Torah make the heart happy, "The precepts of the Lord are right, rejoicing the heart" (Ps. 19:9).

W.   Then [may one say,] just as wine sometimes is bad for the head and the body, so is the case with words of the Torah? Scripture compares words of the Torah to oil. Just as oil is pleasing for the head and body, so words of the Torah are pleasing for the head and body: "Your word is a lamp to my feet" (Ps. 119:105).

X.   May one then say, just as oil is bitter to begin with, and sweet only at the end, so is it the case also with words of Torah? Scripture states, "Honey and milk" (Song 4:11). Just as they are sweet, so words of the Torah are sweet: "Sweeter than honey" (Ps. 19:11).

Y.   May one then say, just as honey has wax cells [that cannot be eaten], so words of the Torah are the same? Scripture says, "...milk" (Song 4:11). Just as milk is pure, so words of the Torah are pure: "Gold and glass cannot equal it" (Job 28:17).

Z.   May one then say, just as milk is [Simon:] insipid, so words of the Torah are the same? Scripture states, "Honey and milk" (Song 4:11). Just as honey and milk, when they are stirred together, do not do any harm to the body, so words of the Torah: "It shall be health to your navel" (Prov. 3:8); "For they are life to those who find them" (Prov. 4:22).

The composition is sustained and perfect. The comparison of "your love," understood as "words of the Torah," to wine persuaded the compositors that the entire piece belongs. But of course it has not be written out to serve our base verse in particular, nor any other as a matter of fact. It is a free-standing and powerful composition, making its own point about its own subject, and not an amplification, in terms of another set of values, of a given verse and its contents.

II:ix
1. A.   Another explanation of the verse, "For your love is better":
    B.   This refers to the patriarchs.
    C.   "...than wine":
    D.   this refers to the princes.
2. A.   Another explanation of the verse, "For your love is better":
    B.   This refers to the the offerings..
    C.   "...than wine":
    D.   this refers to the libations.
3. A.   Said R. Hanina, "If when the Israelites came to that awful deed, Moses had known how precious were the offerings, he would have offered all of the offerings that are catalogued in the Torah.
    B.   "Instead he ran to the merit of the patriarchs: 'Remember Abraham, Isaac, and Israel, your servants' (Ex. 32:13)."
4. A.   Another explanation of the verse, "For your love is better":
    B.   This refers to Israel.
    C.   "...than wine":
    D.   this refers to the gentiles.

E.   [For the numerical value of the letters that make up the word for wine] is seventy,

F.   teaching you that the Israelites are more precious before the Holy One, blessed be He, than all of the nations."

The composition, with its modest interpolation at No. 3, is a powerful triplet, in which the more valuable is compared with the less valuable, first patriarchs as against princes, then offerings as against merit, finally Israel as against the nations. That the whole is inseparable and unitary is shown by the climax, No. 4, and that becomes obvious because of the interpolation at No. 3. So the whole, inclusive of No. 3, is aiming at the final point, 4.F.

3

Song of Songs Rabbah to Song of Songs 1:3

1:3 *Your anointing oils are fragrant,*
your name is oil poured out;
therefore the maidens love you.

III:i

1. A. "Your anointing oils are fragrant":

   B. R. Yannai son of R. Simeon: "All the songs that the patriarchs said before you were fragrances, but as to us, 'your name is oil poured out.

   C. "It is like a man who pours out what is in his jar into the jar of his fellow. [Simon, p. 36, n. 2: our hymns are theirs as the actual ointment to the mere fragrance.]

   D. "All of the religious duties that the patriarchs did before you were fragrances, but as to us, 'your name is oil poured out.'

   E. "[These are] two hundred forty-eight religious actions of commission and three hundred sixty-five religious actions of omission."

2. A. R. Eliezer, R. Joshua, and R. Aqiba:

   B. R. Eliezer says, "If all the seas were ink, and all the reeds were pens, and the heaven and the earth were scrolls, and all people were scribes, they would not be sufficient to write down the Torah that I have learned, but I have taken away from it only so much as a person who dips [Simon:] the point of his pen in the sea."

   C. R. Joshua says, "If all the seas were ink, and all the reeds were pens, and the heaven and the earth were scrolls, and all people were scribes, they would not be sufficient to write down the words of Torah that I have learned, but I have taken away from it only so much as a person who dips [Simon:] the point of his pen in the sea."

   D. R. Aqiba says, "As for me, I do not have the strength to say what my lords have said, but my lords have taken away something from it, while for my part, I have taken away no more than one who

75

smells an etrog. The one who takes the scent enjoys it, but the etrog is not diminished;

    E.   "and like one who fills his jug from a stream, or like one who lights a lamp from another lamp."

3.   A.   One time R. Aqiba delayed coming to the house of study. He came and sat down outside. The question was raised, "Is this the law?"

    B.   They said, "The law is outside."

    C.   Again a question was raised.

    D.   They said, "The law is outside."

    E.   Again a question was raised.

    F.   They said, "Aqiba is outside. Make a place for him."

    G.   He came and sat down at the feet of R. Eliezer.

4.   A.   Now the house of study of R. Eliezer was set up like an arena, and a stone there was designed there for him to sit on.

    B.   One time R. Joshua came in and began kissing that stone.

    C.   He said, "This stone is like Mount Sinai, and this one who sat on it is like the ark of the covenant."

The opening theme, the superiority of the moderns over the ancients, which is evidently invited by the balance between the two clauses of the base verse, accounts for the inclusion of Nos. 2, 3. But these items are of course free-standing and have no bearing upon the whole; so the principle of agglutination is, at best, a very attenuated theme, which, at the slightest pretext, can accommodate pretty much anything.

III:ii

1.   A.   Another interpretation of the verse, "Your anointing oils are fragrant, your name is oil poured out; therefore the maidens love you":

    B.   R. Aha in the name of R. Tanhum b. R. Hiyya: "There are two oils, the oil used to anoint into the priesthood, and the oil used to anoint for the kingship."

    C.   Rabbis say, "There are two Torahs, the Torah that is in writing and the Torah that is memorized."

2.   A.   Said R. Yudan "'...your name is oil poured out': Your name is exalted over all who occupy themselves with the oil of the Torah."

    B.   This is the position of R. Yudan, who said, "'And the yoke shall be destroyed by reason of oil' (Isa. 10:27) [means], the yoke of Sennacherib will be destroyed on account of Hezekiah and his company, who were occupied with the oil of the Torah."

No. 1 is not particular to our base verse, since 1.B, C, are perfectly comprehensible as a free-standing entry, without reference to the base verse. No. 2, by contrast, is narrowly exegetical at A, though here too, 2.B is perfectly comprehensible and does not invoke, or require, our base verse.

III:iii

1. A.   Another interpretation of the verse, "your name is oil poured out":

    B.   just as olive oil is bitter in the beginning but ends up sweet, so "though your beginning was small, yet your end shall greatly increase" (Job. 8:7).

    C.   Just as oil is improved only by crushing in the press, so Israel accomplishes repentance only on account of suffering.

    D.   Just as oil does not mix with other liquids, so Israel does not mix with the nations of the world: "Neither shall you make marriages with them" (Dt. 7:3).

    E.   Just as oil poured into a full cup does not overflow with other liquids [not mixing with them, it overflows on its own], so words of Torah does not flow with trivial words.

    F.   Just as, with oil, if you have a full cup of oil in hand, and into it falls a drop of water, a drop of oil exudes on its account, so if a word of the Torah goes into the heart, correspondingly a word of trivial nonsense goes forth.

    G.   If a word of trivial nonsense goes into the heart, correspondingly a word of the Torah goes forth.

    H.   Just as oil brings light into the world, so Israel is the light of the world: "Nations shall walk at your light" (Isa. 60:3).

    I.   Just as oil is above all other liquids, so Israel is above all the nations: "And the Lord your God will set you on high" (Dt. 28:1).

    J.   Just as oil does not produce an echo [when poured], so Israel does not produce resonance in this world, but in the world to come: "And brought down you shall speak out of the ground" (Isa. 29:4).

Now the "you" of the base verse is Israel, the oil is (in part) Torah-teaching, and the comparison of oil to the beloved is of the relationship of the Torah to Israel. The rest follows.

III:iv

1. A.   [Supply: Another interpretation of the verse, "Your anointing oils are fragrant, your name is oil poured out; therefore the maidens love you":]

    B.   R. Yohanan interpreted the verse to speak of Abraham.

2. A.   [Genesis Rabbah XXXIX:II.1: R. Berekhiah commenced [discourse by citing the following verse of Scripture]: "Your ointments have a good smell" (Song 1:3).]

    B.   "When the Holy One, blessed be He, said to him, 'Leave your land and your birthplace' (Gen. 12:1), what was he like? He was like a flask of myrrh sealed with a tight lid and lying in the corner. The fragrance of that vial does not waft upward. But when someone came and moved it from its place, then its fragrance spreads upward.

    C.   "So said the Holy One, blessed be He, 'Abraham, many good deeds do you have to your credit, many religious duties do you have to your credit. Move yourself about from place to place, so that your name may be made great in the world: "Go out" (Gen. 12:1).'

D. "Written thereafter is the following: 'And I will make of you a great nation' (Gen. 12:2)."

3. A. "...therefore the maidens love you":

B. Said to him the Holy One, blessed be He, "Here are many worlds for you" [the words for maidens and worlds share the same consonants].

C. For it is written, "And Abram took Sarai his wife, and Lot his brother's son, and all their possessions which they had gathered, and the soul that they had made..." (Gen. 12:5).

4. A. [Supply, as at Genesis Rabbah XXXIX:XIV.1:] "And Abram took Sarai his wife, and Lot his brother's son, and all their possessions which they had gathered, and the soul that they had made..." (Gen. 12:5):

B. [Genesis Rabbah XXXIX:XIV.1 attributed the following to R. Eleazar in the name of R. Yosé b. Zimra:] "If all of the nations of the world should come together to try to create a single mosquito, they could not [put a soul into it, and yet you say, 'And the soul that they had made'?] [They could not have created souls.] But this refers to proselytes whom Abraham and Sarah had made. Therefore it is said, 'and the soul that they had made' (Gen. 12:5)."

5. A. Said R. Huniah, "Abraham converted the men and Sarah the women."

B. And what is the sense of the statement, "the souls that they had made in Haran" (Gen. 12:5)?

C. This teaches that our father, Abraham, would bring them home and feed them and give them drink and treat them with love and so draw them near and convert them and bring them under the wings of the Presence of God.

D. This serves to teach you that whoever brings a gentile close [to the worship of the true God] is as if he had created him anew. [Simon, p. 39: had created him and formed him and molded him.]

6. A. Said R. Berekhiah, "Said the Israelites before the Holy One, blessed be He, 'Lord of the world, Since you bring light to the world, your name is exalted in the world.

B. "'And what is the light? It is redemption.

C. "'For when you bring us light, many proselytes come and convert and are added to us, for instance, Jethro and Rahab.

D. "'Jethro heard and came, Rahab heard and came.'"

7. A. Said R. Hanina, "When the Holy One, blessed be He, did a miracle for Hananiah, Mishael, and Azariah, many gentiles came and converted: 'When he sees his children, the work of my hands, in the midst of them, they shall sanctify my name' (Isa. 29:23), and then, 'They also that err in spirit shall come to understanding' (Isa. 29:23)."

The base verse is enriched by a mass of material pertinent to Abraham, solely on account of No. 1. The exposition of Yohanan's reading is accomplished through the insertion of the materials of Genesis Rabbah, as indicated. No. 3 concludes the exposition of the base verse. Then No. 4 works on the materials of Gen. 12:5, and the remainder of the set expands on the theme of conversion. The focus now, however, is not conversion, but, as introduced by No. 6, God's stake in redeeming Israel to expand his own repute in the world. Accordingly, the framers have used materials in a way that serves the purpose they wish to accomplish, which is to make the point that when God saves Israel, God too is served. This material is both preserved in its free-standing condition and also made to serve the compilers' polemic.

III:v

1. A. Another interpretation of the verse, "therefore the maidens love you":
   B. It is because you gave us the spoil of Egypt, the spoil of the [Egyptian army at] the sea, the spoil of Sihon and Og, the spoil of the thirty-one kings [of Canaan] that we love you.
2. A. Another interpretation of the verse, "therefore the maidens love you":
   B. It is because you hid from them the day of death and the day of consolation that they love you [the words for "hid" and "maidens" use the same consonants].
3. A. Another interpretation of the verse, "therefore the maidens love you":
   B. It is with [Simon:] youthful energy and vigor.
4. A. Another interpretation of the verse, "therefore the maidens love you":
   B. This refers to those who repent.
5. A. Another interpretation of the verse, "therefore the maidens love you":
   B. This refers to the third group in the following: "And I will bring the third part through the fire and will refine them as silver is refined" (Zech. 13:9).
6. A. Another interpretation of the verse, "therefore the maidens love you":
   B. This refers to the proselytes: "O Lord, I have heard the report of you and am afraid, O Lord, revive your work in the midst of the years" (Hab. 3:2).
7. A. Another interpretation of the verse, "therefore the maidens love you":
   B. This refers to the generation that lived through the repression [in the time of Hadrian, after the war of Bar Kokhba]: "For your sake we are killed all day long, we are accounted as sheep for slaughter" (Ps. 44:23).
8. A. Another interpretation of the verse, "therefore the maidens love you":
   B. This refers to the Israelites: "But because the Lord loved you and because he would keep the oath" (Dt. 7:8).
9. A. Another interpretation of the verse, "therefore the maidens love you":
   B. This refers to the fact that you hid from them the reward that is coming to the righteous.

C.   For said R. Berekhiah and R. Helbo, "The Holy One, blessed be He, is going to be the lord of the dance for the righteous in the age to come.

D.   "What verse of Scripture indicates it? 'Mark well her ramparts' (Ps. 48:14). Now the word for 'ramparts' is written to be read 'dance.'

E.   "The righteous will be on one side, and the righteous on the other, and the Holy One, blessed be He will be in the middle, and they will dance before him with [Simon:] zest [which uses the same consonants as the word for 'maidens'].

F.   "And they will gesture to one another with their fingers, saying, 'For this is God, our God, for ever and ever. He will guide us eternally' (Ps. 48:15)."

G.   What is the meaning of the word translated "eternally" [which uses the same consonants as the word for 'maidens']? It means, "in two worlds he will guide us," in this world and in the world to come.

10. A.   Another interpretation of the verse, "He will guide us eternally" (Ps. 48:15):

B.   with energy and vigor.

11. A.   Another interpretation of the verse, "therefore the maidens love you":

B.   [Simon:] like those maidens of whom Scripture says, "In the midst of damsels playing upon timbrels" (Ps. 68:26).

12. A.   Another interpretation of the verse, "therefore the maidens love you":

B.   Aqilas translated, "athnasia," meaning, a world in which there is no death.

C.   And they will gesture to one another with their fingers, saying, "For this is God, our God, for ever and ever. He will guide us eternally" (Ps. 48:15)."

D.   He will guide us in two worlds: "For the Lord your God will bless you" (Dt. 15:6), and in the world to come, "And the Lord will guide you continually" (Isa. 58:11).

The second part of the base verse yields a variety of interpretations of words that use the consonants for "maidens." Not all the passages are clear, No. 1 being obscure as to origin, though clear as to intent. Nos. 2, 3 rely on the consonantal hermeneutic. Then come a variety of groups of virtuous persons, who are compared to "the maidens" who love the king, proselytes, martyrs, penitents, and the like. The intersecting verse of No. 9 accounts for the inclusion of some secondary materials, and the rest flows fairly smoothly.

4

Song of Songs Rabbah to Song of Songs 1:4

1:4 *Draw me after you, let us make haste.*
The king has brought me into his chambers.
We will exult and rejoice in you;
we will extol your love more than wine;
rightly do they love you.

IV:i

1. A. "Draw me after you, let us make haste. The king has brought me into his chambers. We will exult and rejoice in you; we will extol your love more than wine; rightly do they love you":

  B. Said R. Meir, "When the Israelites stood before Mount Sinai to receive the Torah, said to them the Holy One, blessed be He, 'Shall I really give you the Torah? Bring me good sureties [Simon: guarantors] that you will keep it, and then I shall give it to you.'

  C. "They said to him, 'Lord of the ages, our fathers are our sureties for us.'

  D. "He said to them, 'Your fathers themselves require sureties.'

  E. "To what is the matter comparable? To someone who went to borrow money from the king. He said to him, 'Bring me a surety, and I shall lend to you.'

  F. "He went and brought him a surety. He said to him, 'Your surety has to have a surety.'

  G. "He went and brought him another surety. He said to him, 'Your surety has to have a surety.'

  H. "When he had brought him yet a third surety, he said to him, 'You should know that it is on this one's account that I am lending to you.'

  I. "So when the Israelites stood to receive the Torah, he said to them, 'Shall I really give you my Torah? Bring me good sureties that you will keep it, and then I shall give it to you.'

  J. "They said to him, 'Lord of the ages, our fathers are our sureties for us.'

K.   "Said to them the Holy One, blessed be He, 'As to your fathers, I have my complaints with them.

L.   "'As to Abraham, I have my complaint against him, for he said, "How shall I know that I shall inherit it?" (Gen. 15:8).

M.   "'As to Isaac, I have my complaint against him, for he loved Esau, while I hated him: 'But Esau I hated' (Mal. 1:3).

N.   "'As to Jacob, I have my complaint against him, for he said, 'My way is hid from the Lord' (Isa. 40:27).

O.   "'Bring me good sureties, and then I shall give it to you.'

P.   "They said to him, 'Lord of the world, our prophets will be our sureties.

Q.   "He said to them, 'I have my complaints against them: 'And the shepherds transgressed against me' (Jer. 2:8); 'Your prophets have been like foxes in ruins' (Ez. 13:4).

R.   "'Bring me good sureties, and then I shall give it to you.'

S.   "They said to him, 'Lo, our children will be our sureties for us.'

T.   "Said to them the Holy One, blessed be He, 'Lo, these are certainly good sureties. On their account I shall give it to you.'

U.   "That is in line with the following verse of Scripture: 'Out of the mouth of babes and sucklings you have founded strength' (Ps. 8:3).

V.   "'Strength' bears the sole meaning of Torah: 'The Lord will give strength to his people' (Ps. 29:11).

W.   "Now when the debtor has to pay up and cannot pay, who is seized? Is it not the surety? That is in line with this verse: 'Seeing that you have forgotten the Torah of your God, I also will forget your children' (Hos. 4:6)."

X.   Said R. Aha, "'I also': it is as if I also am subject to forgetting. [God speaks:] 'Who will see in the Torah before me, "Blessed is the Lord who is to be blessed"? Is it not the youngsters?'"

Y.   [Reverting to Meir's exposition, W:] "It is on account of the weakness of the Torah among you that your children are seized: 'For your faithlessness I have smitten your children' (Jer. 2:30)."

Z.   [The printed text repeats:] "'I also': it is as if I also am subject to forgetting. [God speaks:] 'Who will see in the Torah before me, "Blessed is the Lord who is to be blessed"?'"

AA.   [Reverting to Y:] "Therefore a parent has to introduce one's child to the Torah and to educate the child in learning, so that the child will live a long time in the world: "For by me your days shall be multiplied" (Prov. 9:11).

The prevailing identification of the Song as an account of Israel at Sinai, rather than any specific materials in the base verse, account for the insertion of Meir's utterly free-standing exposition of Israel at Sinai. I do not see a single point in the exposition, inclusive of its own interpolations, at which reference is made to the base verse. Perhaps someone has supposed that "draw me after you" refers to the Torah's speaking to Israel, and the rest follows. But even that seems to me far-fetched. Here is a case in which available materials have been parachuted down for merely thematic reasons. Once we know that the

Song speaks of Israel and God, then any materials pertinent to that general theme are found suitable, and the rest follows.

IV:ii

1. A. [Supply: "Draw me after you, let us make haste]":
   B. R. Yohanan, R. Joshua b. Levi, and Rabbis:
   C. R. Yohanan said, "Because you brought us into a good and spacious land, 'after you let us make haste,' to a good land which is called 'a dwelling place.'"
   D. R. Joshua b. Levi said, "Because you have given us a good and large land which is called 'a dwelling place,' 'after you let us make haste.'"
   E. Rabbis said, "Because you have brought your Presence to dwell in our midst, since it is written, 'And let them make me a sanctuary' (Ex. 25:8), 'after you let us make haste.'"

2. A. And rabbis say further, "Because you have taken away your Presence from our midst, 'after you let us make haste.'
   B. "You should know that that is the case, for all of the sorrows that came upon them on account of the deed involving the golden calf did not bring them to mourning.
   C. "But when Moses said to them, 'For I will not go up in the midst of you' (Ex. 33:3), then forthwith, 'And when the people heard these evil tidings, they mourned' (Ex. 33:4)."

3. A. [Expanding the foregoing,] R. Simeon b. Yohai taught, "The weapon that he had given to the Israelites at Horeb, on which the Ineffable Name of God was incised, when they sinned in the deed of the golden calf, was taken away from them."
   B. How was it taken away from them?
   C. R. Aibu and rabbis:
   D. R. Aibu said, "On its own, the name peeled off."
   E. And rabbis said, "An angel descended and peeled it off."

4. A. [Continuing Simeon b. Yohai, A:] "Said the Israelites before the Holy One, blessed be He, 'Lord of the age, does a woman adorn herself for anyone other than her husband?' [We do not need any ornament any more now that you have left us.]"

5. A. Said R. Joshua b. Levi, "The Israelites greatly desired the Presence of God:
   B. "'[Awake, O north wind, and come, O south wind! Blow upon my garden, let its fragrance be wafted abroad.] Let my beloved come to his garden, [and eat its choicest fruits]' (Song 4:16).
   C. "'...to his garden': 'to his bridal chamber.'"

The exposition of the base verse takes for granted that the subject is Israel's "making haste" after God. No. 1 deals with the land, and, reversing the ground of exposition, No. 2 deals with God's removing his Presence from Israel on account of the golden calf. It was the loss of God's Presence that made the Israelites mourn. No. 4 reverts to No. 2 (though that is hardly a required reading of the matter). No. 5, which serves Song 4:16, is parachuted down because it deals with the theme of

No. 2, which is how much Israel appreciated God's presence. But the passage clearly belongs elsewhere.

IV:iii
1. A.   [Supply: "Draw me after you, let us make haste":]
    B.   R. Yudan and R. Azariah:
    C.   R. Yudan said, "Said the Congregation of Israel before the Holy One, blessed be He, 'Because you have treated my neighbors [a word that uses the same consonants as 'draw me'] in accord with the strict requirements of justice, and me in accord with the requirements of mercy, 'after you, let us make haste.'"

2. A.   For said R. Berekhiah in the name of R. Eleazar, "[Genesis Rabbah XXVIII:V.1:] "From the face of the ground" (Gen. 6:7), Said R. Abba bar Kahana,] "What was done by the ten tribes was not done by the generation of the Flood.
    B.   "With respect to the generation of the Flood, it is written, 'And every imagination of the thoughts of his heart was only evil all day' (Gen. 6:5).
    C.   "With regard to the ten tribes: 'Woe to them that devise iniquity and work evil upon their beds' (Mic. 2:1) which is to say, even by night. And how do we know that they did it by day as well? 'When the morning is light, they execute it' (Mic. 2:1).
    D.   "Nonetheless, of those [of the generation of the Flood] not a remnant was left, while of these [the ten tribes] a remnant was left.
    E.   [Genesis Rabbah XXVIII:V.1:] "It was on account of the merit of the righteous men and righteous women who were destined to emerge from [the ten tribes that a remnant was spared].
    F.   [Genesis Rabbah XXVIII:V.1:] "That is in line with this verse: 'And behold there shall be left a remnant therein that shall be brought forth, both sons and daughters' (Ez. 14:22), that is, on account of the merit of the righteous men and righteous women, the men and women prophets, who were destined to emerge from [the ten tribes a remnant was spared]."

3. A.   Said R. Hanina, "Things were said concerning the cities of the sea that were not said concerning the generation of the Flood: 'Woe to the inhabitants of the seacoast, the nation of the Cherethites' (Zeph. 2:5), indicating by their name [consonants that bear the meaning of extirpation] that they were suitable to be annihilated.
    B.   [Genesis Rabbah XXVIII:V.1:] "On account of what merit do they endure? It is on account of the merit of a singular gentile, who fears heaven, that the Holy One, blessed be He, receives from their hand [that he spares them while having destroyed Sodom and the generation of the Flood]. [There are some good among them.]"
    C.   [Genesis Rabbah XXVIII:V.1:] "The nation of the Cherethites" (Zeph. 2:5): Some explain the name in a positive sense, that is," a nation that enters into a covenant [with God]."
    D.   [Genesis Rabbah XXVIII:V.1:] R. Levi interpreted the verse to speak in a favorable sense: "'Woe to the inhabitants of the seacoast, the nation of the Cherethites' (Zeph. 2:5)': 'Woe to the

nation that has made a covenant,' in line with this usage: 'and made a covenant with him' (Neh. 9:8)."

4. A. R. Joshua b. R. Nehemiah in the name of R. Aha said, "What was said concerning the tribes of Judah and Benjamin was never said concerning Sodom.

B. "In respect to Sodom, it is written, 'And yes, their sin is exceedingly grievous' (Gen. 18:20), but with regard to the tribes of Judah and Benjamin: 'The iniquity of the house of Israel and Judah is *most* exceedingly great' (Ez. 9:9).

C. [Gen. R. continues:] "Nonetheless, of those [of the generation of the Flood] not a remnant was left, while of these [the two tribes] a remnant was left.

D. [Gen. R. continues:] "As to Sodom, 'that was overthrown in a moment' (Lam. 4:6), they never put forth their hands to carry out religious duties, 'Hands therein accepted no duties' (Lam. 4:6), in the line with what R. Tanhuma said, 'No hand joined another hand [to help one another.' [The people did not help one another to carry out their religious duties.]

E. [Gen. R. continues:] "But in regard to the others [of Judah and Benjamin], they extended hands to one another in carrying out religious duties: 'The hands of women full of compassion have sodden their own children and provided the mourner's meal' (Lam. 4:10)."

F. R. Tanhuma said, "We have yet another verse of Scripture in this matter: 'For the iniquity of the daughter of my people is greater than the sin of Sodom' (Lam. 4:6)."

G. Said R. Tanhuma, "They did not assist one another; they did not put out their hands to carry out their religious obligations; but these put out their hands to carry out their religious obligations: 'The hands of women full of compassion' (Lam. 4:6).

H. "Why so? 'So that 'they should have food in the destruction of the daughter of my people' (Lam. 4:6)."

5. A. [As to the verse, "Draw me after you, let us make haste":] said R. Azariah, "Said the Congregation of Israel before the Holy One, blessed be He, 'Because you have given me the spoil of my neighbors, 'after you let us make haste.'

B. "For it is said, 'But every woman shall ask of her neighbor' (Ex. 11:2).

C. "'It is because you gave us the spoil of Egypt, the spoil of the [Egyptian army at] the sea, the spoil of Sihon and Og, the spoil of the thirty-one kings [of Canaan] that 'after you let us make haste.'"

6. A. Another explanation of the verse, "Draw me after you, let us make haste":

B. "We shall make haste because you have incited against me my wicked neighbors."

C. Said R. Abun, "It is comparable to the case of a king who was angry with a royal lady, and so aroused against her her wicked neighbors.

D. "She began to cry out, 'My lord, King, save me.'

	E.	"So the Israelites: 'The Zidonians also and the Amalekites and the Maonites did oppress you, and you cried to me and I saved you out of their hand' (Judges 10:12)."
7.	A.	Another explanation of the verse, "Draw me after you, let us make haste":
	B.	"Endanger me, and 'after you let us make haste.'"
8.	A.	Another explanation of the verse, "Draw me after you, let us make haste":
	B.	Impoverish me and "after you, let us make haste."
	C.	That is in line with what R. Aha said, "When a Jew has to eat carobs, he repents."
	D.	That is also in line with what R. Aqiba says, "Poverty is as appropriate to a daughter of Jacob as a red streak on the neck of a white horse."
9.	A.	Another explanation of the verse, "Draw me after you, let us make haste":
	B.	"Take a pledge from me, and 'after you, let us make haste.'
	C.	"For the great pledge that you have taken from me, 'after you, let us make haste.'"
	D.	That is in line with what R. Menahema said in the name of R. Yohanan, "It is written, 'We have given a pledge to you' (Neh. 1:7):
	E.	"This refers to the first catastrophe [the destruction of the first Temple] and the second catastrophe.
	F.	"For these have been taken as pledges only on our account."
10.	A.	R. Berekhiah in the name of R. Judah b. R. Ilai: "It is written, 'And Moses led Israel onward from the Red Sea' (Ex. 15:22):
	B.	"He led them on from the sin committed at the sea.
	C.	"They said to him, 'Moses, our lord, where are you leading us?'
	D.	"He said to them, 'To Elim, from Elim to Alush, from Alush to Marah, from Marah to Rephidim, from Rephidim to Sinai.'
	E.	"They said to him, 'Indeed, wherever you go and lead us, we are with you.'
	F.	"The matter is comparable to the case of one who went and married a woman from a village. He said to her, 'Arise and come with me.'
	G.	"She said to him, 'From here to where?'
	H.	"He said to her, 'From here to Tiberias, from Tiberias to the Tannery, from the Tannery to the Upper Market, from the Upper Market to the Lower Market.'
	I.	"She said to him, 'Wherever you go and take me, I shall go with you.'
	J.	"So said the Israelites, 'My soul cleaves to you' (Ps. 63:9)."
	K.	Said R. Yosé b. R. Iqa, "And lo, a verse of Scripture itself proclaims the same point: 'Draw me, after you let us make haste.'
	L.	"If it is from one verse of Scripture to another verse of Scripture, if it is from one passage of the Mishnah to another passage of the Mishnah, if it is from one passage of the Talmud to another passage of the Talmud, if it is from one passage of the Tosefta to another passage of the Tosefta, if it is from one aspect of narrative to another aspect of narrative."

Nos. 2-4 are parachuted in; they serve Genesis Rabbah quite well, and serve no purpose here at all. The principal effect of Nos. 2-4 scarcely comes to articulation. It is to link the story of the generation of the Flood to the history of Israel later on. Once the one is brought into juxtaposition with, and compared to, the other, the whole link into a single sustained picture. The composition is somewhat disjointed, in that it deals with both Sodom and the generation of the Flood. But the point made out of diverse cases serves a single polemic. Where you can point to God's sparing generations apparently as wicked as the one(s) whom God destroyed, whether the generation of the Flood or Sodom, there is a reason. God recognized the merit of one or another, but found no merit in the generation of the Flood. What is explained in the base verse, therefore, is the statement that God destroyed the generation of the flood "from the face of the earth," thus leaving no remnant. Then those who survived, even as a remnant, have to be compared to those who did not survive, and the rest follows. Here too the composite draws together materials on a variety of subjects, but all of them serve to make a single point. No. 5 reverts to the original program. Nos. 5 ff. work on the fact that the word for "draw me" and "neighbors" share the same consonants. No. 10 moves on to the shared meaning, already exploited, "take a pledge."

IV:iv
1. A.   "The king has brought me into his chambers":
   B.   We have learned in Tannaite tradition:
   C.   Four entered paradise: Ben Azzai and Ben Zoma, Elisha b. Abuyah and R. Aqiba.
   D.   Ben Azzai gazed and was afflicted: "Have you found honey? Eat so much as is enough for you" (Prov. 25:16).
   E.   Ben Zoma gazed and died, and concerning him it is said in Scripture, "Precious in the sight of the Lord is the death of his saints" (Ps. 116:15).
   F.   Elisha ben Abbuya made cuttings among the plantings.
2. A.   How did he make cuttings among the plantings?
   B.   When he would enter synagogues and school houses and see youngsters succeeding in the Torah, he would say about them a word, and they would be stopped.
   C.   In his regard it is said in Scripture, "Do not let your mouth bring your flesh into guilt" (Qoh. 5:5).
3. A.   [Continuing 1.E:] R. Aqiba went in whole and came out whole.
   B.   And he said, "It is not because I am greater than my colleagues, but this have sages taught in the Mishnah:
   C.   "'Your deeds will draw you near, or your deeds will put you out' [M. Ed. 5:7]."
   D.   And in his regard it is said in Scripture, "The king has brought me into his chambers."

4. A.   R. Yannai said, "The Torah had to be expounded only from the passage, 'This month shall be to you' (Ex. 12:2) [at which point the laws commence].

   B.   "And on what account did the Holy One, blessed be He, reveal to Israel what was on the first day and what was on the second, on to the sixth? It was by reason of the merit gained when they said, 'All that the Lord has spoken we shall do and we shall obey' (Ex. 24:7).

   C.   "Forthwith the rest was revealed to them."

5. A.   R. Berekhiah said, "It is written, 'And he told you his covenant [which he commanded you to perform, even the ten words]' (Dt. 4:13).

   B.   "[Since the word for covenant and the word for creation contained the same letters, it is to be interpreted:] 'And he told you his book of Genesis, which is the beginning of the creation of the world.'

   C.   "'which he commanded you to perform, even the ten words' (Dt. 4:13): this refers to the Ten Commandments.

   D.   "Ten for Scripture, ten for Talmud."

6. A.   And whence was Elihu son of Barachel the Buzite to come and reveal to the Israelites the innermost mysteries of Behemoth and Leviathan,

   B.   and whence was Ezekiel to come and reveal to them the innermost secrets of the divine chariot?

   C.   But that is in line with the following verse of Scripture: "The king has brought me into his chambers."

The inclusion of the whole of Nos. 1-3 is accounted for at 3.D. The pertinent prooftext being the one at hand, the compilers had no reason to omit the entire composition, even though at no point is a point pertinent to our passage as sages read it made to register. No. 4 then continues the general theme of finding out things one did not have to know, which is on account of merit attained in one way or another. That is tacked on, I think, because of Aqiba's allegation. The rest pursue that same theme, and No. 6 confirms the compilers' program.

IV:v

1. A.   "We will exult and rejoice in you":

   B.   The Israelites are described with ten expressions of joy:

   C.   [Simon:] rejoicing, joy, gladness, song, breaking forth, crying aloud, exultation, great rejoicing, gaiety, and shouting.

   D.   rejoicing: "Rejoice greatly, O daughter of Zion" (Zech. 9:9).

   E.   joy: "I will greatly rejoice in the Lord" (Isa. 61:10).

   F.   gladness: "Be glad with Jerusalem" (Isa. 66:10).

   G.   song: "Sing and rejoice, O daughter of Zion" (Zech. 2:14).

   H.   breaking forth: "Break forth into singing and cry aloud" (Isa. 54:1).

   I.   crying aloud: "Cry aloud and shout" (Isa. 12:6).

   J.   exultation: "My heart exults in the Lord" (1 Sam. 2:1).

   K.   great rejoicing: My heart greatly rejoices and with my soul I will praise him" (Ps. 28:7).

   L.   gaiety: "And the children of Israel kept the dedication with gaiety" (Ezra 6:16).

	M.	And shouting: "Shout to the Lord all the earth": (Ps. 98:4).
	N.	Some exclude shouting and include dancing: "Dismay dances before him" (Job 41:14),
	O.	[Simon] leaping like a stranded fish.
2.	A.	Another interpretation of the verse, "We will exult and rejoice in you":
	B.	There we have learned on Tannaite authority: If one has married a woman and lived with her for ten years and not produced offspring, he has not got the right to stop trying.
	C.	Said R. Idi, "There was the case of a woman in Sidon, who lived with her husband for ten years and did not produce offspring.
	D.	They came before R. Simeon b. Yohai and wanted to be parted from one another.
	E.	He said to them, "By your lives! Just as you were joined to one another with eating and drinking, so you will separate from one another only with eating and drinking."
	F.	They followed his counsel and made themselves a festival and made a great banquet and drank too much.
	G.	When his mind was at ease, he said to her, "My daughter, see anything good that I have in the house! Take it and go to your father's house!"
	H.	What did she do? After he fell asleep, she made gestures to her servants and serving women and said to them, "Take him in the bed and pick him up and bring him to my father's house."
	I.	Around midnight he woke up from his sleep. When the wine wore off, he said to her, "My daughter, where am I now?"
	J.	She said to him, "In my father's house."
	K.	He said to her, "What am I doing in your father's house?"
	L.	She said to him, "Did you not say to me last night, 'See anything good that I have in the house! Take it and go to your father's house!' But I have nothing in the world so good as you!"
	M.	They went to R. Simeon b. Yohai, and he stood and prayed for them, and they were answered [and given offspring].
	N.	This serves to teach you that just as the Holy One, blessed be He, answers the prayers of barren women, so righteous persons have the power to answer the prayers of barren women.
	O.	And does this not yield a proposition a fortiori: if a mortal person, on account of saying to another mortal, "I have nothing in the world so good as you!" has prayers answered, the Israelites, who every single day await the salvation of the Holy One, blessed be He, saying, "We have nothing in the world so good as you!" – how much the more so
	P.	Thus":We will exult and rejoice in you."
3.	A.	The matter [of the situation of the Israelites] may be compared to the case of a noble lady, whose husband, the king, and whose sons and sons-in-law went overseas. They came and told her, "Your sons are coming home."
	B.	She said, "What difference does it make to me? Let my daughters-in-law rejoice."
	C.	When her sons-in-law came home, they said to her, "Your sons-in-law are coming."

D.   So she said, "What difference does it make to me? Let my daughters rejoice."

E.   When they told her, "The king, your husband, is coming," she said, "This is the occasion for whole-hearted rejoicing, waves upon waves of joy!"

F.   So in the age to come the prophets will come and say to Jerusalem, "Your sons come from afar" (Isa. 60:4), and she will say, "What difference does that make to me?"

G.   And when they say, "And your daughters are borne on the side" (Isa. 60:4), she will say, "What difference does that make to me?"

H.   But when they said to her, "Lo, your king comes to you, he is triumphant and victorious" Zech. 9:9), she will say, "This is the occasion for whole-hearted rejoicing!"

I.   For so it is written, "Rejoice greatly, O daughter of Zion" (Zech. 9:9); "Sing and rejoice, O daughter of Zion" (Zech. 2:14).

J.   Then she will say, "I will greatly rejoice in the Lord, my soul shall be joyful in my God" (Isa. 61:10).

The point of No. 1 is self-evident and has no bearing upon the base verse, except that two of the ten expressions of joy occur in the base verse. No. 2 is free-standing, drawing back to our base verse only at P; without the allusion to the base verse the point is perfectly well portrayed. No. 3 is another free-standing item, justifiably included because of the theme of rejoicing with the king.

IV:vi

1. A.   Another interpretation of the verse, "We will exult and rejoice in you; [we will extol your love more than wine; rightly do they love you]":

B.   R. Abin commenced discourse by citing the following verse of Scripture: "This is the day that the Lord has made. We will rejoice and be glad in it" (Ps. 118:24).

C.   Said R. Abin, "We do not know in what to rejoice [since "in it" may be read "in him"], whether in the day or in the Holy One, blessed be He.

D.   "Came Solomon and spelled the matter out: 'We will exult and rejoice in you' – in the Holy One, blessed be He.

E.   "'...in you': in your salvation.

F.   "'...in you': in your Torah.

G.   "'...in you': in reverence for you."

2. A.   Said R. Isaac, "[Supply: We will exult and rejoice in you':]

B.   "'...in you': in the twenty-two letters [the numerical value of the word 'in you' being twenty-two] which you wrote for us in the Torah,

C.   "for the B is two, the K [of the Hebrew word 'in you'] stands for twenty, hence twenty-two."

We have what at the head of the matter would have been classified as a *petihta*, that is, an intersecting-verse/base-verse composition; the intersecting verse is particularly well-chosen, as we see, because it requires the clarification of the base verse. No. 2 is tacked on for valid reasons.

IV:vii
1. A.   "...we will extol your love more than wine; [rightly do they love you]":
   B.   More than the wine of the Torah:
   C.   for instance, the laws of Passover on Passover, the laws of Pentecost on Pentecost, the laws of the Festival [of Tabernacles] on the Festival.
2. A.   Another matter concerning the verse, "we will extol your love more than wine; [rightly do they love you]":
   B.   more than the wine of the patriarchs:
   C.   The first Man – what did he do before you?
   D.   Who did deeds before you like Abraham?
   E.   Who did deeds before you like Isaac?
   F.   Who did deeds before you like Jacob? [Simon, p. 50, n. 4: "We will make mention of the love the Patriarchs bore for you; then their merit will stand us in good stead too."]

The glosses of Nos. 1, 2 expand on how "your love" is to be extolled more than wine, and the rest follows. No. 2 seems to me to require the sense, "the love we have for you...." Then the several cases make sense.

IV:viii
1. A.   "...rightly do they love you":
   B.   How upright is their love for you!
   C.   How powerful is their love for you!
2. A.   Said R. Aibi, "With formidable right did our patriarchs act before you in everything that they did."
3. A.   Said R. Hanin, "'Because you have done this thing' (Gen. 22:16):
   B.   "This was the tenth trial, and you call it merely 'a thing'?
   C.   "Lo, if he had not accepted that thing, he would have lost and been deprived of [the merit of] all the earlier deeds.
   D.   "Thus: 'rightly do they love you.'"

The glosses at Nos. 1, 2 seem to me mere amplifications. No. 3 without D is perfectly clear, and the addition of 3.D is merely editorial; but it adds to the meaning of the foregoing the judgment that this is what sincere love requires.

5

Song of Songs Rabbah to Song of Songs 1:5

1:5   *I am very dark, but comely,*
O daughters of Jerusalem,
like the tents of Kedar,
like the curtains of Solomon.

V:i

1. A. "I am very dark, but comely, [O daughters of Jerusalem, like the tents of Kedar, like the curtains of Solomon]" (Song 1:5):

     B. "I am dark" in my deeds.

     C. "But comely" in the deeds of my forebears.

2. A. "I am very dark, but comely":

     B. Said the Community of Israel, "'I am dark' in my view, 'but comely' before my Creator."

     C. For it is written, "Are you not as the children of the Ethiopians to Me, O children of Israel, says the Lord" (Amos 9:7):

     D. "as the children of the Ethiopians" – in your sight.

     E. But "to Me, O children of Israel, says the Lord."

3. A. Another interpretation of the verse, "I am very dark": in Egypt.

     B. "...but comely": in Egypt.

     C. "I am very dark" in Egypt: "But they rebelled against me and would not hearken to me" (Ez. 20:8).

     D. "...but comely" in Egypt: with the blood of the Passover-offering and circumcision, "And when I passed by you and saw you wallowing in your blood, I said to you, In your blood live" Ez. 16:6) – in the blood of the Passover.

     E. "I said to you, In your blood live" Ez. 16:6) – in the blood of the circumcision.

4. A. Another interpretation of the verse, "I am very dark": at the sea, "They were rebellious at the sea, even the Red Sea" (Ps. 106:7).

     B. "...but comely": at the sea, "This is my God and I will be comely for him" (Ex. 15:2) [following Simon's rendering of the verse].

5. A. "I am very dark": at Marah, "And the people murmured against Moses, saying, What shall we drink" Ex. 15:24).

	B.	"...but comely": at Marah, "And he cried to the Lord and the Lord showed him a tree, and he cast it into the waters and the waters were made sweet" (Ex. 15:25).
6.	A.	"I am very dark": at Rephidim, "And the name of the place was called Massah and Meribah" (Ex. 17:7).
	B.	"...but comely": at Rephidim, "And Moses built an altar and called it by the name 'the Lord is my banner' (Ex. 17:15).
7.	A.	"I am very dark": at Horeb, "And they made a calf at Horeb" (Ps. 106:19).
	B.	"...but comely": at Horeb, "And they said, All that the Lord has spoken we will do and obey" (Ex. 24:7).
8.	A.	"I am very dark": in the wilderness, ""How often did they rebel against him in the wilderness" (Ps. 78:40).
	B.	"...but comely": in the wilderness at the setting up of the tabernacle, "And on the day that the tabernacle was set up" (Num. 9:15).
9.	A.	"I am very dark": in the deed of the spies, "And they spread an evil report of the land" (Num. 13:32).
	B.	"...but comely": in the deed of Joshua and Caleb, "Save for Caleb, the son of Jephunneh the Kenizzite" (Num. 32:12).
10.	A.	"I am very dark": at Shittim, "And Israel abode at Shittim and the people began to commit harlotry with the daughters of Moab" (Num. 25:1).
	B.	"...but comely": at Shittim, "Then arose Phinehas and wrought judgment" (Ps. 106:30).
11.	A.	"I am very dark": through Achan, "But the children of Israel committed a trespass concerning the devoted thing" (Josh. 7:1).
	B.	"...but comely": through Joshua, "And Joshua said to Achan, My son, give I pray you glory" (Josh. 7:19).
12.	A.	"I am very dark": through the kings of Israel.
	B.	"...but comely": through the kings of Judah.
	C.	If with my dark ones that I had, it was such that "I am comely," all the more so with my prophets.

The contrast of dark and comely yields a variety of applications; in all of them the same situation that is the one also is the other, and the rest follows in a wonderfully well-crafted composition.

V:ii

1.	A.	"I am very dark":
	B.	Scripture speaks of Ahab: "And it came to pass when Ahab heard those words that he tore his clothing and put sackcloth upon his flesh and fasted and went softly" (1 Kgs. 21:27).
2.	A.	How long did he afflict himself?
	B.	R. Joshua b. Levi said, "For three hours. If he was accustomed to eat his meal at the third hour of the day, he ate it at the sixth, and if he was accustomed to eat at the sixth, he ate at the ninth."
3.	A.	And he lay in sackcloth and went softly" (1 Kgs. 21:27):
	B.	R. Joshua b. Levi said, "He went barefoot."
4.	A.	As to Jehorum, what is written?

B.   "And the people look, and behold, he had sackcloth within, upon his flesh" (1 Kgs. 6:30):

5. A.   [As to the verse, "I am very dark, but comely," R. Levi b. R. Haita gave three interpretations:
    B.   "'I am very dark': all the days of the week.
    C.   "'...but comely': on the Sabbath.
    D.   "'I am very dark': all the days of the year.
    E.   "'...but comely': on the Day of Atonement.
    F.   "'I am very dark': among the Ten Tribes.
    G.   "'...but comely': in the tribe of Judah and Benjamin.
    H.   "'I am very dark': in this world.
    I.   "'...but comely': in the world to come."

Once the verse is made to refer to Ahab, the pertinent verse on Ahab is not only cited but itself spelled out, thus Nos. 1-4. No. 5 then resumes the pattern of the opening composition.

V:iii

1. A.   "O daughters of Jerusalem":
    B.   Rabbis say, "Do not read the letters that spell out "daughters of Jerusalem" as given, but rather, as "builders of Jerusalem" [since the same consonants can yield that other reading].
    C.   This refers to the great sanhedrin of Israel, which goes into session and clarifies every question and matter of judgment. ["Builders" and "clarify" have the same consonants.]

2. A.   Another interpretation of the phrase, "O daughters of Jerusalem":
    B.   Said R. Yohanan, "Jerusalem is destined to be made the metropolitan capital of all cities and [Simon:] draw people to her in streams to do her honor.
    C.   "That is in line with the following passage of Scripture: 'Ashdod, its towns [using the letters that spell out the word for daughters] and villages, Gaza, its towns and its villages until Lesha' (Josh. 15:47)."
    D.   That is the view, then, of R. Yohanan.
    E.   For R. Yohanan said, "It is written, 'I will give them to you for daughters, but not because of your covenant' (Ez. 16:61).
    F.   "What is the sense of 'daughters'? It means towns.
    G.   "What is the sense of, 'but not because of your covenant'? 'Not on account of your contract, but as a gift from me.'"

3. A.   R. Bibi in the name of R. Reuben said, "'Sing, O barren one' (Isa. 54:1).
    B.   "Now is there a song to celebrate barrenness?
    C.   "But 'sing O barren one' for you have not born children for Gehenna."

4. A.   R. Berekhiah in the name of R. Samuel b. R. Nahman said, "The Israelites are compared to a woman.
    B.   "Just as an unmarried women receives a tenth part of the property of her father and takes her leave [for her husband's house when she gets married], so the Israelites inherited the land of the seven peoples, who form a tenth part of the seventy nations of the world.
    C.   "And because the Israelites inherited in the status of a woman, they said a song in the feminine form of that word, as in the

following: 'Then sang Moses and the children of Israel this song [given in the feminine form] unto the Lord' (Ex. 15:1).

D. "But in the age to come they are destined to inherit like a man, who inherits all of the property of his father.

E. "That is in line with this verse of Scripture: 'From the east side to the west side: Judah, one portion...Dan one, Asher one...' (Ez. 48:7), and so throughout.

F. "Then they will say a song in the masculine form of that word, as in the following: 'Sing to the Lord a new song' (Ps. 96:1).

G. "The word 'song' is given not in its feminine form but in its masculine form."

5. A. R. Berekiah and R. Joshua b. Levi: "Why are the Israelites compared to a woman?

B. "Just as a woman takes up a burden and puts it down [that is, becomes pregnant and gives birth], takes up a burden and puts it down, then takes up a burden and puts it down and then takes up no further burden,

C. "so the Israelites are subjugated and then redeemed, subjugated and then redeemed, but in the end are redeemed and will never again be subjugated.

D. "In this world, since their anguish is like the anguish of a woman in childbirth, they say the song before him using the feminine form of the word for song,

E. "but in the age to come, because their anguish will no longer be the anguish of a woman in childbirth, they will say their song using the masculine form of the word for song:

F. "'In that day this song [in the masculine form of the word] will be sung' (Isa. 26:1)."

No. 1 stands all by itself in its reading of "daughters of Jerusalem." No. 2 is likewise free-standing. The remainder address the femininity of Israel in this world in contrast to its masculinity in the world to come. No. 3 sets the stage, though it seems to me not to require what follows. Nos. 4, 5 fully exploit the possibilities of the comparison. My sense is that Solomon's address to the daughters of Jerusalem in particular is what has persuaded the compilers of the appropriate of these materials.

V:iv

1. A. "...like the tents of Kedar, [like the curtains of Solomon]" (Song 1:5):

B. Just as the tents of Kedar, while they appear from the outside to be ugly, black, and tattered, on the inside are made up of precious stones and pearls,

C. so disciples of sages, while they appear in this world to be ugly and black, inside they contain Torah, Scripture, Mishnah, Midrash, laws, Talmud, Tosefta, and lore.

D. Might one say just as the tents of Kedar do not need to be cleaned, so is the case with Israel?

E. Scripture says, "like the curtains of Solomon."

F.   Just as the curtains of Solomon get dirty and are cleaned and then get dirty and are cleaned again, so the Israelites, even though they are dirty with sins all the days of the year, the Day of Atonement comes and makes atonement for them:

G.   "For on this day shall atonement be made for you, to cleanse you" (Lev 16:30); "Though your sins be as scarlet, they shall be white as snow" (Isa. 1:18).

H.   Might one say just as tents of Kedar are moved about from place to place, so is the case with Israel?

I.   Scripture says, "like the curtains of Solomon."

J.   They are like the tents of Him to whom peace belongs, the One at whose word the world came into being,

K.   for from the moment that he stretched [his tents] forth, they never again moved from their place.

2.   A.   R. Eliezer b. Jacob taught on Tannaite authority, "A tent that shall not be removed' (Isa. 33:20):

B.   "the word for 'removed' means, shall not go forth and shall not stir."

3.   A.   Just as in the case of the tents of Kedar, the yoke of no creature is upon them,

B.   so in the case of the Israelites in the age to come, the yoke of no creature will be upon them.

4.   A.   R. Hiyya taught on Tannaite authority, "'And I made you go upright' (Lev. 26:13):

C.   "'upright' means standing erect, fearful of no creature."

5.   A.   R. Yudan said, "[Israel] is like Joseph:

B.   "Just as Joseph was sold to the tents of Kedar, 'And they sold Joseph to the Ishmaelites' (Gen. 37:28), and afterward bought those who had bought him, 'So Joseph bought all the land of Egypt' (Gen. 47:20),

C.   "so the Israelites, 'will take their captors captive' (Isa. 14:2)."

The exposition of the double metaphor, "tents of Kedar, curtains of Solomon," once more appeals to the metaphor to clarity the traits of Israel. The set of No. 1 breaks at D, since the initial comparison is only to disciples of sages, while the continuation moves directly to Israel as a whole. But I think the rhetoric of D and beyond requires us to read No. 1 as a sustained and unitary statement, as I have presented it. But someone who wishes to treat 1.Dff. as a separate entry certainly has good reason to do so. It seems to me that No. 2 is inserted simply because it refers to "tent," but there is no continuity between No. 2 and No. 3. Then No. 3 carries forward the method and thought of No. 1. No. 4 is tacked on because it has the same conception as No. 3, and No. 5 for essentially the same reason. So a single conception, the one of No. 1, with stress upon the freedom of the Israelites in the age to come, holds the whole together (so far as the composition is more than a composite to begin with).

6

Song of Songs Rabbah to Song of Songs 1:6

1:6   *Do not gaze at me because I am swarthy,*
        because the sun has scorched me.
        My mother's sons were angry with me,
        they made me keeper of the vineyards;
        but my own vineyard I have not kept!

VI:i

1. A.   "Do not gaze at me because I am swarthy":
    B.   R. Simon commenced discourse by citing the following verse of Scripture: "'Do not slander a servant to his master' (Prov. 30:10).
    C.   "The Israelites are called servants: 'For to me the children of Israel are servants' (Lev. 25:55).
    D.   "The prophets are called servants: 'But he reveals his counsel to his servants the prophets' (Amos 3:7).
    E.   "Thus said the Community of Israel to the prophets, '"Do not gaze at me because I am swarthy."
    F.   "'None among my sons rejoiced more than Moses, but because he said, "Listen, please, you rebels" (Num. 20:10), he suffered the decree not to enter the land.'"

2. A.   Another interpretation: "'None among my sons rejoiced more than Isaiah, but because he said, "And I dwell in the midst of a people of unclean lips" (Num. 6:5), God said to him, "Isaiah, you can say of yourself, "Because I am a man of unclean lips" (Isa. 6:5), but can you say, "And in the midst of a people of unclean lips I dwell" (Isa. 6:5)?'
    B.   "Note what is written there: 'Then flew to me one of the seraphim with a glowing stone in his hand' (Isa. 6:6)."

3. A.   [Supply: "Then flew to me one of the seraphim with a glowing stone in his hand" (Isa. 6:6):]
    B.   [As to the meaning of the word for glowing stone, since its consonants may be read differently,] said R. Samuel, "The word for glowing stone yields the meaning, break the mouth.
    C.   "'...break the mouth' of the one who has defamed my children."

4. A. Along these same lines:
    B. It is written concerning Elijah, "And he said, I have been very jealous for the Lord, the god of hosts, for the children of Israel have forsaken your covenant" (1 Kgs. 19:14).
    C. Said to him the Holy One, blessed be He, "'...my covenant,' yes, but it is 'your covenant'?"
    D. "They have thrown down your altars" (1 Kgs. 19:14).
    E. He said to him, "They are my altars, are they your altars?"
    F. "They have slain your prophets with the sword" (1 Kgs. 19:14).
    G. He said to him, "They are my prophets, are they your prophets? What business is it of yours!"
    H. "And I, even I alone am left, and they seek my life to take it away" (1 Kgs. 19:14).
    I. Note what is written there: "And he looked and behold there was at his head a cake baked on hot stones" (1 Kgs. 19:6).
5. A. What is the meaning of "hot stones"?
    B. [As to the meaning of the word for hot stones, since its consonants may be read differently,] said R. Samuel, "The word for hot stone yields the meaning, break the mouth.
    C. "'...break the mouth' of the one who has defamed my children."
6. A. R. Yohanan derives the same proposition from the following:
    B. "'The burden of Damascus. Behold Damascus...the cities of Aroer are forsaken' (Isa. 17:1, 2)."
7. A. How come this one deals with Damascus but makes mention of Aroer?
    B. Is not Aroer in the boundaries of Moab?
    C. Now in Damascus were three hundred sixty five temples of idolatry, corresponding to the days of the solar year, and they would worship each one on its day, and they had one day on which all of them would be worshipped at once.
    D. And the Israelites made of all of them a single entity and worshipped them: "And the children of Israel continued to do that which was evil in the sight of the Lord and served the Baalim and the Ashtarot and the gods of Aram and Nidon and Moab" (Judges 10:6). [Simon, p. 57, n. 1: Thus Aram (Damascus) and Moab (Aroer) are mentioned together and for that reason they are coupled in the present verse too.]"
8. A. [Continuing 6.B:] "Now at that moment at which Elijah spoke ill of the Israelites, the Holy One, blessed be He, said to him, 'Elijah, instead of accusing these, come and accuse those!'
    B. "That is in line with this verse: 'Go, return on your way to the wilderness of Damascus' (1 Kgs. 19:15)."
9. A. R. Abbahu and R. Simeon b. Laqish were going to enter the city of Caesarea. Said R. Abbahu to R. Simeon b. Laqish, "How can we go into a city full of cursing and blaspheming?"
    B. R. Simeon b. Laqish got off his ass, took some dirt, and put it into the mouth [of Abbahu].
    C. [Abbahu] said to him, "What's going on?"
    D. [Simeon b. Laqish] said to him, "The Holy One, blessed be He, does not take pleasure in one who defames Israel."

The speaker is still Israel, and she has been defamed, and that yields the repeated insistence that those who speak ill of the people, Israel, suffer punishment. This point is provoked by the opening proposition, No. 1, and the rest spells it all out, so if the indicated units are free-standing, then the compilers have done a fine job of joining discrete materials in making the point that they wanted to make.

VI:ii

1. A. "...because the sun has scorched me":
   B. Said R. Abba b. R. Kahana in the name of R. Hiyya the Elder, "It is written, 'Said R. Abba b. R. Kahana in the name of R. Hiyya the Elder, "It is written, 'For my people have committed two evils' (Jer. 2:13).
   C. "Lo, they neglected many.
   D. "This teaches that they did one that was as bad as two.
   E. "For they worship an idol and turn their backsides toward the house of the sanctuary: 'And he brought me into the inner court of the Lord's house and behold...twenty-five men with their backs toward the Temple of the Lord...and they bowed down toward the sun, toward the east' (Ez. 8:16).
   F. "The use of 'bow down' is the same as in the passage, 'Because their corruption [using some of the same consonants] is in them, there is a blemish in them' (Lev. 22:25)."
2. A. Another interpretation of the verse, "because the sun has scorched me":
   B. It is because I [Simon:] kept stables of horses for the sun:
   C. "And he took away the horses that the kings of Judah had given to the sun at the entrance of the house of the Lord" (2 Kgs. 23:11).
3. A. [Supply: "because the sun has scorched me":]
   B. R. Isaac interpreted the verse to speak of the wars of Midian:
   C. "You find that when the Israelites went to war against Midian, then went in in pairs to a woman. One of them would blacken her face, the other stripped her of her jewelry [to make her repulsive and so prevent themselves from having sexual relations with her].
   D. "But she would say to them, 'Are we too not among the creatures of the Holy One, blessed be He, that you treat us in such a way!'
   E. "And the Israelites would reply, 'Is it not enough for you that we got what was coming to us through you? 'And the Lord said to Moses, Take all the chiefs of the people and hang them up to the Lord in the face of the sun' (Num. 25:4)."
   F. R. Aibu said, "How had they sinned? It was because 'they had joined themselves to Baal Peor' (Num. 25:3)."
5. A. Said R. Isaac, "There was the case of a local noblewoman who had an Ethiopian slave-girl, who went down to draw water from the well with her friend.
   B. "She said to her friend, 'My friend, tomorrow my master is going to divorce his wife and take me as his wife.'
   C. "The other said to her, 'Why?'
   D. "'It is because he saw her hands dirty.'

E.   "She said to her, 'You big fool! Let your ears hear what your mouth
            is saying. Now if concerning his wife, who is most precious to him,
            you say that because he saw her hands dirty one time, he wants to
            divorce her, you, who are entirely dirty, scorched from the day of
            your birth, how much the more so!'

F.   "So too, since the nations of the world taunt the Israelites, saying,
            'This nation has exchanged its glory [for nought],' as in the verse,
            'They exchanged their glory for an ox that eats grass' (Ps. 106:20),

G.   "the Israelites reply to them, 'Now if we who are in that condition
            for an hour and have incurred liability on that account, as for you,
            how much the more so!'

H.   "And not only so, but the Israelites say to the nations of the world,
            'We shall say to you to what we are to be compared:

I.   "It is to a prince who went forth to the wilderness around the town,
            and the sun beat on his head so that his face was darkened. He
            came back to the town, and with a bit of water and a bit of bathing
            in the bath houses, his body turned white and regained its beauty,
            just as before.

J.   "'So it is with me [the Israelites continue]. If the worship of idols
            has scorched us, truly you are scorched from your mother's womb!

K.   "'While you are yet in your mother's womb, you served idols, for
            when a woman is pregnant, she goes into the house of her idol
            and bows down and worships the idol – both she and her child.'"

No. 1 makes sense, in terms of Israel's moral condition, of the
reference to the sun; otherwise I see no point in including the passage. I
translate No. 2 following Simon; here is yet another invocation of the
sun as figurative. I assume that No. 3 at E makes itself pertinent in the
same way. No. 4 is tacked on on account of No. 3. No. 5, assuming that
our passage speaks of Israel, once more takes the bad trait imputed by
Scripture to the one who is speaking and treats it as a trait of Israel,
with the rest of the passage pointing out that the figurative failing of
Israel is what it is, and gentiles are worse.

VI:iii

1.   A.   "My mother's sons were angry with me":

     B.   R. Meir and R. Yosé:

     C.   R. Meir says, "'My mother's sons': the sons of my nation [which
            word uses the same consonants], that is Dathan and Abiram.

     D.   "'...were angry with me': attacked me, filled with wrath the judge
            who [ruled] against me.

     E.   "'...they made me keeper of the vineyards': while he brought
            justice among the daughters of Jethro, could he not bring justice
            between me and my brothers in Egypt?

     F.   "Thus: 'but my own vineyard I have not kept.'"

     G.   R. Yosé says, "'My mother's sons': 'the sons of my nation [which
            word uses the same consonants], that is the spies.'

     H.   "'...were angry with me': 'attacked me, filled with wrath the judge
            who [ruled] against me.

I.   "'...they made me keeper of the vineyards': 'it was because I delayed in the wilderness for forty-two journeys, I did not have the privilege of entering the land of Israel.'

J.   "Thus: 'but my own vineyard I have not kept.'"

2. A.   Another interpretation:

B.   "My mother's sons": the sons of my nation [which word uses the same consonants], that is, Jeroboam b. Nebat.

C.   "...were angry with me": attacked me, filled with wrath the judge who [ruled] against me.

D.   "...they made me keeper of the vineyards": the task of guarding the two golden calves of Jeroboam [1 Kgs. 12:28].

E.   "...but my own vineyard I have not kept": "I did not keep the watch of the priests and Levites."

F.   Thus: "but my own vineyard I have not kept."

3. A.   Said R. Levi, "On the day on which Solomon was married to the daughter of Pharaoh Necho, Michael, the great prince, descended from heaven, and he stuck a large reed into the sea, so that mud came up on either side, and the place was like a marsh. And that was the site of Rome.

B.   "On the day on which Jeroboam b. Nebat set up the two golden calves, two huts were built in Rome.

C.   "And they would build them, but the huts would fall down, build and see the collapse. But there was a sage there, by the name of Abba Qolon. He said to them, 'If you do not bring water from the Euphrates river and mix it with the clay, the building will not stand.'

D.   "They said to him, 'Who will do it?'

E.   "He said to them, 'I.'

F.   "He dressed up like a wine-porter, going into a town and out of a town, into a province and out of a province, until he got there. When he reached there, he went and took water from the Euphrates. They kneaded it into mud and built with it, and the building stood.

G.   "From that time they would say, 'Any town that does not have an Abba Qolon cannot be called a town.'

H.   "And they called Rome Babylon."

I.   On the day on which Elijah, of blessed memory, was taken away, a king arose in Edom: "And there was no king in Edom, a deputy was king" (1 Kgs. 22:48).

4. A.   Another explanation: "My mother's sons were angry with me": the sons of my nation [which word uses the same consonants]. This refers to Ahab.

B.   "...were angry with me": attacked me, filled with wrath the judge who [ruled] against me.

C.   "...they made me keeper of the vineyards": "They made me provide dainties for and feed Zedekiah b. Canaanah and his allies."

D.   But I had one true prophet there, Micaiah, and he ordered them to "feed him with little bread and little water" (1 Kgs. 22:27), thus: "but my own vineyard I have not kept."

5. A.   Another explanation: "My mother's sons": the sons of my nation [which word uses the same consonants]. This refers to Jezebel.
    B.   "...were angry with me": attacked me, filled with wrath the judge who [ruled] against me.
    C.   "...they made me keeper of the vineyards": She was providing dainties for and feeding the prophets of Baal and Asherah.
    D.   But to Elijah, of blessed memory, who was the true prophet, she sent word, "If I do not make your life as the life of one of them by tomorrow" (1 Kgs. 19:2). Thus: "but my own vineyard I have not kept."

6. A.   Another explanation: "My mother's sons": that is Zedekiah the king.
    B.   "...were angry with me": attacked me, filled with wrath the judge who [ruled] against me.
    C.   "...they made me keeper of the vineyards": This is because he gave dainties to Pashhur b. Malkiah and his colleagues.
    D.   One true prophet I had, namely, Jeremiah, about whom it is written, "And they gave him daily a loaf of bread out of the bakers' street" (Jer. 37:21).
    E.   What is the meaning of "the bakers' street"?
    F.   Said R. Isaac, "This is coarse bread, sold outside of the [Simon:] confectioner's shop, and it is blacker than coarse barley bread.
    G.   Thus: "but my own vineyard I have not kept."

7. A.   R. Hiyya in the name of R. Yohanan: "Said the Community of Israel before the Holy One, blessed be He, 'Because I did not observe the law about giving a single dough-offering in the proper manner in the land of Israel, lo, I keep the law concerning setting aside two dough-offerings in Syria [Simon, p. 61, n. 3: one for the priest and one to be burnt, out of doubt.]
    B.   "I was hoping that I might receive the reward for setting aside two, but I receive the reward for only one of them."
    C.   R. Abbah in the name of R. Yohanan: "Said the Community of Israel before the Holy One, blessed be He, 'Because I did not observe the law of keeping a single day holy as the festival in the proper manner in the land of Israel, lo, I keep the law concerning keeping two successive days holy as the festival applicable to the Exiles, outside of the land.
    D.   "I was hoping that I might receive the reward for setting aside two, but I receive the reward for only one of them."
    E.   R. Yohanan cited concerning them the following verse: "Wherefore I gave them also statutes that were not good" (Ez. 20:25).

The clause-by-clause exposition identifies as the speaker a variety of figures. Meir and Yosé concur that it is Moses, but then they differ on the case to which he refers. From No. 2 onward, the speaker is not so clear, since we speak of incidents, rather than persons. Then the speaker should be Israel itself, and that is the upshot at the end. Then at No. 2 we have Israel referring to the golden calves of Jeroboam. The important line is at the end: "My own vineyard I have not kept," now meaning Jerusalem. This precipitates the insertion of No. 3, balancing the decline of Jerusalem with the rise of Rome, a common motif. From Jeroboam we go on to other figures in First Temple times, Ahab, Jezebel, Zedekiah. That the Community of Israel is the speaker – at least in the mind of the compilers – then is underlines at No. 7, which draws a lesson from the cases. Of course No. 7 is autonomous, but including it, the compilers have made explicit the point that they wish to register. This composition as a whole is powerful and unrelenting, cogent and quite particular.

7

Song of Songs Rabbah to Song of Songs 1:7

<table>
<tr><td>1:7</td><td>Tell me, you whom my soul loves,
where you pasture your flock,
where you make it lie down at noon;
for why should I be like one who wanders
beside the flocks of your companions?</td></tr>
</table>

VII:i

1.   A   "Tell me, you whom my soul loves, [where you pasture your flock, where you make it lie down at noon; for why should I be like one who wanders beside the flocks of your companions?]"

      B.   R. Judah b. R. Simon interpreted the verse to speak of Moses:

      C.   "When the Holy One, blessed be He, said to him, 'Come now, therefore, and I will send you to Pharaoh,' (Ex. 3:10),

      D.   "he said to him, 'Lord of the world, "Through me, O Lord" (Ex. 4:13) Can all these things be done? How can I bear all of these vast populations? How many nursing mothers are there among them, how many pregnant women, how many infants! How much good food have you provided for the pregnant women among them? How much parched corn and nuts have you given for the children among them?'

      E.   "Where is this matter made explicit? [It is in the exposition of the following verse:]

      F.   "'Tell me, you whom my soul loves': 'the nation that my soul loves, the nation for which I have given my life.'

      G.   "'...where you pasture your flock': 'in the sunny season.'

      H.   "'...where you make it lie down at noon': 'in the rainy season.'"

2.   A   "...for why should I be like one who wanders [Hebrew: veils herself] beside the flocks of your companions":

      B.   R. Helbo in the name of R. Huna said, "'Do not let me be like a mourner, who covers his lip and weeps.'

      C.   "That is in line with the following usage: 'And he shall cover his upper lip' (Lev. 13:45)."

3. A.   Another explanation for the verse, "for why should I be like one who wanders [Hebrew: veils herself] [besides the flocks of your companions]":

   B.   "So that I may not be like a shepherd whose flock is attacked and ravaged by wolves, and he merely folds his garment and escapes.

   C.   [That interpretation of the letters of the word translated "wanders/veils herself"] is in accord with the following usage: "And he shall fold up the land of Egypt" (Jer. 43:12).

4. A.   "...beside the flocks of your companions":

   B.   [Moses speaks, continuing from 1.H:] "When I go to your companions [the patriarchs], and they ask me about their flocks, what am I going to answer them?"

5. A.   [Supply: "Tell me, you whom my soul loves, where you pasture your flock, where you make it lie down at noon; for why should I be like one who wanders besides the flocks of your companions?]"

   B.   R. Berekhiah interpreted the verse in light of the following: "Let the Lord, the God of the spirits of all flesh, set a man over the congregation" (Num. 27:16).

   C.   "[Moses] said before him, 'Lord of the world, since you are going to remove me from the world, kindly inform me exactly who will be the shepherds that you will appoint over your children.'

   D.   "Where is the matter made explicit? [It is in the exposition of the following verse:]

   E.   "'Tell me, you whom my soul loves': 'the nation for which I have given my life,'

   F.   "'...where you pasture your flock': 'in the time of the pagan kingdoms?'

   G.   "'...where you make it lie down at noon': 'in the subjugation of the pagan nations?'"

   H.   "'...for why should I be like one who wanders [Hebrew: veils herself] beside the flocks of your companions":

   I.   R. Azariah said, "[The letters used in the word 'for why'] may be read, 'so that I may not be made as nothing in the eyes of your companions as they pasture their flocks.'

   J.   "'It would be a profanation of heaven that your children should be afflicted while the flocks of your companions should be prospering.'"

   K.   Said R. Yudan b. R. Simon, "It is so that the nations of the world may not say you have erred in the attribute of justice.

   L.   "He knew that he wanted to slaughter them in the wilderness, and he slaughtered them in the wilderness: 'Therefore he has slain them in the wilderness' (Num. 14:16)."

   M.   Rabbis say, "It is so that your children should not see that they suffer great affliction and so turn away from following you and cleave to 'the flocks of your companions':

   O.   "'Shall the seat of wickedness be your companion' (Ps. 94:20)."

   P.   [Continuing Berekhiah, G:] "At that moment, said the Holy One, blessed be He, to Moses, 'Moses, you say to me, "where you pasture your flock, where you make it lie down at noon"! By your life, if you do not know, in the end you will know: "If you do not

know, O fairest among women, [follow in the tracks of the flock,
and pasture your kids beside the shepherds' tents]' (Song 1:8).

All parties concur that the voice here is Moses'. The issue again is
the context. Judah b. R. Simon has the discourse in beginning of his
mission, Berekhiah at the end. The exposition of the final clause, Nos.
2, 3, turns on the various meanings imputed to the consonants used at the
indicated word. No. 4 then completes No. 1, and No. 5 runs the verse
through the position of Berekhiah. I cannot say I understand 5.K-M.
But the main point is clear, P, and that links our base verse with the
one that follows immediately.

8

Song of Songs Rabbah to Song of Songs 1:8

1:8   *If you do not know,*
O fairest among women,
follow in the tracks of the flock,
and pasture your kids
beside the shepherds' tents.

VIII.i

1. A.   Another interpretation of the verse, "If you do not know, O fairest among women, [follow in the tracks of the flock, and pasture your kids beside the shepherds' tents]":
   B.   "Fairest among women" – fairest among the prophets,
   C.   most eminent among the prophets.
2. A.   Said R. Yosé b. R. Jeremiah, "How come the prophets are compared to women?
   B.   "It is to tell you, just as a woman is not ashamed to demand what her house needs from her husband,
   C.   "so the prophets are not ashamed to demand the needs of the Israelites from their Father who is in heaven."
3. A.   "...follow in the tracks of the flock":
   B.   R. Eliezer, R. Aqiba, and rabbis:
   C.   R. Eliezer says, "From the cakes that the Israelites had taken along from Egypt they eat for thirty-one days."
   D.   For said R. Shila, "Sixty-two meals, you may know, the Israelites had from these cakes."
   E.   [Resuming C:] "[From this you may know] what I am going to do for them in the end, at the conclusion.
   F.   "That is in line with this verse: [Simon:] 'There shall be provision of grain in the land' (Ps. 72:16)." [Simon, p. 64, n. 3: This was the answer to Moses' doubts about providing for Israel in the desert: since I caused a miracle whereby one cake lasted so long, you may rest assured that I can provide for all their wants – in the wilderness and in the Messianic era.]

G.   R. Aqiba says, "From the way in which I surrounded them with clouds of glory, in line with this verse, 'And the Lord went before them by day...the pillar of cloud departed not by day' (Ex. 13:21, 22), you may know what I am going to do for them in the end, at the conclusion.

H.   "That is in line with this verse: 'And there shall be a pavilion for shade in the daytime' (Isa. 4:6)."

I.   Rabbis say, "'From the way in which I fed them in the wilderness [which was through manna,] sweeter than milk and honey, you may know what I am going to do for them in the end, at the conclusion.'

J.   "That is in line with this verse: 'And it shall come to pass in that day that the mountains shall drop down sweet wine' (Joel 4:18)."

We begin with a minor gloss. Following Simon's comment, we must regard No. 2, in its entirety, as a continuation of the theme of the foregoing, that is, the exposition of Berekhiah's account of Moses's doubt about the future of the people. That seems to me well grounded, since, as we noted earlier, the exposition of Song 1:7 ends with the invocation of 1:8, "If you do not know now, in the end you will know." Here is an instance in which my division of the document by its chapters, delineated by the verses of the base-text, yields an infelicitous result. Still, without reference to the prior entry, the whole of No. 3 stands on its own and is entirely comprehensible.

VIII:ii

1. A.   Another interpretation of the verse, "follow in the tracks of the flock, [and pasture your kids beside the shepherds' tents]":

    B.   [God] said to him, "In the end the entire flock will go forth [to death], but you will go forth at the end."

    C.   And it is not that Moses tarried, but when the Israelites were busy with the spoil [of Egypt], Moses was busy with the religious duty involving the bones of Joseph.

    D.   That is in line with this verse: "And Moses took the bones of Joseph with him" (Ex. 13:19).

2. A.   Another interpretation of the verse, follow in the tracks of the flock, [and pasture your kids beside the shepherds' tents]":

    B.   [God] said to him, "In the end the generation will die, and you will be no different from them."

3. A.   How come this came about?

    B.   R. Samuel b. R. Nahman said, "It was on account of the bush."

    C.   For said R. Samuel b. R. Nahman, "All the seven days at the bush, the Holy One, blessed be He, was enticing Moses to go on his mission to Egypt:

    D.   "'And Moses said to the Lord, Oh Lord, I am not a man of words, neither in the yesterday nor the day before nor since you have spoken to your servant' (Ex. 4:10).

    E.   "Lo, that statement encompasses six days, and the day on which the conversation took place makes seven in all.

	F.	"And at the end, to the Holy One, blessed be He, he said, '"Send, I pray you, by the hand of the one whom you will send"' (Ex. 4:10).
	G.	"Said to him the Holy One, blessed be He, 'By your life, I shall bind this up for you in your garment. [I shall exact a penalty from you for your conduct here.]'"
4.	A.	And when did the Holy One, blessed be He, exact that penalty?
	B.	R. Berekhiah, R. Helbo, and R. Levi:
	C.	One said, "During all the seven days of the consecration [of the priesthood], he served as high priest, thinking that the office was his. At the end it was said to him, 'It is not yours, it is Aaron's, your brother's!' 'And it came to pass on the eighth day that Moses called Aaron' (Lev. 9:1)."
	D.	R. Helbo said, "All the seven days of Adar [forty years after the exodus,] Moses was appealing and begging before the Holy One, blessed be He, to let him enter the land. At the end he said to him, 'But you will not cross this Jordan' (Dt. 3:27).
5.	A.	"...and pasture your kids":
	B.	He said to him, "The kids will enter the land, the old goats won't."
6.	A.	"...beside the shepherds' tents":
	B.	Said to him the Holy One, blessed be He, "I shall tell you how long you will take care of my people: 'beside the shepherds' tents.'
	C.	"[Since the words for shepherds and wicked use the same consonants, the meaning is this:] "up to these thorns, that is, until you reach the land of the evil and wicked, that is, Sihon and Og."

It appears that we now have God as the voice of the Song, and Moses is the audience. The point of No. 1 is that Moses was favored to die as the very last of the generation of the Exodus. He follows at the end of the tracks of the flock. But, No. 2, he does not take a different path. Then No. 3 explains why. No. 4 continues No. 3; it is imperfect, since there is no entry for Levi. No. 5 is free-standing, making the same point as No. 2. No. 6 is another autonomous entry, but the several pertinent ones are properly joined, since they do make a single point in a variety of details.

9

Song of Songs Rabbah to Song of Songs 1:9

1:9   *I compare you, my love,*
to a mare of Pharaoh's chariots.

IX:i

1. A. "I compare you, my love, to a mare of Pharaoh's chariots":
   B. R. Pappias interpreted the verse, "'But he is at one with himself, and who can turn him' (Job 23:13):
   C. "He judges on his own everyone who passes through the world, and none can answer the rulings of the One who spoke and brought the world into being."
   D. Said to him R. Aqiba, "It would have been enough for you, Pappias, [not to claim that he rules all alone, which is not true, but only] to say that none can answer the rulings of the One who spoke and brought the world into being. For all is done in truth, and all is done in justice.
   E. "For so it is written, 'I saw the Lord sitting upon a throne high and lifted up' (Isa. 6:1)."
   F. Said R. Simon, "It is the throne that distinguishes between life and death."
   G. [Continuing E:] "'And all the host of heaven were standing by him on his right hand and on his left' (1 Kgs. 22:19).
   H. "Now is there such a thing as left on high? And is not everything on the right? 'Your right hand, O Lord, glorious in power, your right hand, O Lord, dashes in pieces the enemy' (Ex. 15:6).
   I. "Why then does Scripture refer to 'his right hand and his left'?
   J. "But these favor the right, those the left, meaning, these favor acquittal, those a verdict of guilty."
2. A. R. Yohanan in the name of R. Aha derived proof for the same proposition [that God does not judge all by himself] from the following: "And the word was true, even a great host' (Dan. 10:1).
   B. "True is the ruling when a great host is formed."

3. A.   That [same proposition, namely, that God does not judge all by himself] is in line with this verse: "But the Lord God is true" (Jer. 10:10).

     B.   What is the meaning of the word "true"?

     C.   Said R. Ibun, "It means that he is the living God and eternal king."

     D.   Said R. Eleazar, "Every passage in which it is said, 'and the Lord' refers to him and his court.

     E.   "And the generative analogy governing all of them is as follows: 'And the Lord has spoken evil concerning you' (1 Kgs. 22:23). [Here there is an explicit reference to the host of heaven standing by him, as at 1 Kgs. 22:19: 'And all the host of heaven were standing by him on his right hand and on his left.']

     F.   "That is the generative analogy governing all of them."

4. A.   Now how does R. Eleazar interpret this verse of Scripture that is cited by R. Pappias, "But he is at one with himself, and who can turn him'" (Job 23:13)?

     B.   He alone seals the fate of all those who pass through the world, and no other creature seals the document with him.

5. A.   What is the seal of the Holy One, blessed be He?

     B.   R. Bibi in the name of R. Reuben said, "It is truth: 'Howbeit I will declare to you that which is inscribed in the writing of truth' (Dan. 10:21).

     C.   "If 'truth' why then 'writing,' and if 'writing,' then why 'truth'? [Simon, p. 67, n. 4: (truth is) something written, but not necessarily decided upon].

     D.   "But until the document is sealed, it is merely written. When it has been sealed, then the decree is a judgment of truth."

6. A.   Said R. Simeon b. Laqish, "And why is it 'truth'?

     B.   "Since the Hebrew word for truth consists of the letters A, M, and T, the word bears the A at the head of the alphabet, the M in the middle, and the T at the end.

     C.   "This then conveys the message, 'I am the first and I am the Last and besides me there is no god' (Isa. 44:6).

     D.   "'I am the first': 'I did not receive my dominion from anybody else.'

     E.   "'I am the last': 'I am not going to give it over to anybody else, there being no other.'

     F.   "'...and besides me there is no god': 'I have no second.'"

7. A.   [=Genesis Rabbah XXI:V.1] [Concerning the verse, "Behold, the man has become like one of us" (Gen. 3:22),] R. Pappias interpreted the verse as follows: "'Behold, the man has become like one of us' means, like the unique one of the world."

     B.   Said to him R. Aqiba, "That is enough from you, Pappias."

     C.   He said to him, "Then how do you interpret the word, 'like one of us'?"

     D.   He said to him, "Like one of the ministering angels."

     E.   And sages say, "Not in accord with the position of this one, nor in accord with the position of that one. But it teaches the following:

     F.   "The Holy One, blessed be He, set before him two paths, life and death, and he chose the 'other path,' [that of heresy, hence death] and he abandoned the path of life." [Freedman, Genesis Rabbah,

p. 175, n. 1: That which God did not wish him to choose, that is, death. "Behold the man has become as one who knows good and evil of himself, of his own free will, and thereby has himself chosen the path of death."]

8. A.   R. Pappias interpreted the verse, "'Thus they exchanged their glory for the likeness of an ox that eats grass' (Ps. 106:20).

    B.   "Shall I infer that it speaks of the ox that is on high? Scripture says, 'that eats grass.'"

    C.   Said to him R. Aqiba, "That's enough for you, Pappias."

    D.   He said to him, "And how do you interpret the language, 'Thus they exchanged their glory for the likeness of an ox that eats grass' (Ps. 106:20)?"

    E.   "Might it mean, like an ordinary ox? Scripture says, 'that eats grass.'

    F.   "Now as a matter of fact, you have nothing so degraded or disgusting as an ox when it is eating grass."

9. A.   R. Yudan in the name of R. Aha said, "The magicians of Egypt did their enchantments, so that it appeared to be dancing before them.

    B.   "That sense of the letters translated dancing occurs in this verse: 'Damascus has gotten weak, she turns around to flee, and trembling [using the same consonants] has seized her' (Jer. 49:24)."

10. A.   R. Pappias interpreted the verse, "'I compare you, my love, to a mare of Pharaoh's chariots':

    B.   "What is written is, 'at my rejoicing' [since the same letters translated 'to a mare' can be given vowels to make the word read, 'at my rejoicing].'

    C.   "Said the Holy One, blessed be He, 'Just as I rejoiced at the fall of the Egyptians at the sea, so I would have rejoiced to destroy the Israelites. But what saved them?

    D.   "'It was "at their right hand and at their left"' (Ex. 14:22: 'And the waters were a wall to them at their right hand and at their left').

    E.   "That is, it was on account of the merit of the Torah, that they were destined to receive from the right hand of the Holy One, blessed be He, as it is said, 'At his right hand was a fiery law to them' (Dt. 33:2).

    F.   "'...and at their left': this refers to the mezuzah.

    G.   "Another explanation of 'at their right hand and at their left':

    H.   "'at their right hand': this is the recitation of the Shema.

    I.   "'...and at their left': this is the Prayer Said Standing."

    J.   Said to him R. Aqiba, "That is enough from you, Pappias! In every other passage in which the word 'rejoicing' appears, it is written with a sin, but here with a samekh [two different letters with an S-sound]."

    K.   He said to him, "And how do you interpret, 'I compare you, my love, to a mare of Pharaoh's chariots'?"

    L.   [Aqiba said to him,] "Pharaoh rode on a male horse, and, as it were, the Holy One, blessed be He, appeared to him on a male horse: 'And he rode upon a cherub and flew' (Ps. 18:11).

M.   "Said Pharaoh, 'In a battle this male horse can kill its master. Now I'm going to ride on a female horse': "I compare you, my love, to a mare of Pharaoh's chariots.'

N.   "Then Pharaoh went and mounted a red horse, a white horse, a black horse, so the Holy One, blessed be He, as it were, revealed himself on a red, white, and black horse too: 'You have trodden the sea with your horses' (Hab. 3:15), that is, horses of various kinds.

O.   "The wicked Pharaoh came forth wearing a breastplate and helmet, so the Holy One, blessed be He, as it were, revealed himself wearing a breastplate and helmet: 'And he put on righteousness as a coat of mail' (Isa. 59:17).

P.   "The former brought forth naphtha [for chemical warfare], so the Holy One, blessed be He, as it were, did the same: 'his thick clouds passed with hailstones and coals of fire' (Ps. 18:13).

Q.   "He brought forth catapult stones, so the Holy One, blessed be He, as it were, did the same: 'And the Lord sent forth thunder and hail' (Ex. 19:23).

R.   "He produced swords and lances, so the Holy One, blessed be He, as it were, did the same: 'He shot forth lightnings' (Ps. 18:15).

S.   "He brought forth arrows, so the Holy One, blessed be He, as it were, did the same: 'And he sent out his arrows' (Ps. 18:15)."

T.   Said R. Levi, "'He sent out his arrows and scattered them' (Ps. 18:15): the arrows scattered them.

U.   "'...and he shot forth lightnings and discomfited them': this teaches that they threw them into confusion.

V.   "He confused them, frightened them, and took away their standards, so that they did not know what they were doing."

W.   [Reverting to R and Aqiba's exposition:] "Pharaoh came forth in full armor, so the Holy One, blessed be He, as it were, did the same: 'The Lord will go forth as a mighty man' (Isa. 42:13).

X.   "He thundered with his voice, so the Holy One, blessed be He, as it were, did the same: 'The Lord thundered down from heaven' (2 Sam. 22:14).

Y.   "He made his voice loud, so the Holy One, blessed be He, as it were, did the same: 'And the Most High gave forth his voice' (2 Sam. 22:14).

Z.   "Pharaoh came forth in fury, so the Holy One, blessed be He, as it were, did the same: 'You march through the earth in indication' (Hab. 3:12).

AA.   "'...with a bow.' So, as it were: 'You uncover fully your bow' (Hab. 3:9).

BB.   "'...with shield and buckler.' So, as it were: 'Take hold of shield and buckler' (Hab. 3:9).

CC.   "'...with flashing spear.' So, as it were: 'at the shining of your glittering spear' (Hab. 3:11)."

11. A R. Berekhiah in the name of R. Samuel b. R. Nahman: "When Pharaoh had used up all his weapons, the Holy One, blessed be He, began to exalt himself over him.

B.   "He said to him, 'Wicked one! Do you have the winds? Do you have the cherubim? Do you have wings?'

12. A.   And whence did the Holy One, blessed be He, launch them?
    B.   Said R. Yudan, "It was from between the wheels of his chariot.
    C.   "The Holy One, blessed be He, loosened them and threw them onto the sea."
13. A.   Said R. Hanina b. R. Papa, "A mortal who rides on his burden is on something tangible.
    B.   "But the Holy One, blessed be He, is not that way.
    C.   "He carries his chariot and rides on that which is ineffable: 'And he rode upon a cherub and did fly, yes, he swooped down on the wings of the wind' (Ps. 18:11)."
14. A.   [Supply: "And he rode upon a cherub and did fly, yes, he swopped down on the wings of the wind" (Ps. 18:11):]
    B.   One version says, "he swooped," and another version reads, "he was seen" (2 Sam. 22:11) [both versions using some of the same consonants but exchanging the D and R, which are similar in appearance].
    C.   How are the two versions to be reconciled?
    D.   Said R. Aha, "On this basis we learn that the Holy One, blessed be He, had other worlds, and he went forth to make his appearance in them too."

This entire composition has been parachuted down solely because of the appearance of Song 1:9 at No. 10. The focus for the conglomeration of the whole set of course lies with the formula in which Pappias's interpretation is rejected by Aqiba, who offers a better one of his own. There are various secondary accretions, and extensions, e.g., No. 2 for No. 1, No. 3 to No. 2, and so on, are self-evident. But the structure of the whole is visible to the naked eye, and it leaves no doubt that our compilers were perfectly contented to insert a passage with only the most superficial point of contact with the document at hand. Still, Aqiba's extensive comparison of Pharaoh with God, showing the enormous disparity between the earthly and the heavenly ruler, makes ample use of our base verse. But it would have served better without the accretions fore and aft.

IX:ii
1. A.   "I compare you, my love, [to a mare of Pharaoh's chariots]":
   B.   Said R. Eliezer, "The matter may be compared to the case of a princess who was kidnapped, and her father was ready to redeem her.
   C.   "But she gave indications to the kidnappers, saying to them, 'I am yours, I belong to you, and I am going after you.'
   D.   "Said her father to her, 'What are you thinking? Is it that I do not have the power to redeem you? [Simon:] I would have you hold your peace [using the same word as 'compare you'], yes, be silent.'
   E.   "So when the Israelites were encamped at the sea, 'and the Egyptians pursued after them and overtook them in camp by the sea' (Ex. 14:9),

F. "the Israelites, fearful, gave indicates to the Egyptians, saying to them, 'We are yours, we belong to you, and we are going after you.'

G. "Said to them the Holy One, blessed be He, 'What are you thinking? Is it that I do not have the power to redeem you?

H. "For the word 'I have compared you' [bears consonants that yield the meaning,] 'I made you silent.'

I. "Thus: 'The Lord will fight for you, and you will hold your peace' (Ex. 14:14)."

2. A. Another explanation of the verse, "I compare you, my love, to a mare of Pharaoh's chariots":

B. Rabbis say, "Since the Israelites were like mares and the wicked Egyptians like males in heat,

C. "they ran after them until they sunk down in the sea."

D. Said R. Simon, "God forbid that the Israelites should be compared to mares!

E. "But the waves of the ocean appeared like mares, and the Egyptians were like stallions in heat, so they ran after them until they sunk down in the sea.

F. "The Egyptian said to his horse, 'Yesterday I tried to lead you to the Nile, and you would not follow me, but now you are drowning me in the sea.

G. "And the horse said to its rider, 'He has thrown me in the sea' (Ex. 14:10) – [the several consonants being read as individual words, altogether] meaning, see what is in the sea. An orgy [so Simon] has been made ready for you in the sea."

3. A. R. Ishmael taught on Tannaite authority, "'And the Lord overthrew the Egyptians in the midst of the sea' (Ex. 14:27):

B. "this teaches that the horse threw its rider up, and he came down with the horse on top."

C. Said R. Levi, "It is like turning a dish over, so that what is at the bottom is on top, and what is on top is on the bottom."

No. 1 works on the meanings of the consonants in "compare," with stress on the available sense, "silent." Hence the narrative on how God told the Israelites to be silent; then the topic of Pharaoh's chariots is worked out. No. 1 treats the former consideration. No. 2 then moves on to the comparison to the mare of Pharaoh's chariots; this has no bearing on No. 1. No. 3 is tacked on, mainly for thematic considerations, it would seem.

IX:iii

1. A. "[I compare you,] my love, [to a mare of Pharaoh's chariots]":

B. What is the meaning of "my love"?

C. Said R. Jonathan, "The one who feeds me, those who feed me two daily whole-offerings each day: 'The one lamb shall you offer in the morning' (Num. 28:4)."

2. A. For said R. Judah b. R. Simon, "The Israelites would offer two daily whole-offerings every day, one in the morning, one at dusk.

B.   "The one offered in the morning was presented for the transgressions that had been done overnight, and the one at dusk for the transgressions that had been done through the day.

C.   "So no one would ever spend the night in Jerusalem subject to transgression that he might have done [since day and night these were expiated]: 'Righteousness lodged in her' (Isa. 1:21)."

3. A.   Another explanation of "I compare you, my love, [to a mare of Pharaoh's chariots]":

B.   Rabbis say, "The shepherds of my world, who have accepted my Torah.

C.   "For had you not accepted it, I should have made my world revert to formlessness and void."

4. A.   For said R. Hanina in the name of R. Aha, "'When the earth and all the inhabitants thereof are dissolved, I myself establish the pillars of it, selah' (Ps. 75:4).

B.   "Were it not that the Israelites had stood at Mount Sinai and said, 'We shall do and we shall obey' (Ex. 24:7), the world would have melted and reverted to formlessness and void.

C.   "And who laid the foundations for the world? 'When the earth and all the inhabitants thereof are dissolved, I myself establish the pillars of it, selah' (Ps. 75:4).

D.   "This is as if to say, 'on account of 'I am the Lord your God' (Ex. 20:1), 'I myself establish the pillars of it, selah' (Ps. 75:4)."

No. 1 explores the sense of the letters for "love," invoking the meaning available as "feed," so leading to C. No. 2 is a natural addition. No. 3 proceeds to another sense of the same letters, now, shepherd. No. 4 is a stunning conclusion. It also underlines that this compilation really has very little to do with the Song of Songs; it is a compilation devoted to Israel's and God's relationship with one another, with Sinai at the center.

10

Song of Songs Rabbah to Song of Songs 1:10

1:10   *Your cheeks are comely with ornaments,*
your neck with strings of jewels.

X:i

1. A.   "Your cheeks are comely with ornaments":
    B.   just as the cheeks are created only for speech, so Moses and Aaron were created only for speech.
    C.   "...your neck with strings [of jewels]":
    D.   [since the words for jewels and the word for strings use the same consonants, the sense is,] with the two Torahs, the Torah that is in writing and the Torah that is in memory.

2. A.   Another interpretation of "[your neck] with strings [of jewels]":
    B.   with many Torahs: "This is the Torah of the burnt-offering" (Lev. 6:2); "this is the Torah of the sin-offering" (Lev. 7:1); "this is the Torah of the peace-offering" (Lev. 7:11); "this is the Torah when a man shall die in a tent" (Num. 19:14).

3. A.   Another explanation of "with strings":
    B.   with two ornaments [a word using the same consonants],
    C.   with two brothers, speaking of Moses and of Aaron,
    D.   who treat each other with a gracious demeanor.
    E.   This one took pleasure in the achievements of that one, and that one took pleasure in the achievements of this one.

4. A.   Said R. Phineas, "'And he shall be your spokesman to the people, and it shall come to pass that he shall serve you as a mouth, and you shall serve him as God (Ex. 4:16).
    B.   "['Mouth':] means, public interpreter.
    C.   "'...and you shall serve him as God': was Moses turned into Aaron's idol, that you say, 'and you shall serve him as God' (Ex. 4:16)?
    D.   "But this is what the Holy One, blessed be He, said to Moses, 'Moses, just as reverence for me is upon you, so reverence for you will be upon your brother.'
    E.   "But he did not act in that way.

117

F.   "Rather: 'Moses and Aaron went and gathered together all the elders of the children of Israel. And Aaron spoke all the words' (Ex. 4:29-30).

G.   "He put shoulder to shoulder, for even now this one took pleasure in the achievements of that one, and that one took pleasure in the achievements of this one.

H.   "And whence in Scripture do we know that Aaron took pleasure in the achievements of Moses?

I.   "'And also, behold, he comes to meet you, and when he sees you, he will be glad in his heart' (Ex. 4:14)."'

5. A.   Taught on Tannaite authority R. Simeon b. Yohai, "The heart that rejoiced for the achievements of Moses his brother will don the Urim and Thummim:

    B.   "'And you shall put on the breastplate of judgment the Urim and the Thummim, and they shall be upon Aaron's heart' (Ex. 28:30)."

6. A.   [Continuing 4.I:] "And how do we know from Scripture that Moses took pleasure in the achievements of Aaron?

    B.   "'Like the precious oil upon the head, coming down upon the beard; Aaron's beard' (Ps. 133:2)."

7. A.   [Supply: "Like the precious oil upon the head, coming down upon the beard; Aaron's beard" (Ps. 133:2):]

    B.   Said R. Aha, "Now did Aaron have two beards, that Scripture says, 'upon the beard; Aaron's beard'?

    C.   "But when Moses saw the anointing oil dripping down Aaron's beard, it seemed to him as thought it were dripping down his own beard, and he took pleasure, thus: 'upon the beard; Aaron's beard.'"

The metaphor now speaks of Moses and Aaron, and once that conception governs, then the vast and autonomous composition of Nos. 4ff. are appended. The compilers clearly wish to work on themes, rather than on verses of Scripture, and their main interest is in framing a hermeneutic governing the whole, rather than (merely) assembling bits and pieces to shape the reading of the parts.

X:ii

1. A.   "...your neck with strings of jewels":

    B.   This refers to the seventy members of the sanhedrin who were strung out after them [Moses and Aaron] like a string of pearls.

2. A.   Another explanation of the phrase, "your neck with strings of jewels":

    B.   This refers to this refers to those who teach Scripture and repeat Mishnah, instructing children in good faith.

    C.   "...your neck with strings of jewels" refers to children.

3. A.   Another explanation of the verse, "Your cheeks are comely with ornaments":

    B.   This refers to the rabbis.

    C.   "...your neck with strings of jewels":

    D.   This refers to the disciples, who [Simon:] strain their necks to hear the teachings of the Torah from their mouth,

	E.	like someone who has never heard teachings of the Torah in his entire life.
4.	A.	Another explanation of the verse, "Your cheeks are comely with ornaments":
	B.	when they pronounce the law with one another, for instance, R. Abba b. R. Qomi and his colleagues.
	C.	"...your neck with strings of jewels":
	D.	When they make connections among teachings of the Torah, then go on and make connections between teachings of the Torah and teachings of the prophets, teachings of the Prophets and teachings of the Writings, and fire flashes around them, then the words rejoice as when they were given from mount Sinai.
	E.	For the principal point at which they were given was at Mount Sinai with fire: "And the mountain burned with fire to the heart of heaven" (Dt. 4:11).
5.	A.	Ben Azzai was sitting and expounding, and fire burned all around him.
	B.	They went and told R. Aqiba, "My lord, Ben Azzai is sitting and expounding, and fire is burning all around him."
	C.	He went to him and said to him, "I have heard that you are expounding, and fire is burning all around you."
	D.	He said to him, "True."
	E.	He said to him, "Is it possible that you have been occupied with the deepest mysteries of the Chariot?"
	F.	He said to him, "Not at all. I was in session and making connections among teachings of the Torah, then going on and making connections between teachings of the Torah and teachings of the prophets, teachings of the Prophets and teachings of the Writings, so fire flashed around them, and the words rejoiced as when they were given from mount Sinai.
	G.	"For is not the principal point at which they were given was at Mount Sinai with fire: 'And the mountain burned with fire to the heart of heaven' (Dt. 4:11)?"
6.	A.	R. Abbahu was in session and expounding, and fire burned all around him.
	B.	He thought, "Is it possible that I am not making connections among teachings of the Torah as is required for them?"
	C.	For R. Simeon b. Laqish said, "There are those who know how to make connections among words of Torah, but do not know how to penetrate inside of them, and those who know how to penetrate into the depths of the teachings but do not know how to make connections. But I am expert at both making connections and also getting at the heart of matters."

The exposition of the base verse moves from Moses and Aaron to Torah-teaching and the giving of the Torah. The verse works just as well to supply a metaphor to this new theme, which is not to be distinguished in any sharp way from the former one. The strength of the hermeneutic is not its complexity but its simplicity and serviceability to all the intertwined themes that our authorship wishes to set forth in the present context.

X:iii

1. A.   Another explanation of the verse, "Your cheeks are comely with ornaments":
   B.   When people publicly recite teachings of the Torah in their proper turn:
   C.   teachings of the laws of Passover on Passover, the laws of Pentecost on Pentecost, the laws of Tabernacles on Tabernacles,
   D.   [in line with the meaning of the letters of the word for ornaments as in this verse,] "now when the *turn* of every maiden had come" (Est. 3:12).

2. A.   "...your neck with strings of jewels":
   B.   R. Levi in the name of R. Hama b. R. Hanina said, "This refers to the lections of the Torah, which are connected to one another, lead on to one another, or leap from one to the other, or exhibit parallels to one another, or are related to one another."
   C.   Said R. Menahema, "For example, the following:
   D.   "'To these the land shall be divided for an inheritance' (Num. 26:53), followed by, 'Then the daughters of Zelophehad came near' (Num. 27:1); so too: 'The daughters of Zelophehad speak rightly' (Num. 27:7), followed by 'Get you up to this mountain of Abarim' (Num. 27:12).
   E.   "What has one thing to do with the next?
   F.   "Once the land had been divided, the daughters of Zelophehad came to take their share from Moses, and Moses recused himself from their case: 'And Moses brought their case before the Lord' (Num. 27:5).
   G.   "Said to him the Holy One, blessed be He, 'Moses, from their case you recuse yourself, but from my presence you cannot recuse yourself: 'Get you up to this mountain of Abarim.'
   H.   "He said before him, 'Lord of the world, since you remove me from the world, at least let me know what sort of leaders you are going to provide for the Israelites!'
   I.   "Said to him the Holy One, blessed be He, 'Moses, concerning my children you have to have commandments, and concerning the work of my hands do you presume to command me? Instead of giving me instructions concerning my children, give instructions to my children concerning me!'
   J.   "That is in line with this verse: 'Command the children of Israel and say to them' (Num. 28:2)."

3. A.   [Supply: "Command the children of Israel and say to them" (Num. 28:2):]
   B.   The matter provokes a parable: to what may it be compared?
   C.   To the case of a queen who was departing from this life. She said to him, "By the life of my lord, the king, I command you concerning my children!"
   D.   He said to her, "Instead of giving me orders concerning my children, give my children orders concerning me!"

E.   So when Moses said before the Holy One, blessed be He, "Lord of
       the world, since you remove me from the world, at least let me
       know what sort of leaders you are going to provide for the
       Israelites!"

F.   [Supply: Said to him the Holy One, blessed be He, "Moses,
       concerning my children you have to have commandments, and
       concerning the work of my hands do you presume to command
       me? Instead of giving me instructions concerning my children,
       give instructions to my children concerning me!" That is in line
       with this verse: "Command the children of Israel and say to them"
       (Num. 28:2).

No. 1 introduces the third and final theme, moving from study of
Torah to the public teaching of Torah. The point of No. 1 is that each
set of laws must be set forth in proper order, which is taken to be
Passover, Pentecost, Tabernacles. No. 2 then proceeds to compare strings
of jewels with making connections among Torah-teachings, and this is
given concrete meaning forthwith. No. 3 then goes over the ground of
No. 2, saying the same thing but now in the form of a parable. The
comparison derives, of course, from the prevailing perception of court
politics defined by the competition of the children of several wives, on
the one side, and the monarch's quite reasonable fear of his legitimate
heirs, on the other. But I do not think these details of motivation are in
play; the main point is simply the contradictory counsel of queen and
king: worry not about your children's fate with me, but my fate with
them! And that seems to me a very exact and appropriate rebuke for
God to give to Moses, a stunning and apt conclusion. If we see the entire
composition pertaining to Song 1:10 as a unity – and the compilers
require us to do so – then its message is cutting and very concrete.

11

Song of Songs Rabbah to Song of Songs 1:11

1:11   *We will make you ornaments of gold, studded with silver.*

XI:i

1. A. "We will make you ornaments of gold":
   B. this refers to the spoil at the Sea.
   C. "...studded with silver":
   D. this refers to the spoil of Egypt.
2. A. Just as there is a difference between silver and gold, so there is greater value assigned to the money gotten at the Sea than the spoil of Egypt.
   B. For it is said, "And you came with ornaments upon ornaments" (Ez. 16:7):
   C. "...ornaments" refers to the spoil of Egypt.
   D. "...upon ornaments" refers to the spoil at the Sea.
3. A. Another interpretation of "We will make you ornaments of gold":
   B. this refers to the Torah, which [Simon:] Onqelos, the nephew of Hadrian, learned.
   C. "...studded with silver":
   D. R. Abba b. R. Kahana said, "These are the letters."
   E. R. Aha said, "These are the words."
4. A. Another interpretation of "We will make you ornaments of gold":
   B. this is the writing.
   C. "...studded with silver":
   D. this is the ruled lines.
5. A. Another interpretation of "We will make you ornaments of gold":
   B. this refers to the tabernacle: "And you shall overlay the boards with gold" (Ex. 26:29).
   C. "...studded with silver":
   D. "The hooks of the pillars and their fillets shall be silver" (Ex. 27:10).
6. A. R. Berekhiah interpreted the verse to speak of the ark:
   B. "'We will make you ornaments of gold':

	C.	"this refers to the ark, as it is said, 'And you shall overlay it with pure gold' (Ex. 25:11).
	D.	"'...studded with silver':
	E.	"this refers to the two pillars that stand before it, which were made of silver, like [Simon:] columns of a balcony."
7.	A.	How was the ark made?
	B.	R. Hanina and R. Simeon b. Laqish:
	C.	R. Hanina said, "They made three arks, two of gold, one of wood.
	D.	"He put the one of wood around the one of gold, and the other one of gold around the one of wood, and covered its upper rims with gold."
	E.	"R. Simeon b. Laqish said, "They made one ark and covered it on the inside and on the outside: 'within and without you shall overlay it' (Ex. 25:11)."
	F.	How does R. Hanina deal with the verse invoked by R. Simeon b. Laqish?
	G.	"Said R. Phineas, "They put an overlay in the spaces between the boards."
8.	A.	Judah, the son of Rabbi says, "'Your cheeks are comely with ornaments':
	B.	"this refers to the Torah.
	C.	"'...your neck with strings of jewels': this refers to the prophets.
	D.	"'We will make you ornaments of gold':
	E.	"this refers to the Writings.
	F.	"'...studded with silver':
	G.	"this refers to the Song of Songs,
	H.	"[Simon:] something complete and finished off."

The formally-sustained and well-crafted exposition is interesting because it shows us how a repertoire of closely related symbols finds metaphorization in the base verse. Here we see the fully exposed hermeneutical method of the document – not the exegetes that are cited, but the authorship that has assembled the materials, and, I think, done so for its own purposes. The important point is not the detail but the utilization of a complete and fully formed symbolic system in the exposition of the base verse(s), that is, of the Song as a whole – and the appeal to the Song as a whole as a framework in which to hold together and treat as one the symbols. What then are these symbols? In the present instance I catalogue the following: [1] the spoil at the Sea = the Exodus (Nos. 1, 2); [2] the Torah (Nos. 3, 4); [3] the Tabernacle (No. 5); [4] the ark (No. 6, 7). Then comes what is surprising and out of context, No. 8's Song of Songs itself. But of course that is the centerpiece, climax, and key to the whole. As if we could have missed the powerful message of the prior entries, which have walked us through the book of Exodus and its principal components – Exodus, Sinai, tabernacle – the Song of Songs as a whole fully and completely contains the story of the Exodus, Sinai, and the tabernacle, which is to say, the parts contribute to a whole that transcends them;

the parts point to God's love for Israel, the whole expresses that love, vastly exceeding those parts. That seems to me the clear and distinct message of the compilers, and it is, as I said, a message far in excess of what the framers of the individual units have made for us.

12

Song of Songs Rabbah to Song of Songs 1:12

1:12   *While the king was on his couch,*
         my nard gave forth its fragrance.

XII:i

1. A. "While the king was on his couch, [my nard gave forth its fragrance]":

   B. R. Meir and R. Judah:

   C. R. Meir says, "'While the king,' the King of kings of kings, the Holy One, blessed be He, 'was on his couch,' in the firmament, ['my nard gave forth its fragrance'], the Israelites gave forth a bad odor, saying to the calf, 'These are your Gods, O Israel' (Ex. 32:4)."

   D. Said to him R. Judah, "Enough for you, Meir. The Song of Songs is to be interpreted not to the disadvantage, but only to the glory [of Israel].

   E. "For the Song of Songs has been given only for the glory of Israel.

   F. "Then what is the meaning of, 'While the king was on his couch, [my nard gave forth its fragrance]'?

   G. "'While the king,' the King of kings of kings, the Holy One, blessed be He, 'was on his couch,' in the firmament, ['my nard gave forth its fragrance'], the Israelites gave forth a good fragrance before Mount Sinai, saying, 'All that the Lord has said we will do and obey' (Ex. 24:7)."

   H. The position of R. Meir is that "my bad spice" gave its smell.

   I. [Simon, verbatim, p. 77:] Only a tradition was brought by Israel from the Babylonian captivity which they transmitted, that God [in writing the Torah] skipped over the incident of the calf and wrote first the construction of the Tabernacle. [Simon, p. 77, n. 4: This remark seems to be inserted in order to show why on R. Meir's theory the account of the calf does not follow immediately on the account of the giving of the Torah, but is separated from it by the description of the Tabernacle.]

2. A. R. Eliezer, R. Aqiba, and R. Berekhiah:

125

B. R. Eliezer says, "'While the King' of kings of kings, the Holy One, blessed be He, 'was on his couch,' in the firmament, ['my nard gave forth its fragrance'], Mount Sinai was already sending up pillars of smoke: 'And the mountain was burning with fire' (Dt. 4:11)."

C. R. Aqiba says, "'While the King' of kings of kings, the Holy One, blessed be He, 'was on his couch,' in the firmament, ['my nard gave forth its fragrance'], 'already the glory of the Lord abode upon Mount Sinai' (Ex. 24:16)."

D. R. Berekhiah says, "While Moses, who was called king as in the following, 'And there was a king in Jeshurun when the heads of the people were gathered' (Dt. 33:5) 'was at his couch' in the heaven, already 'God spoke all these words' (Ex. 20:1)."

3. A. R. Eliezer b. Jacob and Rabbis:

B. R. Eliezer b. Jacob says, "'While the King' of kings of kings, the Holy One, blessed be He, 'was on his couch,' in the firmament, ['my nard gave forth its fragrance'], Michael, the great prince, had already come down, from heaven and saved Abraham, our father, from the fiery furnace."

C. And Rabbis say, "The Omnipresent, may he be blessed, came down and saved him personally: 'I am the Lord who brought you out of Ur of the Chaldees' (Gen. 15:7).

D. "Then when did Michael come down?

E. "It was in the time of Hananiah, Mishael, and Azariah."

F. Said R. Tabiyomi, "When Jacob, our father, was still reclining on his couch, the Holy Spirit sparkled upon him and he said to his sons, "'God will be with you'" (Gen. 48:21).

G. "He said to them, 'He is destined to bring his Divine Presence to rest among you.'"

4. A. Said R. Nahman, "It is written, 'And Israel journeyed with all that he had and came to Beer-sheba' (Gen. 46:1).

B. "Where was he going?

C. "He went down to cut down the cedars that Abraham, our father, had planted in Beer-sheba: 'And he planted a grove in Beer-sheba' (Gen. 21:33)."

5. A. Said R. Levi, "'And the middle bar in the midst of the boards' (Ex. 26:28):

B. "The bar was thirty-two cubits.

C. "And how at that moment could they get one?

D. "This teaches that they had been stored up with them from the time of Jacob, our father: 'And every man with whom was found with him acacia wood' (Ex. 36:24).

E. "What is written is not 'was found' but 'was found with him,' meaning, from the beginning."

6. A. Said R. Levi b. R. Hiyya, "In Magdala of the Dyers [near Tiberias] they cut them down and took them down with them to Egypt.

B. "The wood contained no knots or cracks."

7. A. There were some acacia trees in Magdala, and the people treated them as prohibited, on account of the sanctity inhering in the ark.

B.   They came and asked R. Hanania, associate of the Rabbis, who said to them, "Do not change the custom that you have received from your forebears."

We have three important readings of the base verse, all of them accomplished through glossing of clauses, No. 1, Meir and Judah, and No. 2, Eliezer, Aqiba, and Berekhiah, then No. 3, Eliezer b. Jacob. All sets of readings adhere to the same conventions until the final imputation of sense, and both of them bear the same basic message; what is subject to dispute then is only the specific event that is subject to metaphorization. And, of course, that is really not a dispute but an effort at encompassing a variety of important events within the single verse. The hermeneutic in fact produces harmonizing and not disjuncture. The secondary accretions, Nos. 4ff., all serve the final entry, and I assume, then, that the order of the entries in the end is governed by the rule that the simplest come first, the more complex later on.

XII:ii

1. A.   R. Phineas in the name of R. Hoshaia said, "'While the king,' the King of kings of kings, the Holy One, blessed be He, 'was on his couch,' in the firmament, ['my nard gave forth its fragrance'], he had already [Simon:] anticipated [his descent on Mount Sinai] [Simon, p. 79, n. 4: by enveloping the mountain in flames and smoke],

    B.   "thus: 'And it came to pass on the third day, while it was yet morning, that there were thunders...upon the mount' (Ex. 19:16)."

2. A.   It may be compared to the case of a king who decreed, "On such and such a day, I shall enter town. The townsfolk slept all night, so when the king came and found them sleeping, he had the trumpets and horns sounded.

    B.   The prince of that town woke the people up and brought them forth to receive the king.

    C.   The king walked before them until he reached his palace.

    D.   Thus the Holy One, blessed be He, anticipated [his descent on Mount Sinai]: "And it came to pass on the third day, while it was yet morning, that there were thunders...upon the mount" (Ex. 19:16).

    E.   But prior: "For the third day the Lord will come down in the sight of all the people" (Ex. 19:11).

    F.   The Israelites had been sleeping all that night, for the sleep of Pentecost is very pleasant, and the night is brief.

    G.   R. Yudan said, "Not a flea bit them."

    H.   Came the Holy One, blessed be He, and found them sleeping. So he had the trumpets and horns sounded.

    I.   That is in line with this verse: "And it came to pass on the third day, while it was yet morning, that there were thunders...upon the mount" (Ex. 19:16).

J.   Moses woke up the Israelites and brought them forth to receive the King of kings of kings, the Holy One, blessed be He: "And Moses brought the people forth to meet God" (Ex. 19:17).

K.   The Holy One went before them until he came to Mount Sinai: "Now Mount Sinai was entirely in smoke" (Ex. 19:18).

L.   Said R. Isaac, "This is why he criticized them through Isaiah: 'Wherefore when I came was there no man? When I called, there was no one to answer? Is my hand shortened at all, that it cannot redeem' (Isa. 50:2)."

3. A.   [Supply: "While the king was on his couch, [my nard gave forth its fragrance]":] Said R. Yudan, "While Hezekiah and his comrades were eating their Passover-offerings in Jerusalem, the Holy One, blessed be He, had already anticipated [their deliverance] on that same night:

B.   "'And it came to pass that night that the angel of the Lord went forth and smote in the camp of the Assyrians' (2 Kgs. 19:35)."

4. A.   [Supply: "While the king was on his couch, [my nard gave forth its fragrance]":] Said R. Abbahu, "While Moses and Israel were eating their Passover-offerings in Egypt, the Holy One, blessed be He, had already anticipated [their deliverance] on that same night:

B.   "'And it came to pass at midnight that the Lord smote all the firstborn in the land of Egypt' (Ex. 12:29)."

5. A.   Then it is the position of R. Abbahu that "my nard gave forth its fragrance" bears a negative meaning: "my bad spice gave forth its stink," for the smell of the blood was bad, but God brought them a good scent of the spices of paradise.

B.   So that made them want to eat.

C.   They said to him, "Our lord, Moses, give us something to eat."

D.   Said to them Moses, "Thus has the Holy One, blessed be He, said to me, 'No foreigner will eat of it' (Ex. 12:43)."

E.   They went and put out the gentiles who were among them, and that made them want to eat.

F.   They said to him, "Our lord, Moses, give us something to eat."

G.   He said to them, "Thus has the Holy One, blessed be He, said to me, 'And every man's servant, bought for money, when you have circumcised him, shall eat thereof' (Ex. 12:44)."

H.   So they went and circumcised their servants, and that made them want to eat.

I.   They said to him, "Our lord, Moses, give us something to eat."

J.   He said to them, "Thus has the Holy One, blessed be He, said to me, 'No uncircumcised persons shall eat of it' (Ex. 12:48)."

K.   Thereupon everyone put his sword on his thigh and circumcised himself.

L.   Who circumcised them?

M.   R. Berekhiah said, "Moses was circumcising them, Aaron was doing the trimming, and Joshua gave them what to drink."

N.   Some say, "Joshua did the circumcising, Aaron did the trimming, and Moses gave them to drink.

O.   "So it is written, 'At that time the Lord said to Joshua, Make knives of flint and again circumcise the children of Israel the second time' (Josh. 5:2).

P.   "Why a second time? Because he was the one who had done it the first time.

Q.   "Forthwith: 'Joshua made knives of flint and circumcised the children of Israel at Gibeat-haaralot' (Josh. 5:3)."

R.   What is the meaning of "at Gibeat-haaralot"?

S.   Rabbi said, "On this basis we learn that they made it a hill of foreskins."

We move on to a fresh statement of essentially the same position as is expressed at XII:i.1ff. The main point is at No. 1. No. 2 restates No. 1 in a powerful parable, which adds nothing new. The reason that the rest is tacked on is the conception of God's anticipating what is going to happen, and that of course is hardly the focus of any of the prior materials. Nos. 3, 4 say the same thing twice, which is that God anticipates the requirements of Israel and redeems them before they know they require redemption or without their knowledge that redemption is taking place. No. 5 then presents a sustained exposition of Ex. 12:43f, with the usual secondary accretions. It is hardly a triumph of the art of compilation.

13

Song of Songs Rabbah to Song of Songs 1:13

1:13   *My beloved is to me a bag of myrrh,*
        that lies between my breasts.

XIII:i

1. A. "My beloved is to me a bag of myrrh, [that lies between my breasts]":
   B. What is the meaning of "a bag of myrrh"?
   C. R. Azariah in the name of R. Judah interpreted the verse to speak of Abraham, our father:
   D. "Just as myrrh is the best of all kinds of spices, so Abraham is the best of all the righteous persons.
   E. "Just as myrrh's fragrance circulates only when brought near fire, so Abraham's deeds were known only when he was thrown into the fiery furnace. And just as whoever collects myrrh finds that his hands get sore, so Abraham afflicted himself and gave himself pain through suffering."
2. A. "...that lies between my breasts":
   B. For he was [Simon:] clasped between the Presence of God and the angel:
   C. "And when he saw he ran to meet them" (Gen. 18:2):
   D. "...he saw": the Presence of God.
   E. "...he ran to meet them": the angel.

Once we have chosen the figure to be treated as having been metaphorized in our base verse, the rest is easy to work out; it is now Abraham. That signals that what will follow will be others of the patriarchs, and Isaac comes next. But there is some disorganization in our document, since Chapter Fourteen contains some materials pertinent to Chapter Thirteen, that is, Song 1:14's set is followed by materials that serve Song 1:13.

14

Song of Songs Rabbah to Song of Songs 1:14

1:14   *My beloved is to me a cluster of*
        henna blossoms,
        in the vineyards of En-gedi.

XIV:i

1. A. "My beloved is to me a cluster of henna blossoms, [in the vineyards of En-gedi]":
    B. "cluster" refers to Isaac,
    C. who was bound on the altar like a cluster [Simon, p. 81, n. 4: he was tied to the wood as a large cluster of grapes is tied to a pole].
    D. "...henna" [also refers to Isaac,]
    E. who atones for the sins of Israel [the words for henna and atone use the same consonants].
2. A. "...in the vineyards of En-gedi":
    B. this speaks of our father, Jacob,
    C. who came into his father [Isaac, to steal the birthright] with a pallid face out of fear and shame, and who wore as his cloak the skin of a goat, and so took the blessings which are the eye of the world [the words for eye and goat use the same consonants as En-gedi].

The application to the patriarchs is now completed. We revert to Song 1:13. Clearly the framers of the passage knew what are now Song 1:13 and 1:14 as a single unbroken verse. There is no important effect upon the meaning.

LIV:ii

1. A. [Supply: "My beloved is to me a bag of myrrh, that lies between my breasts":]
    B. R. Hunia in the name of R. Aha: "You have nothing more prized by a woman than a bundle of perfume.
    C. "Where does she keep it? It is between her breasts."

131

2. A.   And said R. Huna in the name of R. Simeon b. Laqish, "Said the community of Israel before the Holy One, blessed be He, 'You have afflicted the Egyptians through their first born, you have embittered their souls,

    B.   "'but as for me, "that lies between my breasts."'

    C.   "How so? An Egyptian would say to an Israelite, 'Hide this firstborn among your children,' and he would take him and hide him, but the angel would enter and smite him.

    D.   "'But as for me, he "lies between my breasts."'"

The exposition of Song 1:13 works on the second clause of the verse, and No. 2 has God lie between Israel's breasts. In context this is not at all daring.

XIV:iii

1. A.   [Supply: "My beloved is to me a cluster of henna blossoms, in the vineyards of En-gedi":}

    B.   R. Berekhiah said, "Said the Community of Israel before the Holy One, blessed be He, 'When you pain me, when you distress me, "My beloved is mine [and I am his, he pastures his flock among the lilies]" (Song 2:16).

    C.   "'You become my beloved, and you see what man there is in my midst who is so great as can say to the attribute of justice, "Enough," and you take him and make him a pledge on my behalf.'

    D.   "So it is written, '[My beloved is to me] a cluster of henna blossoms, [in the vineyards of En-gedi].'"

2. A.   What is the meaning of "a cluster"?

    B.   [Reading the letters of the word for cluster yields] a man in who is all:

    C.   Scripture, Mishnah, Talmud, Supplements, Lore.

3. A.   "...henna blossoms":

    B.   who atones for the sins of Israel [the words for henna and atone use the same consonants].

4. A.   "...in the vineyards of En-gedi":

    B.   this [En-gedi] refers to the patriarchs of the world, who follow after you like kids and receive the blessings which are the eye of the world [the words for eye and kid use the same consonants as En-gedi].

The two verses read together yield the same metaphorization of the patriarches, pure and simple. So there is no drastic shift in meaning when we join the verse.

XIV:iv

1. A.   [Supply: "My beloved is to me a bag of myrrh, that lies between my breasts. My beloved is to me a cluster of henna blossoms, in the vineyards of En-gedi]":

    B.   R. Yohanan interpreted the verse to speak of the kind of incense that was made by the family of Abtinus:

C.   "'...a bag of myrrh': this is one of the eleven spices that comprised that incense."

2. A.   R. Hunia said [why there were eleven], "Scripture states, 'And the Lord said to Moses, Take for you sweet spices' (Ex. 30:34): two; 'stacte and onycha and galbanum' – five; 'sweet spices' – if you say this is only two more, then this has already been said, so [read the phrase in line with the following] 'of each shall there be a like weight,' thus adding five to the former five, ten; 'with pure frankincense' – eleven.

B.   "In this connection, sages made an inquiry and found that there is nothing better for incense than these eleven spices alone."

3. A.   "...that lies between my breasts":

B.   [the cloud of incense] was held exactly within the two staves of the ark [Simon, p. 83: on the Day of Atonement when burned in the Holy of Holies by the High Priest].

4. A.   "[My beloved is to me] a cluster of henna blossoms":

B.   which atones for the sins of Israel [the words for henna and atone use the same consonants].

C.   Said R. Isaac, "'Cluster' indicates that [the cloud of incense] would spread and ascend to the beams, and then would come down like a cluster [that was hanging on the vine].

D.   "'...henna blossoms' means that it would atone for the sins of Israel [the words for henna and atone use the same consonants]."

5. A.   And said R. Isaac, "'That the cloud of incense may cover' (Lev. 16:13):

B.   "We do not know the purpose of this covering.

C.   "But David came and explained it: 'You have forgiven the iniquity of your people, you have covered all their sin' (Ps. 85:3)."

6. A.   "...in the vineyards of En-gedi":

B.   On account of the merit of the undertakings that I made with your father, Abraham, between the pieces, as it is said, "On that day the Lord made a covenant with Abram saying" (Gen. 15:18).

C.   The verse, "My beloved is to me a cluster of henna blossoms, in the vineyards of En-gedi" speaks of Abraham: "After these things the word of the Lord came to Abram in a vision, saying, Fear not Abram" (Gen. 15:1).

7. A.   [Supply: "After these things the word of the Lord came to Abram in a vision, saying, Fear not Abram" (Gen. 15:1).]

B.   R. Levi in the name of R. Hama said, "At that time there was a measure of uncertainty.

C.   "Who felt uncertain?

D.   "It was Abraham, who felt uncertainty and said before the Holy One, blessed be He, 'Lord of the age, you made a covenant with Abraham that you would not wipe out his seed from the world, and I went and collected good deeds before you, so you gave my covenant precedence over his covenant. Now perhaps someone else is going to come and assemble the merit of religious duties and good deeds more than mine, so the covenant made with him will set aside the covenant made with me!'

E.   "Said to him the Holy One, blessed be He, "'After these things the word of the Lord came to Abram in a vision, saying, Fear not

Abram, I am your shield" (Gen. 15:1). Out of Noah I did not raise up shields and righteous men, but out of you I shall raise up shields and righteous men. And not only so, but if your children should fall into transgression and wicked actions, I shall discern which great man there is among them who can say to the Attribute of Justice, "Enough!" and I shall take him and treat him as the pledge in their behalf.'

F. "For so it is said, 'a cluster,' [reading the letters of the word for cluster yields] a man in who is all, Scripture, Mishnah, Talmud, Supplements, Lore.

G. "'...henna blossoms': who atones for the sins of Israel [the words for henna and atone use the same consonants].

H. "'...in the vineyards of En-Gedi': I take him as a pledge in their behalf."

8. A. Another explanation of "a cluster [of henna blossoms, in the vineyards of En-gedi]":

B. Ben Nezirah said, "This refers to the Holy One, blessed be He, a man in whom is everything.

C. "'...of henna blossoms': who rejected the nations of the world and acknowledged Israel.

D. "When did he reject the nations of the world? One must say, in the war of Jehoshaphat: 'And it came to pass after this that the children of Moab and the children of Ammon and with them some of the Ammonites came against Jehoshaphat to battle' (2 Chr. 20:1).

E. "You note that the Israelites came in the might of Abraham, while Ammon and Moab came in the might of Lot. These fought those, and these fell at the hand of those, and as for Jehoshaphat, his God aided him so he won.

F. "Thus he rejected the nations of the world.

G. "Now if someone should say to you that Scripture does not speak of Jehoshaphat, say to him:

H. "'Here we find a reference to En-gedi and elsewhere the same: "In Hazazon-tamar, the same is En-gedi" (2 Chr. 20:1). Just as En-gedi in the latter passage speaks of the war of Jehoshaphat, so the reference here means that Scripture speaks of Jehoshaphat.'"

9. A. Said R. Levi b. R. Zechariah, "Now if in connection with this world, it is written concerning the Holy One, blessed be He, 'the Lord your God is a devouring fire, a jealous God' (Dt. 4:24), he rejects the nations of the world and recognizes Israel,

B. "in the age to come, how much the more so!"

Nos. 1, 2 work on the matter of myrrh. Then we proceed to the uses of the incense, and that introduces the motif of forgiveness, such as the henna/atone intersection invites, so, No. 4. Nos. 5, 6 complete the exposition of the theme of incense. The exposition moves smoothly into the theme of Abraham, No. 6. But that starts an entirely new inquiry, since what is now subject to the verse's metaphor is Abraham. So we move on to treat the verse as a metaphorization of Abraham, yielding, however, yet another affirmation of Israel. This is surely justified by the possibility of reading the verse as we do, point by point in connection with Abraham. No. 8 finds yet a third point, the verse now speaks of God; the same theme – the rejection of the nations, the affirmation of Israel – is played through again. No. 9 then provides a suitable finis.

15

Song of Songs Rabbah to Song of Songs 1:15

1:15   *Behold, you are beautiful, my love;*
        behold, you are beautiful;
        your eyes are doves.

XV:i

1. A.   "Behold, you are beautiful, my love; behold, you are beautiful; [your eyes are doves]":
    B.   "Behold you are beautiful" in religious deeds,
    C.   "Behold you are beautiful" in acts of grace,
    D.   "Behold you are beautiful" in carrying out religious obligations of commission,
    E.   "Behold you are beautiful" in carrying out religious obligations of omission,
    F.   "Behold you are beautiful" in carrying out the religious duties of the home, in separating priestly ration and tithes,
    G.   "Behold you are beautiful" in carrying out the religious duties of the field, gleanings, forgotten sheaves, the corner of the field, poor person's tithe, and declaring the field ownerless.
    H.   "Behold you are beautiful" in observing the taboo against mixed species.
    I.   "Behold you are beautiful" in providing a linen cloak with woolen show-fringes.
    J.   "Behold you are beautiful" in [keeping the rules governing] planting,
    K.   "Behold you are beautiful" in keeping the taboo on uncircumcised produce,
    L.   "Behold you are beautiful" in keeping the laws on produce in the fourth year after the planting of an orchard,
    M.   "Behold you are beautiful" in circumcision,
    N.   "Behold you are beautiful" in trimming the wound,
    O.   "Behold you are beautiful" in reciting the Prayer,
    P.   "Behold you are beautiful" in reciting the Shema,

	Q.	"Behold you are beautiful" in putting a mezuzah on the doorpost of your house,
	R.	"Behold you are beautiful" in wearing phylacteries,
	S.	"Behold you are beautiful" in building the tabernacle for the Festival of Tabernacles,
	T.	"Behold you are beautiful" in taking the palm branch and etrog on the Festival of Tabernacles,
	U.	"Behold you are beautiful" in repentance,
	V.	"Behold you are beautiful" in good deeds,
	W.	"Behold you are beautiful" in this world,
	X.	"Behold you are beautiful" in the world to come.
2.	A.	"...your eyes are doves":
	B.	"...your eyes" stand for the sanhedrin, which is the eyesight of the community.
	C.	That is in line with this verse: "If it is hid from the eyes of the community" (Num. 15:24).
	D.	There are two hundred forty-eight limbs in a human being, and all of them function only through eyesight.
	E.	So the Israelites can function only in line with their sanhedrin.
3.	A.	"Doves":
	B.	Just as a dove is innocent, so the Israelites are [Simon supplies: innocent; just as the dove is beautiful in its movement, so Israel are] beautiful in their movement, when they go up for the pilgrim festivals.
	C.	Just as a dove is distinguished, so the Israelites are distinguished: not shaving, in circumcision, in show-fringes.
	D.	Just as the dove is modest, so the Israelites are modest.
	E.	Just as the dove puts forth its neck for slaughter, so the Israelites: "For your sake are we killed all day long" (Ps. 44:23).
	F.	Just as the dove atones for sin, so the Israelites atone for other nations.
	G.	For all those seventy bullocks that they offer on the Festival of Tabernacles correspond to the nations of the world, so that the world should not become desolate on their account: "In return for my love they are my adversaries, but I am all prayer" (Ps. 109:4).
	H.	Just as the dove, once it recognizes its mate, never again changes him for another, so the Israelites, once they recognized the Holy One, blessed be He, never exchanged him for another.
	I.	Just as the dove, when it enters its nest, recognizes its nest and young, fledglings and apertures, so the three rows of the disciples of the sages, when they take their seats before them, knows each one his place.
	J.	Just as the dove, even though you take its fledglings from under it, does not ever abandon its cote, so the Israelites, even though the house of the sanctuary was destroyed, never nullified the three annual pilgrim festivals.
	K.	Just as the dove renews its brood month by month, so the Israelites every month renew Torah and good deeds.
	L.	Just as the dove [Simon:] goes far afield but returns to her cote, so do the Israelites: "They shall come trembling as a bird out of Egypt" (Hos. 11:11), this speaks of the generation of the

wilderness; "and as a dove out of the land of Assyria" (Hos. 11:11), this speaks of the Ten Tribes.

M.   And in both cases: "And I will make them dwell in their houses, says the Lord" (Hos. 11:11).

4. A.   Rabbi says, "There is a kind of dove, who, when it is being fed, attracts her fellows, who smell her scent and come to her cote.

    B.   "So when an elder is in session and expounding, many proselytes convert at that time, for example, Jethro, who heard and came, and Rahab, who heard and came.

    C.   "Likewise on account of Hananiah, Mishael, and Azariah, many converted: 'For when he sees his children...sanctify my name...they also that err in spirit shall come to understanding' (Isa. 29:23)."

5. A.   Rabbi was in session and expounding, but the community's attention wandered, so he wanted to wake them up. He said, "A single woman in Egypt produced six hundred thousand at a single birth."

    B.   Now there was present a disciple, named R. Ishmael b. R. Yosé, who said to him, "Who was this?"

    C.   He said to him, "This was Jochebed, who produced Moses, and he was numbered as the equal to six hundred thousand Israelites: 'Then sang Moses and the children of Israel' (Ex. 15:1); 'And the children of Israel did according to all that the Lord has commanded Moses' (Num. 1:54); 'And there has not arisen a prophet in Israel like Moses' (Dt. 34:10)."

6. A.   "...your eyes are doves":
    B.   they are like doves.
    C.   Your likeness is similar to that of the dove:
    D.   Just as a dove brought light to the world, so you bring light to the world: "And nations shall walk at your light" (Isa. 60:3).
    E.   When did a dove bring light to the world?
    F.   In the time of Noah: "And the dove came in to him in the evening, and lo, in her mouth was an olive leaf, freshly plucked" (Gen. 8:11).

7. A.   [Supply: "And the dove came in to him in the evening, and lo, in her mouth was an olive leaf, freshly plucked" (Gen. 8:11):] What is the meaning of "freshly plucked"?
    B.   It was killed: "Joseph is without doubt torn in pieces" (Gen. 37:33).
    C.   Said R. Berekhiah, "Had she not killed it, it would have turned into a great tree."

8. A.   [=Genesis Rabbah **XXX:VI.3:**] Whence did the dove bring the olive branch?
    B.   R. Levi [Gen. R.: Abba] said, "She brought it from the young shoots in the Land of Israel."
    C.   [Gen. R.: R. Levi said, "She brought it from the mount of Olives,] for the Land of Israel had not been submerged in the flood. That is in line with what the Holy One, blessed be He, said to Ezekiel, 'Son of man, say to her: "You are a land that is not cleaned nor rained upon in the day of indignation"' (Ez.. 22:24)."
    D.   R. Yohanan said, "Even millstone cases dissolved in the water of the flood."

E.   R. Tarye [Gen. R.: Birai] said, "The gates of the garden of Eden opened for the dove, and from there she brought it."

F.   Said to him R. Abbahu, "If she had brought it from the garden of Eden, should the dove not have brought something of greater value, such as cinnamon or balsam? But in choosing the olive leaf, the dove gave a signal to Noah, saying to him, 'Noah, better is something bitter from this [source, namely,] the Holy One, blessed be He, than something sweet from you.'"

The pattern of No. 1 derives from the hermeneutic that treats our poem as a source of metaphors for Israel's religious reality. No. 2 follows suit. No. 3 reverts to the metaphor of the dove for Israel. No. 4 is attached with good reason, and No. 5 is parachuted down because it was attached to No. 4 before No. 4 entered our document; the principle of agglutination prior to the making of documents clearly was the making of collections in the names of authorities. No. 6 then reverts to our base verse, and it also introduces the inevitable appearance of the dove in the story of Noah. The rest then is attached for thematic reasons.

16

Song of Songs Rabbah to Song of Songs 1:16

1:16   *Behold, you are beautiful, my beloved,*
truly lovely.
Our couch is green...

XVI:i

1. A. "Behold, you are beautiful, my beloved, truly lovely. [Our couch is green]":
   B. R. Abbahu and R. Hanina:
   C. R. Abbahu said, "He praised her with repetition, but she praised him with plain speech.
   D. "He praised her with repetition: 'Behold, you are beautiful, my love; behold, you are beautiful; [your eyes are doves]' (Song 1:15). For he he wanted to make himself another nation, he can do it.
   E. "She praised him with plain speech, 'Behold, you are beautiful, my beloved, truly lovely.'"
   F. R. Hanina said to him, "She too praised him with repetition: 'Behold, you are beautiful, my beloved, truly lovely.'
   G. "She said to him, 'Lord of the age, the anger that you bring upon me is pleasant. Why? For you bring me back and carry me to better ways.'" [The words for anger and truly use the same consonants.]

2. A. Another explanation of the clause, "Our couch is green":
   B. This refers to the house of the sanctuary: "With his nurse in his bed chamber, he was hid in the house of the Lord" (2 Kgs. 11:2).

3. A. [Supply: "With his nurse in his bed chamber, he was hid in the house of the Lord" (2 Kgs. 11:2):]
   B. What is the meaning of "bed chamber?
   C. R. Eleazar and R. Samuel b. R. Nahman:
   D. R. Eleazar said, "in the [Simon:] side chambers.
   E. R. Samuel b. R. Nahman said, "in the upper chambers."
   F. There is no disagreement.

G. One who said "in the side chambers" speaks of the rainy season, and one who said, "in the upper chambers" speaks of the dry season.

4. A. Another explanation of the clause, "Our couch is green":

B. R. Azariah in the name of R. Judah b. R. Simon: "The matter is to be compared to the case of a king who went out to the wilderness, and they brought him a short bed. He began to find it uncomfortable and it cramped his limbs.

C. "When they got to town, they brought him a good-sized bed. He began to stretch himself out and loosen his limbs.

D. "So before the house of the sanctuary was built, the Presence of God was cramped in between the two staves of the ark.

E. "When the house of the sanctuary was built, 'and the staves were lengthened' (1 Kgs. 8:8)."

5. A. Another explanation of the clause, "Our couch is green":

B. Just as a bed is made only for comfort, so before the house of the sanctuary was built, the Presence of God was moved from place to place:

C. "But I have walked in a tent and in a tabernacle" (1 Sam. 7:6).

D. After the house of the sanctuary was built, "This is my resting place forever" (Ps. 132:14).

6. A. Another explanation of the clause, "Our couch is green":

B. Just as a bed is made only for comfort, so Israel, before the house of the sanctuary was built, were moved from place to place: "they journeyed and they encamped."

C. Once the house of the sanctuary was built: "And Judah and Israel dwelt safely" (1 Kgs. 5:5).

7. A. Another explanation of the clause, "Our couch is green":

B. Just as a bed is only for sexual propagation, so before the house of the sanctuary was built: "Go, count Israel" (1 Chr. 21:2).

C. Once the house of the sanctuary was built: "Judah and Israel were many, as the sand" (1 Kgs. 4:20).

8. A. Another explanation of the clause, "Our couch is green":

B. Just as a bed is only for sexual propagation, so before the house of the sanctuary was built: "The whole congregation was forty two thousand" (Ezra 2:64).

C. Once the house of the sanctuary was built, they were fruitful and multiplied.

9. A. For R. Yohanan said, "From Gabbata to Antipatris were six hundred thousand villages, and they would count a population twice as numerous as the Israelites who went out of Egypt.

B. "And now if you tried to stick in six hundred thousand reeds, it could not hold them."

C. Said R. Hanina, "The land of Israel has shrunk."

Song 1:15, 16 are assigned by Abbahu to God and Israel, respectively; one verse repeats its adjective, the other does not. Hanina's message is separate; he works on the meanings imputed to the letters that spell "anger." We proceed to the second half of the base verse, which is taken to speak of the house of the sanctuary; the

Temple then is where God and Israel are joined. Once that point registers, at No. 2, we work on its deeper meanings, from No. 4 to the end. The Temple is God's resting place, so Nos. 4, 5, and also Israel's, No. 6; the Temple is the source of Israel's fecundity, Nos. 7, 8. So the sequence from No. 3 to the end is in good order and the necessary themes well exposed.

17

Song of Songs Rabbah to Song of Songs 1:17

1:17   *...the beams of our house are cedar,*
        our rafters are pine.

XVII

1. A. "...the beams of our house are cedar, [our rafters are pine]":
   B. R. Menahama in the name of R. Berekhiah: "The stones on which our father, Jacob, slept were turned beneath him into feather beds.
   C. "What [Simon:] sprung from them?
   D. "'...the beams of our house are cedar.'"

2. A. Another interpretation of the phrase, "the beams of our house are cedar":
   B. This refers to the righteous men and women, the prophets and prophetesses, who came from him.

3. A. "...our rafters are pine":
   B. Said R. Yohanan, "No one can derive any use of pine. Why? Because it bends."
   C. So too is the view of R. Yohanan, for R. Yohanan said, "'I am like a leafy cypress tree' (Hos. 14:9): 'I am the one who bowed down so as to uproot the desire to serve idolatry.'
   D. "'Ephraim shall say, what have I to do with idols' (Hos. 14:9): 'What have I to do with the impulse to worship idols?'
   E. "'As for me I respond' (Hos. 14:9): 'I raise up my voice to him.'
   F. "'And look on him' (Hos. 14:9): 'did I not sing a song to you?'
   G. "Thus: 'I am the one who bowed down so as to uproot the desire to serve idolatry.'"

4. A. Another explanation of the clause, "our rafters are pine":
   B. the place on which the priests ran was made of pine: "And he covered the floor of the house with pine boards" (1 Kgs.6:15).

5. A. Said R. Yohanan, "The Torah thereby teaches good policy: a person should make his ceiling with cedars and his floor with pine wood:
   B. "'the beams of our house are cedar, our rafters are pine.'"

The exposition is somewhat diffuse. The opening point recalls that the temple is built on the spot on which Jacob used a stone for a pillow. No. 2 sustains the same metaphor of the Temple for Jacob's house. No. 3 moves from metaphor to moral, and No. 4 from metaphor to a concrete allusion to the Temple; but that of course rests upon the established reading of this "bower" for God's and Israel's life as metaphor for the Temple.

Part Two
PARASHAH TWO

Song of Songs Chapter Two

2:1   *I am a rose of Sharon,*
  a lily of the valleys.

2:2   *As a lily among brambles,*
  so is my love among maidens.

2:3   *As an apple tree among the trees of the wood,*
  so is my beloved among young men.
  With great delight I sat in his shadow,
  and his fruit was sweet to my taste.

2:4   *He brought me to the wine cellar,*
  and his banner over me was love.

2:5   *Sustain me with raisins,*
  refresh me with apples;
  for I am sick with love.

2:6   *O that his left hand were under my head,*
  and that his right hand embraced me!

2:7   *I adjure you, O daughters of Jerusalem,*
  by the gazelles or the hinds of the field,
  that you not stir up nor awaken love
  until it please.

2:8   *The voice of my beloved!*
  Behold he comes,
  leaping upon the mountains,
  bounding over the hills.

2:9   *My beloved is like a gazelle,*
  or a young stag.
  Behold, there he stands
  behind our wall,
  gazing in at the windows,
  looking through the lattice.

2:10   *My beloved speaks and says to me,*
  "Arise, my love, my fair one,
  and come away;

2:11   *"for lo, the winter is past,*
         the rain is over and gone.
2:12   *"The flowers appear on the earth,*
         the time of singing has come,
         and the voice of the turtledove is heard in our land.
2:13   *"The fig tree puts forth its figs,*
         and the vines are in blossom;
         they give forth fragrance.
         "Arise, my love, my fair one,
         and come away.
2:14   *"O my dove, in the clefts of the rock,*
         in the covert of the cliff,
         "let me see your face,
         let me hear your voice,
         "for your voice is sweet,
         and your face is comely.
2:15   *"Catch us the foxes,*
         the little foxes,
         that spoil the vineyards,
         for our vineyards are in blossom."
2:16   *My beloved is mine and I am his,*
         he pastures his flock among the lilies.
2:17   *Until the day breathes*
         and the shadows flee,
         turn my beloved, be like a gazelle,
         or a young stag upon rugged mountains.

18

Song of Songs Rabbah to Song of Songs 2:1

2:1   *I am a rose of Sharon,*
       a lily of the valleys.

XVIII.i

1. A.   "I am a rose of Sharon, [a lily of the valleys]":

     B.   Said the Community of Israel, "I am the one, and I am beloved.

     C.   "I am the one whom the Holy One, blessed be He, loved more than the seventy nations."

2. A.   "I am a rose of Sharon":

     B.   "For I made for him a shade through Bezalel [the words for shade and Bezalel use the same consonants as the word for rose]: 'And Bezalel made the ark' (Ex. 38:1)."

3. A.   "...of Sharon":

     B.   "For I said before him a song [which word uses the same consonants as the word for Sharon] through Moses:

     C.   "'Then sang Moses and the children of Israel' (Ex. 15:1)."

4. A.   Another explanation of the phrase, "I am a rose of Sharon":

     B.   Said the Community of Israel, "I am the one, and I am beloved.

     C.   "I am the one who was hidden in the shadow of Egypt, but in a brief moment the Holy One, blessed be He, brought me together to Raamses, and I [Simon:] blossomed forth in good deeds like a rose, and I said before him this song: 'You shall have a song as in the night when a feast is sanctified' (Isa. 30:29)."

5. A.   Another explanation of the phrase, "I am a rose of Sharon":

     B.   Said the Community of Israel, "I am the one, and I am beloved.

     C.   "I am the one who was hidden in the shadow of the sea, but in a brief moment I [Simon:] blossomed forth in good deeds like a rose, and I pointed to him with the finger [Simon:] (opposite to me): 'This is my God and I will glorify him' (Ex. 15:2)."

6. A.   Another explanation of the phrase, "I am a rose of Sharon":

     B.   Said the Community of Israel, "I am the one, and I am beloved.

     C.   "I am the one who was hidden in the shadow of Mount Sinai, but in a brief moment I [Simon:] blossomed forth in good deeds like a lily in hand and in heart, and I said before him, 'All that the Lord has said we will do and obey' (Ex. 24:7)."

7. A. Another explanation of the phrase, "I am a rose of Sharon":
    B. Said the Community of Israel, "I am the one, and I am beloved.
    C. "I am the one who was hidden and downtrodden in the shadow of the kingdoms. But tomorrow, when the Holy One, blessed be He, redeems me from the shadow of the kingdoms, I shall blossom forth like a lily and say before him a new song: 'Sing to the Lord a new song, for he has done marvelous things, his right hand and his holy arm have wrought salvation for him' (Ps. 98:1)."

8. A. R. Berekhiah said, "This verse ["I am a rose of Sharon, a lily of the valleys"] was said by the wilderness.
    B. "Said the wilderness, 'I am the wilderness, and I am beloved.
    C. "'For all the good things that are in the world are hidden in me: 'I will plant in the wilderness a cedar, an acacia tree' (Isa. 41:19).
    D. "'The Holy One, blessed be He, has put them in me so that they may be guarded in me. And when the Holy One, blessed be He, seeks them from me, I shall return to him unimpaired the bailment that he has left with me.'
    E. "'And I shall blossom in good deeds and say a song before him: "The wilderness and parched land shall be glad" (Isa. 35:1).'"

9. A. In the name of rabbis they have said, ""This verse ["I am a rose of Sharon, a lily of the valleys"] was said by the land [of Israel].
    B. "Said the land, 'I am the land, and I am beloved.
    C. "'For all the dead of the world are hidden in me: "Your dead shall live, my dead bodies shall arise" (Isa. 26:19).
    D. "'When the Holy One, blessed be He, will ask them from me, I shall restore them to him.
    E. "'And I shall blossom in good deeds and say a song before him: "From the uttermost parts of the earth we have heard songs" (Isa. 24:16).'"

This stunning and cogent exposition metaphorizes Israel in Egypt, at the Sea, at Sinai, and subjugated by the gentile kingdoms, and coherently explains how the redemption will come. The Song therefore has Israel singing to God. The voices change, but the basic motif of the metaphorization of Israel's life remains constant. The formal requirements are shown at No. 4, and are readily retrojected into Nos. 1-3; the rest is entirely coherent. I find no special significance in the fact that we have five go-arounds. The development of the formal program and motif at No. 8, 9 in no way diminishes from the power of the whole but only adds to it.

XVIII:ii

1. A. [Concerning the verse, "I am a rose of Sharon, a lily of the valleys,"] R. Yudan and R. Eliezer:
    B. R. Yudan said, "'I am a rose': does not the word for rose mean the same as the word for lily, and the word for lily the same as the word for rose?

C.   "But when it is in the early stages of growth, it is called rose, but when full-grown, lily.

D.   "And as to the word for rose, why is it called rose? Because it is hidden in its own shadow [the words for hidden in its own shadow use the letters for the word for rose] [Simon, p. 93, n. 1: its many petals creating a shadow for itself]."

2.   A.   Said R. Eliezer, "The righteous are compared to the most beautiful of plants, and among the most beautiful of plants, the most beautiful species. The most beautiful of plants is the lily,. and the most beautiful species of that plant is the lily.

B.   "And not to the lily of the mountains, which easily withers, but the lily of the valley, which continues to bloom.

C.   "But the wicked are compared to the most vile of things, and to the most vile species of that thing.

D.   "They are compared to the most vile of things, which is chaff, and not to the chaff of the valley, which has some wetness, but: 'And they shall be chased as the chaff of the mountains before the wind' (Isa. 17:13)."

The two statements of course do not match, since No. 1 talks of one thing, No. 2 of another. Yudan's entry deals with the use of two words for the same species, and Eliezer's point is essentially autonomous of our verse altogether.

XVIII:iii

1.   A.   R. Abba b. Kahana said, "[With reference to 'a lily of the valleys'], said the Community of Israel before the Holy One, blessed be He, 'I am the one, and I am beloved.

B.   "'For I am [Simon} plunged into the valley of troubles.

C.   "'But when the Holy One, blessed be He, will draw me up from my sorrows, I shall blossom in good deeds like a lily and say before him a song.'

D.   "Is it not the one that says, 'Lord in trouble they have sought you' (Isa. 26:3) [Simon, p. 93, n. 3: in consequence of their trouble, having been released therefrom, they have sought thee with song.]"

2.   A.   Said R. Aha, "[With reference to 'a lily of the valleys'], said the Community of Israel before the Holy One, blessed be He, 'When you [Simon:] look piercingly at me, I shall blossom in good deeds like a lily and say a song:

B.   "'"A song of ascents: out of the depths I have called you O Lord" (Ps. 130:1).'"

3.   A.   Rabbis say, "[With reference to 'a lily of the valleys'], said the Community of Israel before the Holy One, blessed be He, 'I am the one, and I am beloved.

B.   "'For I am [Simon} plunged into the valley of Gehenna.

C.   "'But he Holy One, blessed be He, will draw me up from the depths: "He brought me up also out of the tumultuous pit" (Ps. 40:3).

D.   "'Then I shall blossom forth in good deeds and say a song:

E.   "'"And he has put a new song in my mouth" (Ps. 40:4).'"

4.   A.   The statement of Rabbis accords with the view of R. Eleazar the Modite: "In the age to come the angels in charge of the other nations will come to accuse Israel before the Holy One, blessed be He,

      B.   "saying to him, 'Lord of the world, these have worshipped idolatry, and those have worshipped idolatry.

      C.   "'These have practiced fornication and those have practiced fornication.

      D.   "'These have shed blood and those have shed blood.

      E.   "'How come these go down to Gehenna, while those do not go down?'

      F.   "And the Holy One, blessed be He, will answer them, saying, 'If so, then let all of the nations go to Gehenna with their gods.'

      G.   "That is in line with this verse: 'For let all the peoples walk each one in the name of its god' (Mic. 4:5)."

5.   A.   Said R. Reuben, "If the matter were not expressly written out in Scripture, it would not be possible to say it at all:

      B.   "'For in fire will the Lord be judged' (Isa. 66:16).

      C.   "What is written is not 'judges' but 'is judged'!

      D.   "So too David by the Holy Spirit said, 'Yes, though I walk in the valley of the shadow of death I will fear no evil, for you are with me' (Ps. 23:4) [that is, God is in Gehenna with David]."

6.   A.   [Supply: "Yes, though I walk in the valley of the shadow of death I will fear no evil, for you are with me; your rod and your staff comfort me; only goodness and mercy shall follow me all the days of my life, and I shall dwell in the house of the Lord forever" (Ps. 23:4-6]:

      B.   Another comment on "your road and your staff comfort me":

      C.   "your rod" refers to suffering.

      D.   "...your staff" refers to the Torah.

      E.   "...comfort me": shall I claim, without suffering? No, for Scripture says, "only."

      F.   Might one say, "in this world"?

      G.   Scripture says, "only goodness and mercy shall follow me all the days of my life, and I shall dwell in the house of the Lord forever."

This profound composite works on the word "valley," which means also, "depths," and therefore calls to mind suffering and sorrow. That accounts for No. 1, which replays the familiar form in the new key. No. 2 then works on ascending from the depths, with the same result, and No. 3 follows suit. While No. 4 looks as though it were tacked on without good reason, in fact the basic theme is the same: now Gehenna. And the same is to be said for Nos. 5, 6, which deal with passage through the valley. So the common theme serves to unite quite disparate materials, but also to make of them a single cogent composite.

19

Song of Songs Rabbah
to Song of Songs 2:2

2:2   *As a lily among brambles,*
     so is my love among maidens.

XIX:i

1. A.   "As a lily among brambles, [so is my love among maidens]":

     B.   R. Isaac interpreted the verse to speak of Rebecca: "'And Isaac was forty years old when he took as his wife Rebecca, daughter of Bethuel, the Aramaean of Paddan-aram, sister of Laban the Aramaean' (Gen. 25:20).

     C.   "Why does Scripture find it necessary to say that she was the sister of Laban the Aramaean? Has not the fact that she was the daughter of Bethuel the Aramaean already been stated? Whey does Scripture find it necessary to say that she was the daughter of Bethuel? Has not the fact that she was the sister of Laban the Aramaean already been stated?

     D.   "It is necessary to indicate that her father was a deceiver, her brother a deceiver, the people of her place where she grew up deceivers.

     E.   "This righteous woman has emerged from their midst. To what may she be compared? To 'a lily among brambles.'"

     F.   R. Phineas in the name of R. Simon: "'And Isaac sent Jacob away, and he went to Paddan-aram, to Laban, son of Bethuel, the Aramaean, brother of Rebecca, mother of Jacob and Esau' (Gen. 28:5).

     G.   "He included them all in the same circle of deception."

2. A.   R. Eleazar interpreted the same verse to speak of those who came forth from Egypt: "'a lily among brambles':

     B.   "Just as it is difficult to pick a rose among thorns, so it was hard to redeem the Israelites from Egypt.

     C.   "That is in line with the following verse of Scripture: 'Or has God tried to come to take a nation for himself from the midst of another nation' (Dt. 4:34)."

151

3. A.   R. Joshua in the name of R. Hanan: "'A nation from the midst of a people' is not written here, nor 'a people from the midst of a nation,' but 'a nation from the midst of a nation.'

    B.   "For the Egyptians were uncircumcised and the Israelites were uncircumcised, the Egyptians grew ceremonial locks and so did the Israelites, the Egyptians wore garments made of mixed species and so did the Israelites.

    C.   "Therefore by the measure of strict justice, the Israelites ought not to have been redeemed from Egypt."

    D.   Said R. Samuel b. R. Nahman, "If the Holy One, blessed be He, had not bound himself by an oath, the Israelites would never have been redeemed from Egypt.

    E.   "'Therefore say to the children of Israel, I am the Lord, and I shall take you out of the burdens of Egypt' (Ex. 6:6).

    F.   "The language, 'therefore,' can refer only to an oath, as it is said, 'Therefore I take an oath concerning the house of Eli' (1 Sam. 3:14)."

4. A.   Said R. Berekhiah, "'You have redeemed your people with your arm' (Ps. 77:6) – with naked power."

    B.   Said R. Yudan, "From the phrase, 'to go and take a nation from the midst of another nation' to the phrase 'great terrors' (Dt. 4:34) are seventy-two letters.

    C.   "Should you claim that there are more, you should deduct from the count the last reference to 'nation,' which does not count."

    D.   R. Abin said, "It was for the sake of his name that he redeemed them, and the name of the Holy One, blessed be He, consists of seventy-two letters."

5. A.   R. Azariah in the name of R. Judah in the name of R. Simon [interpreted the cited verse to speak of Israel before Mount Sinai].

    B.   ["'a lily among brambles':] The matter may be compared to a king who had an orchard. He planted in it rows upon rows of figs, grapevines, and pomegranates. After a while the king went down to his vineyard and found it filled with thorns and brambles. He brought woodcutters and cut it down. But he found in the orchard a single red rose. He took it and smelled it and regained his serenity and said, 'This rose is worthy that the entire orchard be saved on its account.'

    C.   "So too the entire world was created only on account of the Torah. For twenty-six generations the Holy One, blessed be He, looked down upon his world and saw it full of thorns and brambles, for example, the Generation of Enosh, the generation of the Flood, and the Sodomites.

    D.   "He planned to render the world useless and to destroy it: 'The Lord sat enthroned at the flood' (Ps. 29:10).

    E.   "But he found in the world a single red rose, Israel, that was destined to stand before Mount Sinai and to say before the Holy One, blessed be He, 'Whatever the Lord has said we shall do and we shall obey' (Ex. 24:7).

    F.   "Said the Holy One, blessed be He, [Lev. R.:] 'Israel is worthy that the entire world be saved on its account.'" [Song: "for the sake of the Torah and those who study it...."]

6. A.   R. Hanan of Sepphoris interpreted the verse to speak of acts of loving kindness [that one may do by helping others carry out their liturgical obligations]:

    B.   "Ten men entered a synagogue to say their prayers, but they did not know how to say the Shema and go before the ark to recite the Prayer. But there was among them one who did know how to say the Shema and to go before the ark.

    C.   "Among them, he was 'like a lily among brambles.'

    D.   "Ten men went in to greet the bride, but did not know how to say the blessings for the bride and groom. But there was among them one who knew how to say the blessing for bride and groom.

    E.   "Among them, he was 'like a lily among brambles.'

    F.   Ten went into a house of mourning but did not know how to say the blessing for mourners. But among them one did know how to say the blessing for mourners.

    G.   "Among them, he was 'like a lily among brambles.'

7. A.   R. Eleazar Hisma went to a certain place. The people said to him, "Does my lord know how to recite the Shema's blessings?"

    B.   He said to them, "No."

    C.   They said to him, "Does my lord know how to come near to recite the prayer before the ark?"

    D.   He said to them, "No."

    E.   They said to him, "Is this R. Eleazar, the man for whom people make such a fuss? It is for nothing that people call you 'my lord!'"

    F.   His face turned white. He went to R. Aqiba, and he looked sick. He said to him, "What's with you? You look sick."

    G.   He told the story to him.

    H.   He said to him, "Does my lord wish to learn?"

    I.   He said to him, "Yes."

    J.   After he had learned, he went to the same place. They said to him, "Does my lord know how to recite the Shema's blessings?"

    K.   He said to them, "Yes."

    L.   They said to him, "Does my lord know how to come near to recite the prayer before the ark?"

    M.   He said to them, "Yes."

    N.   They said to him, "Lo, Eleazar has regained the power of speech," and they called him R. Eleazar Hisma [=who can speak].

    O.   R. Jondah would teach his disciples even the blessing for bride and groom and even the blessing for mourners, saying to them, "You should be masters in every detail."

8. A.   R. Huna interpreted the verse to speak of the kingdoms [who now rule Israel]:

    B.   "['As a lily among brambles':] just as, when the north wind blows on the lily, it bends southward, and a thorn pricks it, and when the south wind blows, it bends northward, and a thorn pricks it, and all the while, the heart [of its stem[points upward,]

    C.   "so even though Israel is enslaved among the nations of the world by surcharges, head taxes, and confiscations, nonetheless their heart points upward toward their father in heaven.

    D.   [So did David say,] 'My eyes are always toward the Lord' (Ps. 25:15).

9. A. R. Abihu interpreted the cited verse to speak of the coming redemption:

    B. "['As a lily among brambles':] when the lily is among the brambles, it is hard for the farmer to pick it, so what does he do? He burns the thorns around it and plucks it.

    C. "So: 'The Lord has commanded concerning Jacob that those who are around him should be his enemies' (Lam. 1:17),

    D. "for example, Halamo [which is gentile, is enemy] to Naveh [which is Israelite], Susita to Tiberias, Qastra to Haifa, Jericho to Nauran, Lud to Ono.

    E. "That is in line with the following verse of Scripture: 'This is Jerusalem. I have est her in the midst of the gentiles' (Ez. 5:5).

    F. "Tomorrow, when redemption comes to Israel, what will the Holy One, blessed be He, do to them? He will bring a flame and burn the area around Israel.

    G. "That is in line with this verse: 'And the peoples will be as burnings of lime, as thorns cut down that are burned in fire' (Isa. 33:12).

    H. "And in the same connection: 'The Lord alone shall lead him' (Dt. 32:12)."

10. A. R. Abun said, "Just as a lily wilts so long as the hot spell persists, but when the dew falls on it, the lily thrives again,

    B. "so Israel, so long as the shadow of Esau falls across the world, Israel wilts,

    C. "but when the shadow of Esau passes from the world, Israel will once more thrive:

    D. "'I shall be like the dew for Israel. It will blossom as the lily' (Hos. 14:6)."

11. A. Just as the lily expires only with its scent, so Israel expires only with religious acts and good deeds.

    B. Just as the lily is only for the scent, so the righteous were created only for the redemption of Israel.

    C. Just as the lily is placed on the table of kings at the beginning and end of a meal, so Israel will be in both this world and the world to come.

    D. Just as it is easy to tell a lily from the thorns, so it is easy to tell the Israelites from the nations of the world.

    E. That is in line with this verse of Scripture: "All those who see them will recognize them" (Isa. 61:9).

    F. Just as a lily is made ready for Sabbaths and festivals, so Israel is made ready for the coming redemption.

    G. R. Berekhiah said, "Said the Holy One, blessed be He, to Moses, 'Go and say to Israel My children, when you were in Egypt, you were like a lily among brambles. Now that you come into the land of Israel, you shall be like a lily among brambles.

    H. "'"Be careful not to do deeds like those of this party or that.'"

    I. "Thus [Moses admonished Israel, saying to them, 'You shall not do as they do in the land of Egypt, where you dwelt, and you shall not do as they do in the land of Canaan, to which I am bringing you. You shall not walk in their statutes'" (Lev. 18:3).

This entire composition, originally Leviticus Rabbah XXIII:I-VII, is parachuted down nearly verbatim. The reason it has been chosen is obvious: the intersecting verse of that composition is our base verse. But the base verse here is Lev. 18:3, with which we conclude, and there can be no doubt that the compilers have chosen the whole thing only because of its general thematic pertinence.

20

Song of Songs Rabbah
to Song of Songs 2:3

2:3   *As an apple tree among the trees of the wood,*
so is my beloved among young men.
With great delight I sat in his shadow,
and his fruit was sweet to my taste.

XX:i

1. A.   "As an apple tree among the trees of the wood":
    B.   R. Huna and R. Aha in the name of R. Yosé b. Zimra, "Just as in the case of an apple tree, everybody avoids it in extreme heat, since it has no shade in which to sit,
    C.   "so the nations of the world fled from sitting in the shade of the Holy One, blessed be He on the day on which the Torah was given.
    D.   "Might one suppose that the same was so of Israel?
    E.   "Scripture states, 'With great delight I sat in his shadow,'
    F.   "'I took delight in him and I sat.'
    G.   "'I am the one who desired him, and not the nations of the world.'"

2. A.   R. Aha b. R. Zeira made two statements.
    B.   "First: an apple produces blossoms before leaves,
    C.   "so the Israelites in Egypt [Simon:] declared their faith before they heard the message:
    D.   "'And the people believed, and they heard that the Lord had remembered' (Ex. 4:31)."

3. A.   R. Aha b. R. Zeira made a second statement:
    B.   "Just as an apple produces blossoms before leaves,
    C.   "so the Israelites at Mount Sinai undertook to do even before they had heard what they were supposed to do:
    D.   "'We will do and we will hear' (Ex. 24:7)."

4. A.   R. Azariah made two statements:
    B.   "Just as an apple completes the ripening of its fruit only in Sivan,
    C.   "so the Israelites gave forth a good fragrance only in Sivan."

5. A.   R. Azariah made a second statement:

156

B. "Just as in the case of an apple tree, from the moment that it blossoms until its fruit ripens is a span of fifty days,

C. "so from the time that the Israelites went forth from Egypt until they accepted the Torah was a span of fifty days.

D. "When did they receive it?

E. "'In the third month after the children of Israel had gone forth' (Ex. 19:1)."

6. A. R. Judah b. R. Simon made two statements:

B. "Just as an apple costs only a penny, but you can smell its fragrance any number of times,

C. "So said Moses to the Israelites, 'If you wish to be redeemed, you may be redeemed for a simple matter.'

D. "They may be compared to someone who had sore feet and he went to all the physicians for healing and was not healed. Then he came to one, who said to him, 'If you want to be healed, you can be healed in a simple way. Plaster your feet with bullshit.'

E. "So said Moses to the Israelites, 'If you wish to be redeemed, you may be redeemed for a simple matter.'

F. "'"And you shall take a bunch of hyssop and dip it"' (Ex. 12:22).

G. "They said to him, 'Our lord, Moses, how much does this bundle of hyssop cost? Four or five cents?'

H. "He said to them, 'Even a penny. But it will make it possible for you to inherit the spoil of Egypt, the spoil at the Sea, the spoil of Sihon and Og, and the spoil of the thirty-one kings [of Canaan].'

I. "The palm-branch [for the Festival of Tabernacles], which costs someone a good dollar, and through which one carries out a variety of religious duties, all the more so!

J. "Therefore Moses admonishes Israel, 'And you shall take for yourself on the first day' (Lev. 23:40)."

7. A. R. Judah b. R. Simon made another statement:

B. "The matter may be compared to the case of a king who had a precious stone and a pearl. His son came along and said to him, 'Give it to me.'

C. "He said to him, 'It is yours, it belongs to you, and I give it over to you.'

D. "So said the Israelites before the Holy One, blessed be He, '"The Lord is my strength and my song"' (Ex. 15:2).

E. "Said to them the Holy One, blessed be He, 'It is yours, it belongs to you, and I give it over to you.'

F. "For 'strength' refers only to the Torah: 'The Lord will give strength to his people' (Ps. 29:11). [Simon, p. 100, n. 3: So the Community of Israel said, "I longed for his shadow," i.e. "I longed for the Torah and the Divine protection it affords – and I did indeed sit there, God freely giving it to me, declaring it altogether mine.]

8. A. Said R. Levi, "Three good hopes did the Israelites form at the Sea.

B. "They hoped for the Torah, they hoped for the standards, and they hoped for the tabernacle.

C. "They hoped for the Torah: 'With great delight I sat in his shadow.'

D. "They hoped for the standards: 'with great delight.'

E. "They hoped for the tabernacle: 'I sat....'

F. "That is in line with this verse: 'For I have not dwelled in a house since the day that I brought up the children of Israel out of Egypt' (2 Sam. 7:6)."

9. A. That accords with the view of R. Menaheman: "'And they went out into the wilderness of Shur' (Ex. 15:22):

B. "This teaches that they prophesied in their own regard that they were going to be organized in camps, with standards and rows, like a vineyard."

The formal traits of the whole are rather more uniform than we should expect, with "X made two statements" the governing formula, even when the formula does not fit. No. 1 begins the exploitation of the apple as metaphor for Israel, deriving the several lessons from the interplay of the clauses of our base verse, that is, "apple tree" and "delight in sitting in his shadow." These comparisons run through Nos. 2, 3, 4, 5, 6. Clearly, No. 6 preserves language that has no purpose here but belongs to Lev. R. XXX:I. The invocation of the metaphorization of Israel having been worked out, we move on at No. 7 to the Torah. Now we stress the second clause, concerning sitting in the shadow of the beloved; this now involves the Torah and then the organization by standards and the tabernacle. No. 8 completes the matter. We now proceed to the remainder of our base verse. As we shall see, the metaphor remains fairly consistent: Sinai and Torah, in one form or another.

XX:ii

1. A. "...and his fruit was sweet to my taste":

B. Said R. Isaac, "This refers to the twelve months that the Israelites spent before Mount Sinai, [Simon:] regaling themselves with teachings of the Torah.

C. "What verse of Scripture makes that point? 'and his fruit was sweet to my taste.

D. "'...to my taste' it was sweet, but to the taste of the seventy nations of the world it was bitter like wormwood."

2. A. [=Leviticus Rabbah I:X:] "Out of the tent of meeting" (Lev. 1:1):

B. Said R. Eleazar, "Even though Torah had been given earlier to Israel, at Sinai [Lev. R.: as a fence, restricting their actions], they were liable to punishment on account of violating it only after it had been repeated for them in the tent of meeting.

C. "This may be compared to a royal decree that had been written and sealed and brought to the province. The inhabitants of the province became liable to be punished on account of violating the decree only after it had been proclaimed to them in a public meeting in the province.

D. "Along these same lines, even though the Torah had been given to Israel at Sinai, they bore liability for punishment on account of violating its commandments only after it had been repeated for them in the tent of meeting.

E.   "This is in line with the following verse of Scripture: 'Until I had brought him into my mother's house and into the chamber of my teaching (Song 3:4).

F.   "'...into my mother's house' refers to Sinai.

G.   "'...and into the chamber of my teaching' refers to the tent of meeting, from which the Israelites were commanded through instruction in the Torah."

3. A.   [=Lev. R. I:XI.1:] Said R. Joshua b. Levi, "If the nations of the world had known how valuable the tent of meeting was to them, they would have sheltered it with tents and balustrades.

     B.   "You note that before the tabernacle was erected, the nations of the world used to hear the sound of God's word and [fearing an earthquake] they would rush out of their dwellings.

     C.   "That is in line with this verse: 'For who is there of all flesh, who has heard the voice of the living God speaking out of the midst' (Dt. 5:23)."

4. A.   [=Lev. R. I:XI.2:] Said R. Simon, "The word of God went forth in two modes, for Israel as life, for the nations of the world as poison.

     B.   "'...as you have and lived; (Dt. 4:33) – you heard and lived.

     C.   "for the nations of the world as poison: you hear the voice of God and live, while the nations of the earth hear and die.

     D.   "'That is in line with this verse: 'Under the apple tree I awakened' (Song 8:5)."

     E.   "'...out of the tent of meeting":

     F.   R. Hiyya taught, "The sound was cut off from that point and did not go beyond the tent of meeting."

5. A.   [=Lev. R. I:XII.1:] Said R. Isaac, "Before the tent of meeting was set up, prophecy was common among the nations of the world. Once the tent of meeting was set up, prophecy disappeared from among them. That is in line with this verse: 'I held it' [the Holy spirit, producing], 'and would not let it go [until I had brought it...into the chamber of her that conceived me' (Song 3:4)."

     B.   Should you object, "Lo, Balaam later on practiced prophecy –

     C.   the answer is, "He did so for the good of Israel: 'Who has counted the dust of Jacob (Num. 23:10); 'No one has seen iniquity in Jacob' (Num. 23:21); 'For there is no enchantment with Jacob' (Num. 23:23); 'How goodly are your tents, O Jacob' (Num. 24:5); 'There shall go forth a star out of Jacob' (Num. 24:17); 'and out of Jacob shall one have dominion' (Num. 24:19).

Why this vast insertion from Leviticus Rabbah Parashah One has been parachuted down I cannot say. It seems to me that beyond No. 1, the compilers have simply inserted whole materials that bear out the proposition that the seventy nations of the world lost out at Sinai. But that point is hardly primary to the inserted materials, since the point of those materials, itself not prominent, is simply that if the nations had understood what would happen in the tent of meeting, they would have been concerned. In all, it is difficult to defend the decision of the compilers, if that was their decision, to borrow so heavily upon available materials of no exceptional pertinence to their case.

21

Song of Songs Rabbah
to Song of Songs 2:4

2:4   *He brought me to the wine cellar,*
         and his banner over me was love.

XXI:i

1.   A.   "He brought me to the wine cellar, [and his banner over me was love]":

       B.   R. Meir and R. Judah:

       C.   R. Meir says, "Said the Congregation of Israel, 'The impulse to do evil took hold of me through wine, and I said to the calf, "These are your gods, Israel'" (Ex. 32:4).

       D.   "'When wine gets into someone, it mixes up his mind.'"

       E.   Said to him R. Judah, "That's enough for you, Meir! People interpret the Song of Songs not in a derogatory way but only in a praiseworthy way [for Israel],

       F.   "for the Song of Songs was given only for Israel's praise.

       G.   "And what is the meaning of, 'He brought me to the wine cellar'?

       H.   "Said the Congregation of Israel, 'The Holy One, blessed be He, "brought me" to the great wine cellar, meaning, to Sinai.

       I.   "'["and his banner over me was love"]: and he placed over me there banners of the Torah, religious duties, and good deeds.

       J.   "'And with great love did I accept them.'"

2.   A.   R. Abba in the name of R. Isaac said, "Said the Congregation of Israel, 'The Holy One, blessed be He, "brought me" to the great wine cellar, meaning, to Sinai.

       B.   "'And he gave me the Torah there, which is interpreted in forty-nine different ways to yield a ruling of cleanness, and in forty-nine different ways to yield a ruling of uncleanness.'

       C.   "How come? Because the numerical value of the letters in the word for 'and his banner' is forty-nine.

       D.   "'And with great love did I accept them.'

       E.   "Thus: 'and his banner over me was love.'"

3.   A.   R. Jonah said, "In the case of two associates occupied in teachings of law,

> B. "with this one citing the generative source of the law, while that one does not cite the generative source of the law [as he reads it], –

> C. "said the Holy One, blessed be He, 'and his banner over me was love.'" [Simon, p. 103, n. 4: his array of words is beloved, although they are not in accord with the true law, since his intention is good.]

4. A. Said R. Aha, "An ignorant person who reads the word 'love' as 'enmity,' for instance, 'and you will love' as 'and you will hate' –

   B. "said the Holy One, blessed be He, 'His mistake [using the same letters as the word for banner] is beloved to me.'"

5. A. Said R. Issachar, "A child who reads for Moses, 'Muses,' and for Aaron 'Arun,' and for Efron 'Efran' –

   B. "said the Holy One, blessed be He, 'His babble [using some of the same letters as the word for banner] is beloved to me.'"

6. A. Said R. Hunia, "In the past if someone would point to an icon [of the king] with his finger, he would be punished, but now, someone can leave his entire hand any number of times upon the name of God [in the scroll] and is not punished.

   B. "Said the Holy One, blessed be He, 'His thumb [using the same letters as the word for banner] is beloved to me.'"

7. A. And Rabbis say, "Even in the case of a child who skips the name of God any number of times is not punished.

   B. "Not only so, but said the Holy One, blessed be He, 'His omission [using the same letters as the word for banner] is beloved to me.'"

8. A. [Supply: "and his banner over me was love"]:

   B. Said R. Berekhiah, "Even concerning those banners with which Jacob deceived his father, 'And she put the skins of the kids of the goats upon his hands' (Gen. 27:16),

   C. "the Holy One, blessed be He, said, 'Even on them I shall bring my Presence to rest.'

   D. "Thus: 'And you shall make curtains of goats' hair' (Ex. 26:7).

   E. "Not only so, but further, said the Holy One, blessed be He, 'and his banner over me was love': 'his deceiving of me was beloved.'"

9. A. [Supply: "He brought me to the wine cellar, and his banner over me was love"]:

   B. R. Joshua of Sikhnin in the name of R. Levi: "Said the Congregation of Israel, 'The Holy One, blessed be He, "brought me" to the great wine cellar, meaning, to Sinai.

   C. "'And there I saw Michael and his banner, Gabriel and his banner, and my eyes saw the arrangements on high, and I loved them.'

   D. "At that moment said the Holy One, blessed be He, to Moses, 'Since it is the wish of my children to encamp by banners [as in heaven], let them encamp by banners: 'Every man with his own banner, according to the ensigns' (Num. 2:2)."

The dispute at No. 1 of course is fundamental, because of Judah's rebuke to Meir. But the basic point is clear. The second clause of our base verse is introduced at the end, H-I, and that proves to be the focus for the rest. The entire composition from No. 2 onward simply works on

various senses and meanings to be imputed to the letters for the word
"banner." It is clear that, in the present exegetical framework, a keen
interest in the possible meanings of rearranging the letters for words
defines a principal exegetical concern, and that accounts for No. 2 –
numerical value – and then the various plays on the letters DGL, all of
them in the same pattern, from No. 3 through No. 7. The present set
seems to have escaped the attention of the Judaic academy. Nos. 8, 9
present no surprises.

22

Song of Songs Rabbah
to Song of Songs 2:5

2:5   *Sustain me with raisins,*
       refresh me with apples;
       for I am sick with love.

XXII:i
1. A.   "Sustain me with raisins, [refresh me with apples; for I am sick
         with love:]"
   B.   [With reference to letters of the word for raisins, we interpret the
         opening clause:] with two fires, the fire above, the fire below [the
         heavenly fire, the altar fire].
2. A.   Another explanation: "Sustain me with raisins":
   B.   with two fires, the Torah in Writing, the Torah in Memory.
3. A.   Another explanation: "Sustain me with raisins":
   B.   with many fires, the fore of Abraham, the fire of Moriah, the fire of
         the bush, the fire of Elijah, and the fire of Hananiah, Mishael, and
         Azariah.
4. A.   Another explanation: "Sustain me with raisins":
   B.   This refers to the well-founded laws.
5. A.   "...refresh me with apples":
   B.   this refers to the lore, the fragrance and taste of which are like
         apples.
6. A.   "...for I am sick with love":
   B.   Said the Congregation of Israel before the Holy One, blessed be
         He, "Lord of the world, all of the illnesses that you bring upon me
         are so as to make me more beloved to you."
7. A.   Another interpretation of the phrase, "for I am sick with love":
   B.   Said the Congregation of Israel before the Holy One, blessed be
         He, "Lord of the world, all of the illnesses that you bring upon me
         are because I love you."
8. A.   Another interpretation of the phrase, "for I am sick with love:]"
   B.   "Even though I am sick, I am beloved unto him."

The word-studies continue through No. 4, and Nos. 5, 6, 7 go on to interpret the base verse by reference to sense, rather than the rearrangements of the letters.

XXII:ii

1. A.   It has been taught on Tannaite authority: when a person is not ill, he eats whatever he finds. When he gets sick, he wants to eat all sorts of sweets.

   B.   Said R. Isaac, "In the past, the Torah was worked out in encompassing principles, [Simon: the main outlines of the Torah were known to all], so people wanted to hear a teaching of the Mishnah or of the Talmud.

   C.   "Now that the Torah is not worked out in encompassing principles, [Simon: the main outlines of the Torah are not known] people want to hear a teaching of Scripture or a teaching of lore."

   D.   Said R. Levi, "In the past, when money was available, people wanted to hear a teaching of the Mishnah or law or Talmud.

   E.   "Now that money is scarce, so that people are sick on account of subjugation, people want to hear only words of blessing and consolation."

2. A.   R. Simeon b. Yohai taught on Tannaite authority, "When the Israelites came forth from Egypt, what were they like?

   B.   "They were comparable to a prince who recovered from an illness.

   C.   "Said his tutor [to the king], 'Let your son go to school.'

   D.   "Said the king to him, 'My son has not yet recovered his full color. For he has become pale because of his illness. Let my son take it easy and enjoy himself for three months with food and drink, and then he can go back to school.'

   E.   "So when the Israelites went forth from Egypt, there were among them those who had been deformed through the slave labor of mortar and bricks.

   F.   "The ministering angels said to him, 'Lo, the time has come. Give them the Torah.'

   G.   "Said to them the Holy One, blessed be He, 'My children have not yet recovered their full color on account of the slave labor of mortar and bricks.

   H.   "'But let my children take it easy for three months at the well and with the quail, and then I will give them the Torah.

   I.   "'And when is that? "In the third month"' (Ex. 19:1)." [Simon, p. 106, n. 1: Hence now in the third month has the time come for you to 'Sustain me with raisins, refresh me with apples; for I am sick with love.']

3. A.   At the end of the repression our masters gathered in Usha, and these are they:

   B.   R. Judah, R. Nehemiah, R. Meir, R. Yosé, R. Simeon b. Yohai, R. Eliezer b. R. Yosé the Galilean, and R. Eliezer b. Jacob.

   C.   They sent word to the sages of Galilee and said to them, "Whoever has learned, let him come and teach. And whoever has not learned, let him come and learned."

   D.   So they met and learned and did what was necessary.

E. Now when it came time to depart, they said, "Is this place, in which we have been received, going to be left empty? [Simon: 'We cannot leave a place where we have been thus entertained without a parting blessing.']

F. They gave the place of honor to R. Judah, who was a local resident. It is not because he was greater than the others in Torah-learning, but it is the residence of a person that endows him with the honor of precedence. [His task, like that of all the others, was to speak in praise of hospitality.]

4. A. R. Judah came forward and interpreted this verse: "'Now Moses used to take the tent and pitch it outside the camp, afar off from the camp. [And it came to pass that everyone who sought the Lord]' (Ex. 33:7):

B. "Here the word 'afar off' is used, and the same word is used elsewhere: 'Yet there shall be a space afar off between you and it, about two thousand cubits by measure' (Josh. 3:4).

C. "Just as the sense of the word in that latter passage is explicitly two thousand cubits, so here too 'afar off' means two thousand cubits.

D. "[The verse proceeds:] 'And it came to pass that everyone who sought' not Moses but 'every one sought the Lord.'

E. "On this basis we learn that whoever hospitably receives associates is as though he receives the Presence of God.

F. "And you, my brothers, my lords, great authorities of the Torah, who among you has taken the trouble to travel ten mils [a mil being two thousand cubits], or twenty, or thirty, or forty, so as to hear words of the Torah, all the more so that the Holy One, blessed be He, will not hold back your reward in this world and in the coming one!"

5. A. R. Nehemiah came forward and interpreted this verse: "'An Ammonite or a Moabite shall not enter into the assembly of the Lord' (Dt. 23:4):

B. "It has been taught, 'Two great nations were excluded from entering the congregation of the Lord.

C. "'Why was this so? "Because they did not meet you with bread and water" (Dt. 23:5).'

D. "Now were the Israelites really in need at that moment? And is it not the fact that all the forty years that the Israelites were in the wilderness, the well would bubble for them and the manna would come down for them and the quail was available to them and the clouds of glory surrounded them and the pillar of cloud traveled before them?

E. "And yet you say, 'Because they did not meet you with bread and water'!"

F. Said R. Eleazar, "It is a matter of proper conduct that one who comes in from a trip is met with food and drink."

G. [Resuming E:] "Come and see how the Holy One, blessed be He, exacted a penalty from those two nations.

H. "It is written in the Torah, 'An Ammonite and a Moabite shall not enter the assembly of the Lord' (Dt. 23:4).

I.   "But you, people of Usha, who greeted our lords with your food and your drink and your beds, how much the more so will the Holy One, blessed be He, provide for you a good reward!"

6. A.   R. Meir came forward and interpreted this verse: "'Now there dwelled an old prophet in Bethel' (1 Kgs. 13:11):

B.   "And who was it? This was Amaziah, priest of Bethel [Amos 7:10]."

C.   Said to him R. Yosé, "Meir, you're making scrambled eggs! Who was he really? He was Jonathan son of Gershom son of Moses: 'Jonathan, son of Gershom, son of Manasseh' (Judges 18:30).

D.   "Now the N in the name Manasseh is suspended, indicating that if he attained merit, he would be deemed the son of Moses, and if not, then he would be deemed the son of Manasseh [2 Kgs. 21]."

E.   Associates asked before R. Samuel b. R. Nahman, saying to him, "How come a priest for an idol lived all those years?"

F.   He said to them, "It was because he was stingy with the idol. [Simon: he tried to discourage idolatry.]

G.   "How so? [Cf. Gen. R. XXXVIII:XIII.1: Said R. Hiyya (in explanation of how Haran died in his father's presence) "Terah was an idol manufacturer. Once he went off on a trip and put Abraham in charge of the store. Someone would come in and want to buy an idol.] If someone came to worship the idol, he would say to him, 'How old are you?'

H.   "He would say, 'Forty or fifty or sixty or seventy or eighty years old.'

I.   "He would, 'Woe to that man, who is forty or fifty or sixty or seventy or eighty years old and this idol was made only five or twelve years ago, and you are going to abandon your God and worship it? That is a come-down!"

J.   "So the man would be ashamed and go his way.

K.   "A smartass came and said this to him, 'Then why do you stay here and serve it?'

L.   "He said to him, 'I collect my salary and blind its eye.'

M.   "When David heard about this, he sent word to him and brought him and said to him, 'Are you really the grandson of that righteous man and are worshipping idolatry?'

N.   "He said to him, 'Indeed, I have a tradition from the household of my father's father: "Sell yourself for idolatry, but do not fall into need from other people!"'

O.   "He said to him, 'God forbid! That is not the point. But: "Sell yourself to work that is alien to you, but do not fall into need from other people!"'

P.   "Since David saw that he loved money, he went and made him secretary of the treasury.

Q.   "They say that when David died, he reverted to his corruption: 'And he said to him, I also am a prophet as you are...he lied to him' (1 Kgs. 13:18).

R.   "What is the meaning of 'lied'?

S.   "He deceived him.

T.   "And what was the deceit?

U.   "He fed him food in a spirit of deceit [Simon, p. 108, n. 7: by his lies he persuaded him to accept his hospitality, notwithstanding that he had been ordered strictly to eat nothing in that place].

V.   "'And it came to pass, as they sat at the table, that the word of the Lord came to the prophet who brought him back' (1 Kgs. 13:20).

W.   "Now this yields an argument *a fortiori:*

X.   "If this one, who lied to him and fed him food in a spirit of deceit, had the merit that the Holy Spirit would come to rest upon him, you, our brothers, people of Usha, who have received our lords with food in a spirit of sincerity and drink and a bed, how much the more so will the Holy One, blessed be He, provide for you a good reward!"

7. A.   R. Yosé came forward and interpreted this verse: "'And the ark of the Lord remained in the house of Obed-edom the Gittite...and it was told to king David, saying, The Lord has blessed the house of Obed-edom and all that belongs to him' (2 Sam. 6:11f.):

    B.   "How come? It was because of the ark of God.

    C.   "And how did he bless him?

    D.   "With children: 'Ammiel the sixth, Issachar the seventh' (1 Chr. 26:5); 'all these were of the children of Obed-edom, they and their children' (1 Chr. 26:5).

    E.   "They say: he had eight sons and eight daughters-in-law, and every one of them had two children each month.

    F.   "How did this work?

    G.   "She was unclean for seven days [of her menstrual period], then clean for seven days, and then she gave birth, then unclean for seven days [of her menstrual period], then clean for seven days, and then she gave birth, this sixteen per month, forty-eight in three months, and with six of his own, there were fifty-four, and the initial eight bring the count to sixty-two: 'Sixty-two of Obed-edom' (1 Chr. 26:5)."

    H.   Colleagues asked before R. Yohanan, saying to him, "What is the meaning of this statement: 'Peullethai the eighty, for God blessed him" (1 Chr. 26:55)?

    I.   He said to them, "[Referring to the letters in the name of Peullethai, which can yield the following meaning:] 'He did a great service for the Torah."

    J.   [Reverting to G:] "And what was the great service that he performed for the Torah?

    K.   "He would light before the ark a single candle in the morning, and a single candle at dusk.

    L.   "Now this yields an argument *a fortiori:* if because he lit a single candle before the ark of God, which neither eats nor drinks nor speaks, but merely contains the two tablets of stone, he acquired the merit of being blessed on account of the honor paid to it,

    M.   "you, our brothers, people of Usha, how much the more so!"

8. A.   R. Simeon b. Yohai came forward and interpreted this verse: "'And it fell on a day that Elisha passed to Shunem, where there was an important woman, and she insisted that he eat bread' (2 Kgs. 4:8)."

    B.   Said to him R. Judah b. R. Simon, "Merely because it is written of her that 'she insisted that he eat bread' did she gain the merit that her son be resurrected?"

C.	R. Yudan in the name of R. Zeira and R. Yohanan in the name of R. Simeon b. Yohai said, "Great is supporting the poor, for it brings about the resurrection of the dead not in its appointed time."
D.	[Reverting to B, supply: said to him R. Simeon b. Yohai,] "The women of Zarephath, because she fed Elijah, had the merit that her son was resurrected from the dead.
E.	"The Shunammite woman, because she fed Elisha, had the merit that her son was resurrected from the dead."
F.	Said R. Judah b. R. Ilai, "Even candles and even wicks did Elijah bring from place to place, so as not to impose bother upon people."
G.	R. Judah b. R. Simon said, "Now did he really eat her food? And is it not the fact that both she and he ate his food [and not hers]? 'And she and he...ate' (1 Kgs. 17:15) – so what is written is he and she [Simon, p. 110, n. 2: which implies that he was the principal, the food being his].
H.	"But because she welcomed him in a cordial way and served him, she had the merit of having her son resurrected from the dead.
I.	"Now you, people of Usha, who have accorded such grace to us, all the more so!"
9. A.	R. Eliezer b. R. Yosé the Galiean came forward and interpreted this verse: "'And Saul said to the Kenites, Go, depart, leave the Amalekites, lest I destroy you with them, for you showed kindness to all the children of Israel when they came up out of Egypt' (1 Sam. 15:6):
B.	"Now did Jethro show kindness to all Israel? But is it the fact that Jethro showed kindness only with Moses alone?"
C.	Said R. Eleazar, "Jethro surely showed kindness to Moses: 'Call him that he may eat bread' (Ex. 2:20)."
D.	Said R. Simon, "That is not so, but he gave him food only for pay: 'And moreover he drew water for us' (Ex. 2:19)."
E.	R. Judah, R. Nehemiah, and rabbis:
F.	R. Judah said, "'...he drew water for us' and for our parents."
G.	R. Nehemiah said, "'...he drew water for us' and for our shepherds."
H.	Rabbis said, "'...he drew water for us' on account of the merit accrued by our fathers. He drew water for the shepherds so as to keep the peace among them."
I.	[Reverting to B, Eliezer b. R. Yosé continues,] "And yet you say that Jethro showed kindness to all Israel?
J.	"But this serves to teach you that whoever shows kindness to a single one of the eminent persons of Israel is credited as though he had done it for all Israel.
K.	"Now you, our brothers, people of Usha, how much the more so!"
10. A.	R. Eliezer b. Jacob came forward and interpreted this verse: "'And Moses and the priests the Levites spoke to all Israel, saying, Keep silence and hear, O Israel: this day you have become a people' (Dt. 27:9):
B.	"Now was that the day on which they received the Torah? And had they not received it forty years earlier, and yet you say, 'this day'!

C.   "This teaches that once Moses repeated the Torah to them and they received it cordially, it was credited to them as though they had received it that very day from Sinai.

D.   "That is why it is said, 'this day you have become a people' (Dt. 27:9).

E.   "Now you, our brothers, people of Usha, who have received our lords so cordially – how much the more so!"

The sequence, as Simon suggests, seems parachuted down onto the target of a verse that speaks of coddling the patient for a while until he gets better. Otherwise I can make no sense of including this enormous exercise in praise of hospitality to sages. But how the passages make a point relative to the general theme of the situation of a just-recovered patient I cannot say; Israel after the oppression defines the occasion for including the collection, not the cause, for making it. Here again we see the clear-cut point of differentiation between compilation and composition, and the composition is surely temporally prior.

23

Song of Songs Rabbah
to Song of Songs 2:6

2:6   *O that his left hand were under my head,*
        and that his right hand embraced me!

XXIII:i

1. A.   "O that his left hand were under my head":
    B.   this refers to the first tablets.
    C.   "...and that his right hand embraced me":
    D.   this refers to the second tablets.
2. A.   Another interpretation of the verse, "O that his left hand were under my head":
    B.   this refers to the show-fringes.
    C.   "...and that his right hand embraced me":
    D.   this refers to the phylacteries.
3. A.   Another interpretation of the verse, "O that his left hand were under my head":
    B.   this refers to the recitation of the *Shema.*
    C.   "...and that his right hand embraced me":
    D.   this refers to the Prayer.
4. A.   Another interpretation of the verse, "O that his left hand were under my head":
    B.   this refers to the tabernacle.
    C.   "...and that his right hand embraced me":
    D.   this refers to the cloud of the Presence of God in the world to come: "The sun shall no longer be your light by day nor for brightness will the moon give light to you" (Isa. 60:19). Then what gives light to you? "The Lord shall be your everlasting light" (Isa. 60:20).
5. A.   Another interpretation of the verse, "O that his left hand were under my head":
    B.   this refers to the mezuzah.
6. A.   It has been taught on Tannaite authority by R. Simeon b. Yohai, "'And you shall write them on the doorposts of your house' (Dt. 6:9).

B. "[Since the words for house and coming use the same consonants,] 'when you come into your house from the street [you should have the mezuzah on the doorpost that you will see at your right, so it is affixed on the right doorpost as one enters the house]."

7. A. Said R. Yohanan, "'And you shall set the table outside the veil and the candlestick...toward the south' (Ex. 26:35). [That is, the candlestick is to be set on the left of someone entering from the east (Simon, p. 112, n. 3)].

B. "And is that not the way? For does a person not put the candlestick down at the left, so that it will not impede his right hand?

C. "[And, with reference to the verse, 'O that his left hand were under my head, and that his right hand embraced me,"] does not a man put his left hand under the head and caress with the right?"

8. A. Said R. Aha, "R. Yohanan derives the evidence from this verse: 'to love the Lord your God...and to cleave to him' (Dt. 11:22).

B. "And what is this cleaving? It is with 'his left hand under my head.'"

The layout seems to me rather typical, in that the disciplined and well-composed materials come first, repeating their point through a standard sequence of topics available for metaphorization, then appending other, more miscellaneous items. Why we invoke, as our candidates for the metaphor at hand, the Ten Commandments, show-fringes and phylacteries, recitation of the Shema and the Prayer, the tabernacle and the cloud of the Presence of God, and the mezuzah, seems to me clear from the very catalogue. These reach their climax in the analogy between the home and the tabernacle, the embrace of God and the Presence of God. So the whole is meant to list those things that draw the Israelite near God and make the Israelite cleave to God, as the base verse says, hence the right hand and the left stand for the most intimate components of the life of the individual and the home with God. The remainder is tacked on and does not spoil the effect of the extraordinary metaphorization effects at Nos. 1-4+5. (I see No. 5 as essentially secondary, tacked on because of the reference to God's tabernacle, with its counterpart, the Jew's home.)

24

Song of Songs Rabbah
to Song of Songs 2:7

2:7   *I adjure you, O daughters of Jerusalem,*
by the gazelles or the hinds of the field,
that you not stir up nor awaken love
until it please.

XXIV:i

1. A. "I adjure you, O daughters of Jerusalem, [by the gazelles or the hinds of the field, that you not stir up nor awaken love until it please]":

   B. By what did he impose the oath? [That is, By what did God impose an oath upon Israel]?

   C. R. Eliezer says, "He imposed the oath by heaven and earth.

   D. "'...by the gazelles': [since the word for gazelle and the word for host use the same consonants], it was by the host above and by the host below, by two hosts. That is, by the hosts."

2. A. "...or the hinds of the field":

   B. this is the beasts of the field: "For you shall be in league with the stones of the field, and the beasts of the field shall be at peace with you" (Job 5:23).

3. A. R. Hanina b. R. Pappa and R. Judah b. R. Simon:

   B. R. Hanina said, "He imposed the oath by the patriarchs and matriarchs.

   C. "For 'by the gazelles,' [since the word for gazelle and the word for will use the same consonants], it was by the patriarchs, who carried out my will, and through whom I accomplished my will.

   D. "'...or the hinds of the field,' [since the word hind occurs here and in the verse to be cited,] it was by the tribal progenitors, in line with the usage of the word for hind in this verse: 'Naphtali is a hind let loose' (Gen. 49:21)."

   E. R. Judah b. R. Simon said, "He imposed the oath upon them by the circumcision, since the word for 'gazelles' refers to the host that bears a sign.

F.   "And it was by 'the hinds of the field' because they pour out their blood for the sanctification of my Name like the blood of a deer or a hind."

4. A.   Rabbis said, "He imposed the oath upon them by the generation of the repression, specifically:

    B.   "'by the hosts that carried out my will in the world, and through whom I carried out my will.

    C.   "And it was by 'the hinds of the field' because they pour out their blood for the sanctification of my Name like the blood of a deer or a hind: 'For your sake we are killed all day long' (Ps. 44:23)."

5. A.   Said R. Hiyya b. R. Abba, "If someone should say to me, 'Give your life for the sanctification of the Name of the Holy One, blessed be He, I should readily give it up, on condition that he kill me immediately.

    B.   "But in the generation of the repression, I should not have been able to bear the torment.

    C.   "For what did they do in the generation of the repression?

    D.   "They would bring iron discs and make them white-hot in fire, and then put them under the armpits and took away their lives through them.

    E.   "They would bring needles of reeds and put them under their fingernails and remove their lives through them.

    F.   "That is in line with what David said, 'To you, O Lord, do I lift up my soul' (Ps. 25:1),

    G.   "that is written, 'I give up,' which is to say, they gave up their souls for the sanctification of the Name of the Holy One, blessed be He."

6. A.   Said R. Hoshaiah, "Said the Holy One, blessed be He, to Israel, 'Wait for me, and I shall make you like the host above.'"

7. A.   R. Yudan in the name of R. Meir: "Said the Holy One, blessed be He, to Israel, 'If you keep my oath, I shall make you like the host above,

    B.   "and if not, I shall make you like the host below."

The mention of an oath of course demands that we identify the oath and by what it was imposed, Nos. 1ff. We of course take for granted that since the address is to "the daughters of Jerusalem," the oath can only be that imposed by God, since there are only two parties to this discourse. Nos. 1-2, then 3, 4 then appeal to the "gazelles" and "hinds," working on the words that share the consonants of the former word, the verses in which the latter occurs. Once we invoke the martyrs who carried out God's will, a metaphor invited by the results of the philological inquiry, the rest follows, Nos. 5, 6.

XXIV:ii

1. A.   R. Yosé b. R. Hanina said, "The two oaths [Song 2:7: 'I adjure you, O daughters of Jerusalem,' and Song 3:5, 'I adjure you, O daughters of Jerusalem, by the gazelles or the hinds of the field'] apply, one to Israel, the other to the nations of the world.

B.   "The oath is imposed upon Israel that they not rebel against the yoke of the kingdoms.

C.   "And the oath is imposed upon the kingdoms that they not make the yoke too hard for Israel.

D.   "For if they make the yoke too hard on Israel, they will force the end to come before its appointed time."

2.   A.   Said R. Levi, "It is written, 'Behold a king shall reign in righteousness' (Isa. 32:1).

B.   "The Holy One, blessed be He, does not place a tyrannical king over his nation before he [Simon] first exacts their debt and completely liquidates it. [Simon, p. 114, n. 5: The setting up of a tyrant is a sign that God is now about to liquidate Israel's debt, i.e., punish Israel for all their sins, so that the redemption may come all the sooner.]"

3.   A.   R. Abbahu in the name of R. Tanhum said, "What did the Israelite officials say to Pharaoh? 'There is no straw given to your servants...but the fault is in your own people' (Ex. 5:16).

B.   "'You sin against your people, and you sin against your nation, and through your own actions your kingdom will be taken away from you and given to another nation.'"

4.   A.   R. Helbo says, "There are four oaths that are mentioned here [Song 2:7, 'I adjure you, O daughters of Jerusalem,' Song 3:5, 'I adjure you, O daughters of Jerusalem, by the gazelles or the hinds of the field,' Song 5:8, 'I adjure you, O daughters of Jerusalem, if you find my beloved, that you tell him I am sick with love,' Song 8:4, 'I adjure you, O daughters of Jerusalem, that you not stir up nor awaken love until it please'], specifically,

B.   "he imposed an oath on Israel not to rebel against the kingdoms and not to force the end [before its time[, not to reveal its mysteries to the nations of the world, and not to go up from the exile [Simon:] by force.

C.   "For if so [that they go up from the exile by force], then why should the royal messiah come to gather together the exiles of Israel?"

5.   A.   R. Onia said, "The four oaths he imposed upon them corresponded to the four generations that forced the end before its time and stumbled in the effort.

B.   "And what are they?

C.   "Once in the days of Amram, once in the days of Dinai, once in the days of Kosiba, and once in the days of Shutelah son of Abraham: 'The children of Ephraim were as archers handling the bow' (Ps. 78:9)."

D.   Some say, "One in the days of Amram, once in the generation of the repression, once in the days of the son of Kosiba, and once in in the days of Shutelah son of Abraham: 'The children of Ephraim were as archers handling the bow' (Ps. 78:9)."

E.   "For they were reckoning the hour from the time that the Holy One, blessed be He, made the decree when he speak with our father, Abraham, between the pieces [Gen. 15:13-17], but the time actually commenced from the moment at which Isaac was born.

F.   "[Basing their actions upon this erroneous reckoning,] they assembled and went forth to battle and many of them fell slain.

G.   "How come? 'Because they did not believe in the Lord and did
         not trust in his salvation' (Ps. 78:9),
H.   "but they forced the end and violated the oath."

Now we work on the several verses that run parallel to this one,
that is, passages in which "I adjure you, daughters of Jerusalem," occur.
Here too we spoke of God's oath upon Israel, but the framework shifts
dramatically. Now our interest is in Israel and the nations, and the
point is repeated that Israel must not hasten the messianic coming but
must accept the yoke of the nations until God removes it. Nos. 1, 2 make
this point and one more: the nations must not make things too hard on
Israel. No. 4 repeats this same proposition, now making explicit the
consideration that God must be free to act by grace, through the
messiah.

XXIV:iii
1.   A   "...that you not stir up nor awaken love until it please":
     B.   R. Yudan and R. Berekiah:
     C.   R. Yudan said, "It is the love ['nor awaken love'] that Isaac had for
           Esau: 'Now Isaac loved Esau' (Gen. 25:8).
     D.   "What is then the sense of, 'until it please'?
     E.   "Until the pleasure of the old man has been done."
2.   A   R. Berekhiah said, "It is the love that the Holy One, blessed be
           He, had for Israel: 'I have lord you, says the Lord' (Mal. 1:2).
     B.   "What is then the sense of, 'until it please'?
     C.   "The 'it' refers to the dominion of heaven, and bears this meaning:
           'until the Attribute of Justice will be pleased on its own.'
     D.   "'[But then,] I shall bring it with great thunders, and I shall not
           delay.'
     E.   "That is why it is written, 'until it please.'"

Esau, No. 1, of course stands for Rome. Simon, p. 115, n. 7, explains
No. 1 as follows: "Until Esau has exhausted the blessings bestowed on
him by Isaac. Then shall Israel be redeemed from Esau's yoke, but
before that, Israel must not attempt to throw off the yoke. The fruitless
revolts against the Romans with their terrible consequences naturally
inspired these sentiments." It seems to me what No. 1 explains,
however, is the success of Esau, who by this time stands for Christian
Rome, and the point is that the success of Esau too is the will of God,
and God's will must be done. No. 2 complements No. 1. This entire
exposition of the base verse is simply stunning.

25

Song of Songs Rabbah
to Song of Songs 2:8

2:8   *The voice of my beloved!*
Behold he comes,
leaping upon the mountains,
bounding over the hills.

1. A.   "The voice of my beloved! Behold he comes [leaping upon the mountains, bounding over the hills]":

    B.   R. Judah and R. Nehemiah and Rabbis:

    C.   R. Judah says, "'The voice of my beloved! Behold he comes': this refers to Moses.

    D.   "When he came and said to the Israelites, 'In this month you will be redeemed,' they said to him, 'Our lord, Moses, how are we going to be redeemed? And did not the Holy One, blessed be He, say to Abraham, "And they shall work them and torment them for four hundred years" (Gen. 15:13), and now we have in hand only two hundred and ten years!'

    E.   "He said to them, 'Since he wants to redeem you, he is not going to pay attention to these reckonings of yours.

    F.   "'But: "leaping upon the mountains, bounding over the hills." The reference here to mountains and hills in fact alludes to calculations and specified times. "He leaps" over reckonings, calculations, and specified times.

    G.   "'And in this month you are to be redeemed: "This month is the beginning of months" (Ex. 12:1).'"

2. A.   R. Nehemiah says, "'The voice of my beloved! Behold he comes': this refers to Moses.

    B.   "When he came and said to the Israelites, 'In this month you will be redeemed,' they said to him, 'Our lord, Moses, how are we going to be redeemed? We have no good deeds to our credit.'

    C.   "He said to them, 'Since he wants to redeem you, he is not going to pay attention to bad deeds.'

D.   "'And to what does he pay attention? To the righteous people among you and to their deeds,

E.   "'for example, Amram and his court.

F.   "'"leaping upon the mountains, bounding over the hills": mountains refers only to courts, in line with this usage: "I will depart and go down upon the mountains" (Judges 11:37).

G.   "'And in this month you are to be redeemed: "This month is the beginning of months" (Ex. 12:1).'"

3. A.   Rabbis say, "'The voice of my beloved! Behold he comes': this refers to Moses.

B.   "When he came and said to the Israelites, 'In this month you will be redeemed,' they said to him, 'Our lord, Moses, how are we going to be redeemed? And the whole of Egypt is made filthy by our own worship of idols!'

C.   "He said to them, 'Since he wants to redeem you, he is not going to pay attention to your worship of idols.

D.   "'Rather, "leaping upon the mountains, bounding over the hills": mountains and hills refer only to idolatry, in line with this usage: "They sacrifice on the tops of the mountains and offer upon the hills" (Hos. 4:13).

E.   "'And in this month you are to be redeemed: "This month is the beginning of months" (Ex. 12:1).'"

4. A.   R. Yudan and R. Hunia:

B.   R. Yudan in the name of R. Eliezer son of R. José the Galilean, and R. Hunia in the name of R. Eliezer b. Jacob say, "'The voice of my beloved! Behold he comes': this refers to the royal messiah.

C.   "When he says to the Israelites, 'In this month you are to be redeemed, they will say to him, 'How are we going to be redeemed? And has not the Holy One, blessed be He, taken an oath that he would subjugate us among the seventy nations.'

D.   "Now he will reply to them in two ways.

E.   "He will say to them, 'If one of you is taken into exile to Barbary and one to Sarmatia, it is as though all of you had gone into exile.

F.   "'And not only so, but this state conscripts troops from all of the world and from every nation, so that if one Samaritan or one Barbarian comes and subjugates you, it is as though his entire nation had ruled over you and as if you were subjugated by all the seventy nations.

G.   "'In this month you are to be redeemed: "This month is the beginning of months" (Ex. 12:1).'"

Nos. 1-3 form a perfectly matched set; remove one and you lose the whole. They go over the trilogy of the timing of redemption, the moral condition of those to be redeemed, and the past religious misdeeds of those to be redeemed. Against these three arguments Moses argues that God will redeem at God's own time, as an act of grace and forgiveness. The theological message emerges with enormous power through invoking the love of God for Israel, God "leaping upon the mountains." I cannot point to a better or more telling example of the rewards accruing to the framers of the document from their decision to work on just this part of Scripture. The obvious necessity of No. 4 to complete the message requires no comment. Any conception that first comes the individual units, then the completed composition, seems to me to take second place before the notion that the plan of the whole – as a theological statement, I mean – came prior to the formation of the parts. Then it hardly matters whose names are tacked on to the formally matched and perfect components.

26

Song of Songs Rabbah to Song of Songs 2:9

2:9   *My beloved is like a gazelle,*
or a young stag.
Behold, there he stands
behind our wall,
gazing in at the windows,
looking through the lattice.

[2:10   *My beloved speaks and says to me,*
"Arise, my love, my fair one,
and come away..."]

XXVI:i

1. A.   "My beloved is like a gazelle":

      B.   Said R. Isaac, "Said the Congregation of Israel before the Holy One, blessed be He, 'Lord of the world, you have said to us, [Simon:] "My love, my love." You are the one who says, "My love, my love" to us first.' [Simon, p. 118: *Dew* is an exclamation of affection. Jastrow: Thou art sighing for us first, instead of our aspiring for Thee.]

2. A.   "My beloved is like a gazelle":

      B.   Just as a gazelle leaps from mountain to mountain, hill to hill, tree to tree, thicket to thicket, fence to fence,

      C.   so the Holy One, blessed be He, lept from Egypt to the sea, from the sea to Sinai, from Sinai to the age to come.

      D.   In Egypt they saw him: "For I will go through the land of Egypt" (Ex. 12:12).

      E.   At the sea they saw him: "And Israel saw the great hand" (Ex. 14:31); "This is my God and I will glorify him" (Ex. 15:2).

      F.   At Sinai they saw him: "The Lord spoke with you face to face in the mountain" (Dt. 5:4); "The Lord comes from Sinai" (Dt. 33:2).

3. A.   "...or a young stag":

      B.   R. Yosé b. R. Hanina said, "Meaning, like young deer."

4. A.   "Behold, there he stands behind our wall":

	B.	behind our wall at Sinai: "For on the third day the Lord will come down" (Ex. 19:11).
5.	A.	"...gazing in at the windows":
	B.	"And the Lord came down upon mount Sinai, at the top of the mountain" (Ex. 19:11).
6.	A.	"...looking through the lattice":
	B.	"And God spoke all these words" (Ex. 20:1).
7.	A.	"My beloved speaks and says to me, ['Arise, my love, my fair one, and come away] (Song 2:10)'":
	B.	What did he say to me?
	C.	"I am the Lord your God" (Ex. 20:2).

No. 1 appears to be free-standing and narrowly exegetical. But in the rerun that follows, it is shown to be integral to the whole. Nos. 2-7 form a sustained and coherent unit, reading the clauses of the verse as an allusion to Israel at Sinai and God's expression of his love. So now it is God who is talking.

XXVI:ii

1.	A.	Another explanation of the verses, "My beloved is like a gazelle":
	B.	Said the Community of Israel before the Holy One, blessed be He, "Lord of the world, you have said to us, [Simon:] "My love, my love." You are the one who says, "My love, my love" to us first.' [Simon, p. 118: *Dew* is an exclamation of affection. Jastrow: Thou art sighing for us first, instead of our aspiring for Thee.]
2.	A.	"My beloved is like a gazelle":
	B.	Just as a gazelle leaps from mountain to mountain, hill to hill, tree to tree, thicket to thicket, fence to fence,
	C.	so the Holy One, blessed be He, leaps from synagogue to synagogue, school house to school house.
	D.	All this why? So as to bestow blessing upon Israel.
	E.	And on account of what merit?
	F.	It is for the merit accruing to Abraham: "And the Lord appeared to him by the terebinths of Mamre and he was sitting" (Gen. 18:1).
3.	A.	R. Berekhiah in the name of R. Simeon b. Laqish: "While read as 'sitting,' the word is written as, 'sat.'
	B.	"Abraham intended to stand up. Said to him the Holy One, blessed be He, 'Remain seated, Abraham. You provide a model for your children. Just as you sit while I stand, so your children will be when they enter the synagogue and the school house and recite the Shema: they will sit, while my Glory will stand among them.
	C.	"What verse of Scripture indicates it? 'God stands in the congregation of God' (Ps. 82:1)."
4.	A.	[Supply: "God stands in the congregation of God" (Ps. 82:1):]
	B.	R. Haggai in the name of R. Isaac said, "What is written here is not, 'God is standing,' but rather, 'God stands.'
	C.	"What is the meaning of 'God stands'?
	D.	"It is, [Simon:] 'ready to attention,' as it says: 'And present yourself there to me on the top of the mount' (Ex. 34:2); 'And it shall come to pass that before they call, I will answer' (Isa. 65:24)."

5. A.   Rabbi in the name of R. Hanina: "Upon the occasion of every expression of praise with which the Israelites praise the Holy One, blessed be He, the Holy One, blessed be He, sits among them:

   B.   "'You are holy, enthroned upon the praises of Israel' (Ps. 22;4)."

6. A.   "...or a young stag":

   B.   R. Yosé b. R. Hanina said, "Meaning, like young deer."

7. A.   "Behold, there he stands behind our wall":

   B.   behind the walls of the synagogues and schoolhouses.

8. A.   "...gazing in at the windows":

   B.   from between the shoulders of the priests.

9. A.   "...looking through the lattice":

   B.   from between the fingers of the priests.

10. A.   "My beloved speaks and says to me":

   B.   What did he say to me?

   C.   "The Lord bless you and keep you" (Num. 6:24).

We go over the same matter as before, moving on from the redemption at Sinai to the union of synagogue, schoolhouse, and Temple, with the priestly blessing at the climax.

XXVI:iii

1. A.   Another explanation of the verse, "My beloved is like a gazelle":

   B.   Said the Community of Israel before the Holy One, blessed be He, "Lord of the world, you have said to us, [Simon:] "My love, my love." You are the one who says, "My love, my love" to us first.' [Simon, p. 118: *Dew* is an exclamation of affection. Jastrow: Thou art sighing for us first, instead of our aspiring for Thee.]

2. A.   "...or a young stag":

   B.   Just as a stag appears and then disappears, appears and then disappears,

   C.   so the first redeemer [Moses] came but then disappeared and then reappeared.

3. A.   How long did he disappear?

   B.   R. Tanhuma said, "Three months: 'And they met Moses and Aaron' (Ex. 5:20)."

   C.   Judah b. Rabbi said, "Intermittently."

   D.   So the final redeemer will appear to them and then disappear from sight.

   E.   And how long will he disappear from them?

   F.   Forty-five days: "And from the time that the continual burnt-offering shall be taken away and the detestable thing that causes abomination be set up, there shall be a thousand and two hundred ninety days" (Dan. 12:11); "Happy is he who waits and comes to the thousand three hundred and thirty-five days" (Dan. 12:13).

   G.   What are the additional days?

   H.   R. Yohanan, the laundrywoman's son, said in the name of R. Jonah, "These are the forty-five days on which he will disappear from them."

I.   In those days the Israelites will pick saltwort and juniper roots for food: "They pluck saltwort with wormwood and the roots of the broom are their food" (Job 30:3).

J.   Where will he led them?

K.   Some say, "To the wilderness of Judah."

L.   Some say, "To the wilderness of Sihon and Og."

M.   Those who say, "To the wilderness of Judah," cite the following: "I will yet again make you dwell in tents as in the days of the appointed season" (Hos. 12:10).

N.   Those who say, "To the wilderness of Sihon and Og cite the following: "Therefore behold I will allure her and bring her into the wilderness and speak tenderly to her. And I will give her vineyards from there" (Hos. 2:16-17).

O.   And whoever believes in him and follows him and waits for him will live.

P.   But whoever does not believe in him and follow him and wait for him but goes over to the nations of the world in the end will be killed by them.

Q.   Said R. Isaac b. R. Merion, "In the end of the forty-five days [H-I above], he will reappear to them and bring down manna for them.

R.   "For 'there is nothing new under the sun.'"

4. A.   "...or a young stag":

    B.   meaning, like young deer.

5. A.   "Behold, there he stands behind our wall":

    B.   behind the Western Wall of the house of the sanctuary.

    C.   Why so?

    D.   Because the Holy One, blessed be He, took an oath to him that it would never be destroyed.

    E.   And the Priests' Gate and the Huldah gate will never be destroyed before the Holy One, blessed be He, will restore them.

6. A.   "...gazing in at the windows":

    B.   through the merit of the matriarchs.

7. A.   "My beloved speaks and says to me":

    B.   What did he say to me?

    C.   "This month shall be for you the beginning of the months" (Ex. 12:2).

Obviously overwhelmed by interpolations, this next reading of our base verses introduces the messianic theme, the third in line as we have now come to expect. The secondary accretions of No. 3 do not spoil the exegetical program, which resumes and is completed at Nos. 4ff., despite the erroneous, "another interpretation". The opening of the next unit repeats that error.

27

Song of Songs Rabbah
to Song of Songs 2:10

2:10   My beloved speaks and says to me,
        "Arise, my love, my fair one,
        and come away..."

XXVII:i

1. A.   Another interpretation of the verse, "My beloved speaks and says
          to me":
    B.   R. Azariah said, "Are not 'speaking' and 'saying' the same thing?
    C.   "But 'he spoke to me' through Moses, and 'said to me' through
          Aaron."
2. A.   What did he say to me?
    B.   "Arise, my love, my fair one":
    C.   "Arise" means, "get up."
3. A.   Another interpretation of "arise my love":
    B.   "Arise, daughter of Abraham," of whom it is written, "Get you up
          out of your country and from your kin" (Gen. 12:1).
4. A.   "Arise, my love, my fair one":
    B.   Daughter of Isaac, who became my friend and beautified me on
          the altar.
5. A.   "...and come away":
    B.   Daughter of Jacob, who obeyed his father and mother: "And
          Jacob obeyed his father and his mother and went away to Paddan-
          aram" (Gen. 28:7).

The phrase-by-phrase amplification replays a familiar theme in a
new key. This entire matter will be reworked through Chapter Thirty.

28

Song of Songs Rabbah
to Song of Songs 2:11

2:11   *"...for lo, the winter is past,*
the rain is over and gone."

XXVIII:i
1.   A.   "...for lo, the winter is past":
     B.   this refers to the four hundred years that were decreed for our ancestors in Egypt.
     C.   "...the rain is over and gone":
     D.   this refers to the two hundred and ten years [of actual duress].
2.   A.   [Supply: "for lo, the winter is past, the rain is over and gone":]
     B.   are not winter and rain the same thing?
     C.   Said R. Tanhuma, "The principal duress [of winter] is the rain.
     D.   "So the principal subjugation of the Israelites in Egypt took place in the eighty-six years from the time of the birth of Miriam."
3.   A.   The explanation [of her name] is that it was on that account that she was called "Miriam,"
     B.   on account of the fact that "they made their lives bitter" (Ex. 1:14),
     C.   for the name Miriam bears the meaning of bitterness.

No. 1 invokes the point made already about the disparity between the four hundred years of God's message to Abraham and the calculation of the two hundred ten years actually spent in Egypt. On Tanhuma's statement, Simon adds (p. 11, n. 1:), "But not the whole of winter is unpleasant. Similarly, not the entire period of 210 years was spent in bondage." But that then ignores D, and the comment is possible only if we assume that Nos. 1 and 2 are a single unitary statement. No. 3 clearly is tacked on.

29

Song of Songs Rabbah to Song of Songs 2:12

2:12   *"The flowers appear on the earth,*
       the time of singing has come,
       and the voice of the turtledove is heard in our land."

XXIX:i

1. A.   "The flowers appear on the earth":
   B.   the conquerors [a word that uses some of the same consonants as the word flowers] appear on the earth.
   C.   To whom does this refer?
   D.   to Moses and Aaron: "And the Lord spoke to Moses and Aaron in the land of Egypt, saying" (Ex. 12:1).
2. A.   "...the time of singing has come":
   B.   The time has come for Israel to be redeemed.
   C.   The time has come for the foreskin to be cut off [a word that uses the same consonants as singing].
   D.   The time has come for the Canaanites to be cut off.
   E.   The time has come for their idolatry to be uprooted: "And against all the gods of Egypt I will execute judgments" (Ex. 12:12).
   F.   The time has come for the sea to have its waters cleaved in two: "And the waters were divided" (Ex. 14:21).
   G.   The time has come for the Song [at the sea] to be said: "Then sang Moses" (Ex. 15:1).
3. A.   R. Tanhuma said, "The time has come for songs should be made for the Holy One, blessed be He: 'The Lord is my strength and my song' (Ex. 15:2),
   B.   "meaning, 'the songs of the Lord [are my strength].'"
4. A.   [Supply (Simon, p. 122, n. 5:) "the time has come for the Torah to be given":]
   B.   Said R. Bibi, "'Your statutes have been my songs' (Ps. 119:54)."
5. A.   "...and the voice of the turtledove is heard in our land":
   B.   Said R. Yohanan, "'The voice of the good pioneer is heard in our land' [the words for turtledove and pioneer or explorer using the same consonants].

C.   "This refers to Moses when he said, 'And Moses, says, thus says the Lord, at about midnight' (Ex. 11:4)."

Nos. 1-2, 5 work out the way in which the Song celebrates the Exodus, a familiar motif. The speaker is now not so self-evidently assumed to be God.

30

Song of Songs Rabbah
to Song of Songs 2:13

2:13   *"The fig tree puts forth its figs,*
        and the vines are in blossom;
        they give forth fragrance.
        "Arise, my love, my fair one,
        and come away."

XXX:i

1. A.   "The fig tree puts forth its figs":
    B.   this refers to the Israelite sinners who perished during the three days of darkness: "And there was thick darkness...they did not see one another" (Ex. 10:22-23).
    C.   "...and the vines are in blossom; they give forth fragrance":
    D.   this refers to the survivors, who repented and were redeemed.
    E.   Moses came along to them and said to them, "All this good fragrance is wafted about you, and yet you sit here!
    F.   "'Arise, my love, my fair one, and come away.'"

The Exodus supplies the conclusion of the treatment of the successive verses. We now rework the entire set in several fresh ways.

XXX:ii

1. A.   Another comment on the verses, "My beloved speaks and says to me, ['Arise, my love, my fair one, and come away, for lo, the winter is past, the rain is over and gone. The flowers appear on the earth, the time of singing has come, and the voice of the turtledove is heard in our land. The fig tree puts forth its figs, and the vines are in blossom; they give forth fragrance. Arise, my love, my fair one, and come away]'" (Song 2:10-13):
    B.   "My beloved speaks and says to me":
    C.   R. Azariah said, "Are not 'speaking' and 'saying' the same thing?
    D.   "But 'he spoke to me' through Moses, and 'said to me' through Aaron."

187

2. A.   What did he say to me? "Arise, my love, my fair one, and come away, for lo, the winter is past":
   B.   This refers to the forty years that the Israelites spent in the wilderness.
3. A.   "the rain is over and gone":
   B.   This refers to the thirty-eight years that the Israelites were as though excommunicated in the wilderness.
   C.   For the Word did not speak with Moses until that entire generation had perished: "And the days in which we came from Kadesh-barnea...moreover the hand of the Lord was against them...so it came to pass that when all the men of war were consumed...the Lord spoke to me saying" (Dt. 2:14-17).
4. A.   "The flowers appear on the earth":
   B.   the conquerors appear on the earth,
   C.   that is, the princes: "Each prince on his day" (Num. 7:11).
5. A.   "...the time of singing has come":
   B.   The time for the foreskin to be removed.
   C.   The time for the Canaanites to be cut off.
   D.   The time for the land of Israel to be split up: "Unto these the land shall be divided" (Num. 26:53).
6. A.   "...and the voice of the turtledove is heard in our land":
   B.   Said R. Yohanan, "'The voice of the good pioneer is heard in our land' [the words for turtledove and pioneer or explorer using the same consonants].
   C.   "This refers to Joshua when he said, 'Pass in the midst of the camp.'"
7. A.   "The fig tree puts forth its figs":
   B.   this refers to the baskets of first fruits.
8. A.   "...and the vines are in blossom; they give forth fragrance":
   B.   this refers to drink-offerings.

The form is now established and will be followed quite carefully. The first set of applications deals with the Exodus and the conquest of the land.

XXX:iii
1. A.   Another reading of the verse, "My beloved speaks and says to me":
   B.   He "spoke to me" through Daniel,
   C.   and "said to me" through Ezra.
   D.   And what did he say to me?
2. A.   "Arise, my love, my fair one, and come away, for lo, the winter is past":
   B.   this refers to the seventy years that the Israelites spent in Exile.
3. A.   "...the rain is over and gone":
   B.   this is the fifty-two years between the time that the first Temple was destroyed and the kingdom of the Chaldaeans was uprooted.
   C.   But were they not seventy years?
   D.   Said R. Levi, "Subtract from them the eighteen years that an echo was circulated and saying to Nebuchadnezzar, 'Bad servant! Go

up and destroy the house of your Master, for the children of your Master have not obeyed him.'"

4. A.   "The flowers appear on the earth":

     B.   For example, Mordecai and his colleagues, Ezra and his colleagues.

5. A.   "...the time of singing has come":

     B.   The time for the foreskin to be removed.

     C.   The time for the wicked to be broken: "The Lord has broken off the staff of the wicked" (Isa. 14:5),

     D.   the time for the Babylonians to be destroyed,

     E.   the time for the Temple to be rebuilt: "And saviors shall come up on Mount Zion" (Obad. 1:21); "The glory of this latter house shall be greater than that of the former" (Hag. 2:9).

6. A.   "...and the voice of the turtledove is heard in our land":

     B.   Said R. Yohanan, "'The voice of the good pioneer is heard in our land' [the words for turtledove and pioneer or explorer using the same consonants].

     C.   "This refers to Cyrus: 'Thus says Cyrus, king of Persia...all the kingdoms of the earth...whoever there is among you of all his people...let him go up...and build the house of the Lord' (Ezra 1:2-3)."

7. A.   "The fig tree puts forth its figs":

     B.   this refers to the baskets of first-fruits.

8. A.   "...and the vines are in blossom; they give forth fragrance":

     B.   this refers to drink-offerings.

The second reading carries us to the second redemption, with the restoration of Israel to Zion. The decision to create the entire composition comes prior to the inquiry into what materials may serve, since the repetitions fill obvious gaps. These are not then mistakes (pace Simon, p. 124, n. 2, on my No. 5: "This is really out of place here and is repeated from above").

XXX:iv

1. A.   Another explanation of the verse, "My beloved speaks and says to me":

     B.   He "spoke" through Elijah,

     C.   and "said to me" through the Messiah.

     D.   What did he say to me?

2. A.   "Arise, my love, my fair one, and come away, for lo, the winter is past":

     B.   Said R. Azariah, "'...for lo, the winter is past': this refers to the kingdom of the Cutheans [Samaritans], which deceives [the words for winter and deceive use some of the same consonants] the world and misleads it through its lies: 'If your brother, son of your mother...entices you' (Dt. 13:7)."

3. A.   "...the rain is over and gone":

     B.   this refers to the subjugation.

4. A.   "The flowers appear on the earth":

     B.   the conquerors appear on the earth.

     C.   Who are they?

	D.	R. Berekhiah in the name of R. Isaac: "It is written, 'And the Lord showed me four craftsmen' (Zech. 2:3),
	E.	"and who are they? Elijah, the royal Messiah, the Melchizedek, and the military Messiah."
5.	A.	"...the time of singing has come":
	B.	The time for the Israelites to be redeemed has come,
	C.	the time for the foreskin to be removed.
	D.	The time for kingdom of the Cutheans to perish,
	E.	the time for the kingdom of Heaven to be revealed: "and the Lord shall be king over all the earth" (Zech. 14:9).
6.	A.	"...and the voice of the turtledove is heard in our land":
	B.	What is this? It is the voice of the royal Messiah,
	C.	proclaiming, "How beautiful upon the mountains are the feet of the messenger of good tidings" (Isa. 52:7).
7.	A.	"The fig tree puts forth its figs":
	B.	Said R. Hiyya b. R. Abba, "Close to the days of the Messiah a great pestilence will come to the world, and the wicked will perish."
8.	A.	"...and the vines are in blossom; they give forth fragrance":
	B.	this speaks of those who will remain, concerning whom it is said, "And it shall come to pass that he who is left in Zion and he who remains in Jerusalem" (Isa. 4:3).
9.	A.	Said R. Yohanan, [B. Sanhedrin 97A: Our Rabbis have taught on Tannaite authority]:
	B.	"The seven year cycle in which the son of David will come:
	C.	"As to the first one, the following verse of Scripture will be fulfilled: 'And I will cause it to rain upon one city and not upon another' (Amos 4:7).
	D.	"As to the second year, the arrows of famine will be sent forth.
	E.	"As to the third, there will be a great famine, in which men, women, and children will die, pious men and wonder-workers alike, and the Torah will be forgotten in Israel.
	F.	"As to the fourth year, there will be plenty which is no plenty.
	G.	"As to the fifth year, there will be great prosperity, and people will eat, drink, and rejoice, and the Torah will be restored to those that study it.
	H.	"As to the sixth year, there will be rumors.
	I.	"As to the seventh year, there will be wars.
	J.	"As to the end of the seventh year [the eighth year], the son of David will come."
	K.	Said Abbaye, "Lo, how many septennates have passed like that one, and yet he has not come."
2.	A.	The Messiah will come only in the conditions described in that which was said by R. Simeon b. Laqish:
	B.	[M. Sot. 9:15AA-GG:] R. Judah says, "In the generation in which the son of David will come, the gathering place will be for prostitution, Galilee will be laid waste, Gablan will be made desolate, and the men of the frontier will go about from town to town, and none will take pity on them; and the wisdom of scribes will putrefy; and those who fear sin will be rejected; and the truth will be herded away.
	C.	"And the generation will be brazen-faced like a dog.

    D.   "How do we know that truth will be abandoned?

    E.   "For it is said, 'And the truth will be herded away [and he who departs from evil makes himself a prey' (Isa. 59:15)."

    F.   And where does truth go?

    G.   The school of R. Yannai said, "It will be divided into herds and herds, each going its way.

3. A.   Rabbis say, "In the generation in which the son of David will come, the sages of the generation will die,

    B.   "and the eyes of those who remain will grow dim because of sorrow and anguish,

    C.   "and much trouble and many evils will come upon the community.

    D.   "Harsh decrees will be renewed and sent forth.

    E.   "Before the first has been carried out, another will come and add to it."

4. A.   Said R. Nehorai, "In the generation in which the son of David will come, the youth will humiliate the elders,

    B.   "the elders will stand up before the youth.

    C.   "'The daughter rises up against her mother, the daughter-in-law against her mother-in-law, a man's enemies are the men of his own house' (Mic. 7:6).

    D.   "And a son will not be ashamed before his father."

5. A.   R. Nehemiah says, "Before the days of the Messiah poverty will increase, there will be inflation, while the vine will give its fruit, the wine will sour.

    B.   "The entire kingdom will turn to heresy.

    C.   "And there will be no reproof."

6. A.   Said R. Abba b. Kahana, "The son of David will come only in a generation the leadership of which is in the hands of dogs."

7. A.   Said R. Levi, "The son of David will come only in a generation the leadership of which is impudent and liable to annihilation."

8. A.   Said R. Yannai, "If you see one generation after another cursing and blaspheming, expect the Messiah:

    B.   "'Wherewith your enemies have taunted, O Lord, wherewith your enemies have taunted the footsteps of your anointed' (Ps. 89:52); then 'Blessed be the Lord forevermore, amen and amen' (Ps. 89:53)."

The trilogy now comes to its climax with the third and final redemption, the Exodus and conquest, the return to Zion, and the ultimate salvation then forming the entire corpus for which the language of the Song serves as metaphor. The remainder is tacked on for obvious reasons. It is an anthology of materials that find a more natural place in the Talmud of Babylonia, as indicated.

31

Song of Songs Rabbah to Song of Songs 2:14

2:14   *"O my dove, in the clefts of the rock,*
in the covert of the cliff,
"let me see your face,
let me hear your voice,
"for your voice is sweet,
and your face is comely"

XXXI:i

1.   A.   "O my dove, in the clefts of the rock, [in the covert of the cliff, let me see your face, let me hear your voice, for your voice is sweet, and your face is comely]":

B.   What is the meaning of "my dove, in the clefts of the rock"?

C.   Said R. Yohanan, "Said the Holy One, blessed be He, 'I call Israel a dove: "And Ephraim has become like a silly dove, without understanding" (Hos. 7:11).

D.   "'To me they are like a dove, but to the nations of the world they are like wild beasts: "Judah is a lion's whelp" (Gen. 49:9); "Naphtali is a hind let loose" (Gen. 49:21); "Dan shall be a serpent in the way" (Gen. 49:17); "Benjamin is a wolf that ravages" (Gen. 49:27).'

E.   "For the nations of the world make war on Israel and say to Israel, 'What do you want with the Sabbath and with circumcision?'

F.   "And the Holy One, blessed be He, strengthens Israel and before the nations of the world they become like wild beasts so as to subdue them before the Holy One, blessed be He, and before Israel.

G.   "But as to the Holy One, blessed be He, they are like a dove that is without guile, and they obey him: 'And the people believed, and when heard that the Lord had remembered' (Ex. 4:31)."

2.   A.   [Supply: "And the people believed, and when heard that the Lord had remembered" (Ex. 4:31):]

B.   Said the Holy One, blessed be He, to Moses, "Moses, are you standing and crying out? I have already heard Israel and their cry: 'Wherefore do you cry out to me' (Ex. 14:25).

	C.	"The children of Israel do not need you."
3.	A.	[Reverting to 1.G:] "Therefore said the Holy One, blessed be He, '"...my dove, in the clefts of the rock."'"
4.	A.	Said R. Judah b. R. Simon, Yohanan, "Said the Holy One, blessed be He, 'To me they are like a dove, but to the nations of the world they are as cunning as snakes.'
	B.	"Thus: 'Shadrach, Meshach and Abed-nego answered and said to the king, O Nebuchadnezzar' (Dan. 3:16).
	C.	"If 'to the king' then why 'Nebuchadnezzar,' and if 'Nebuchadnezzar,' then why 'king'?
	D.	"But this is what they said to him: 'If it is for the purposes of taxes, head-taxes, crop-taxes, or corvée, you are king over us: "to the king, Nebuchadnezzar."
	E.	"'But if it is for this matter [of worshipping an idol] that you tell us to bow down to your idol, you are simply Nebuchadnezzar, and your name is Nebuchadnezzar, you are a mere man, and we regard you as no more than a dog.
	F.	"'[The name Nebuchadnezzar yields letters with this sense:] 'bark like a dog, bubble with rage like a pot, chirp like a cricket.'
	G.	"Forthwith he barked like a dog, boiled like a pot, and chirped like a cricket."
5.	A.	"I advise you, obey the command of the king" (Qoh. 8:2):
	B.	Said R. Levi, "'I obey the command of the King of kings of kings,
	C.	"'the command that instructed at Sinai, "I am the Lord your God" (Ex. 20:2).
	D.	"'And with special reference to the statement of the oath of God (Qoh. 8:2): "You shall not take the name of the Lord your god in vain" (Ex. 20:7)."
6.	A.	It was taught on Tannaite authority by the house of R. Ishmael, "When the Israelites went forth from Egypt, to what were they to be compared?
	B.	"To a dove that fled from a hawk and flew into the cleft of a rock and found a serpent hidden there.
	C.	"It went in but could not, because the snake was hidden there, and it tried to go backward but could not, because the hawk was standing outside.
	D.	"What did the dove do? It began to cry out and beat its wings, so that the owner of the dovecote should hear and come and save it.
	E.	"That is what the Israelites were like at the sea.
	F.	"To go down into the sea they could not do, because the sea had not yet been split before them.
	G.	"To retreat they could not do, because Pharaoh was already drawing near.
	H.	"So what did they do?
	I.	"'And they were afraid, and the children of Israel cried out to the Lord' (Ex. 14:10).
	J.	"Forthwith: 'Thus the Lord saved Israel that day' (Ex. 14:30)."
7.	A.	R. Judah in the name of R. Hama of Kefar Tehumin: "The matter may be compared to the king who had an only daughter and wanted to listen to her converse.
	B.	"What did he do?

C.   "He circulated an announcement and said, 'Let everybody assemble in the piazza.'

D.   "When they had come forth, what did he do? He made a gesture to his servants, and they suddenly fell on her like thugs.

E.   "She began to cry out, 'Father, father, save me.'

F.   "He said, 'Had I not treated you in this way, you would not have cried out and said, "Father, save me."'

G.   "So when the Israelites were in Egypt, the Egyptians enslaved them, and they begin to cry out and look upward to the Holy One, blessed be He: 'And it came to pass in the course of those many days that the king of Egypt died, and the children of Israel signed by reason of the bondage, and they cried' (Ex. 2:23).

H.   "Forthwith: 'And God heard their groaning' (Ex. 2:24).

I.   "The Holy One, blessed be He, heard their prayer and brought them out with am mighty hand and with an outstretched arm.

J.   "But the Holy One, blessed be He, wanted to listen to their voice, and they did not want it.

K.   "What did the Holy One, blessed be He, do?

L.   "He hardened Pharaoh's heart and he pursued after them: 'And the Lord hardened the heart of Pharaoh, king of Egypt, and he pursued' (Ex. 14:8); 'And Pharaoh brought near' (Ex. 14:10)."

8. A.   [Supply: "And Pharaoh brought near" (Ex. 14:10):]

    B.   What is the meaning of "brought near"?

    C.   He brought the Israelites near to repentance.

9. A.   [Continuing 7.L:] "When they saw them, they raised their eyes to the Holy One, blessed be He: 'The children of Israel lifted up their eyes, and behold, the Egyptians were marching after them, and they were much afraid, and the children of Israel cried out to the Lord' (Ex. 14:10).

    B.   "This was in the same way that they had cried out in Egypt.

    C.   "Now when the Holy One, blessed be He, heard, he said to them, 'If I had not treated you in this way, I should not have heard your voice.

    D.   "It is in connection with that moment that he said, 'O my dove, in the clefts of the rock.'

    E.   "What is says is not 'let me hear a voice,' but 'let me hear your voice.'

    F.   "For 'I have already heard it in Egypt.'

    G.   "And when the children of Israel cried out before the Holy One, blessed be He, forthwith: 'thus the Lord saved Israel that day' (Ex. 14:30).

The amplification of the base verse of course has God speaking of Israel. The opening inquiry has God take the view that while to him they are like a dove, to the nations they are dangerous. That is the point of No. 1, with a minor gloss, and No. 3. The same comparison is worked out at No. 4. That seems to me essentially cogent with the foregoing, since the issue is still Israel as both dove and beast to the nations of the world: dove in obedience to law, beast in defiance of idolatry. I do not see how No. 5 fits in; it seems to me parachuted down with no good reason, essentially to complement No. 4's obedience to the king's command when it is lawful. No. 6 begins an essentially new treatment of the metaphor of the dove, one that does not draw near our base verse but simply works on why Israel is like a dove; naturally we revert to the Exodus, a familiar motif by now. The point is very clear, and No. 7 (+8) and 9 present no surprises either. Once we have interpreted the verse in this framework, we must expect a replay of the same motif: the sea, Sinai, the nations of the world; the cult; and so forth and so on.

XXXI:ii

1. A. [Supply: "my dove, in the clefts of the rock, in the covert of the cliff, let me see your face, let me hear your voice, for your voice is sweet, and your face is comely":

   B. R. Eleazar interpreted the verse to speak of Israel when it stood at the sea:

   C. "'...my dove, in the clefts of the rock, in the covert of the cliff': for they were hidden in the [Simon:] recess of the sea.

   D. "'...let me see your face': 'Stand still and see the salvation of the Lord' (Ex. 14:13).

   E. "'...let me hear your voice': that is, the song, 'Then sang Moses' (Ex. 15:1).

   F. "'...for your voice is sweet': this refers to the song.

   G. "'...and your face is comely': for the Israelites were making a gesture of glorification with their finger and saying, 'This is my God and I will glorify him' (Ex. 15:2)."

2. A. R. Aqiba interpreted the verse to speak of Israel when it stood at Mount Sinai:

   B. "'...my dove, in the clefts of the rock, in the covert of the cliff': for they were hidden in the [Simon:] recess of the Sinai.

   C. "'...let me see your face': 'And all the people saw the thundering' (Ex. 20:15).

   D. "'...let me hear your voice': this is the voice that was before the Ten Commandments: 'All that the Lord has spoken we shall do and obey' (Ex. 24:7).

   E. "'...for your voice is sweet': this is the voice after the Ten Commandments: 'And the Lord heard the voice of your words...and said...they have said well all that they have spoken' (Dt. 5:25)."

3. A. [Supply: "And the Lord heard the voice of your words...and said...they have said well all that they have spoken" (Dt. 5:25):]

   B. What is the meaning of "they have said well all that they have spoken"?

   C. Hiyya b. R. Ada and Bar Qappara:

   D. One said, "It was like the act of trimming [which uses the same consonants as the word well] in the trimming of the lamps."

   E. The other said, "It was like the act of preparation in the preparation of the incense."

4. A. [Continuing 2.E:] "'...and your face is comely': 'And when the people saw it, they trembled and stood afar off' (Ex. 20:15)."

5. A.   R. Yosé the Galilean interpreted the verse to speak of the [subjugation of Israel to the] kingdoms:

   B.   "'...my dove, in the clefts of the rock, in the covert of the cliff': they were hidden in the shadow of the kingdoms.

   C.   "'...let me see your face': this refers to study.

   D.   "'...let me hear your voice': this refers to a good deed."

6. A.   Now they took a vote one time in the upper room of Aris in Lydda saying, "What is the more important? Study or deed?"

   B.   R. Tarfon says, "Greater is deed."

   C.   R. Aqiba says, "Greater is study."

   D.   They voted and reached the decision that study is the greater, since it brings about deed.

7. A.   [Continuing 5.D:] "'...for your voice is sweet': this refers to study.

   B.   "'...and your face is comely': this refers to deed."

8. A.   R. Huna and R. Aha in the name of R. Aha b. Hanina, following the theory of R. Meir, interpreted the verse to speak of the tent of meeting:

   B.   "'...my dove, in the clefts of the rock, in the covert of the cliff': for they were shadowed in the shade of the tent of meeting.

   C.   "'...let me see your face': 'And the congregation was assembled at the door of the tent of meeting' (Lev. 8:4).

   D.   "'...let me hear your voice': 'And when all the people saw it, they shouted' (Lev. 9:24).

   E.   "Since they saw something new, therefore they proclaimed a new song.

   F.   "'...for your voice is sweet': this refers to the song.

   G.   "'...and your face is comely': 'And all the congregation drew near and stood before the Lord' (Lev. 9:5)."

9. A.   Said R. Tanhuma, "They [R. Huna and R. Aha in the name of R. Aha b. Hanina] in the theory of R. Meir, interpreted it to refer to the tent of meeting. I will will interpret it, in line with the position of rabbis, [who hold that it speaks of] the eternal house [the temple]:

   B.   "'...my dove, in the clefts of the rock, in the covert of the cliff': for they were shadowed in the shade of the eternal house.

   C.   "'...let me see your face': 'Then Solomon assembled' (1 Kgs. 8:1).

   D.   "'...let me hear your voice': 'It came even to pass, when the trumpeters and singers were as one' (2 Chr. 5:13)."

10. A.   R. Abin in the name of R. Abba, the Priest, son of Daliah: "It is written, 'And all the people answered together' (Ex. 19:8), but also, 'And all the people answered with one voice and said' (Ex. 24:3).

    B.   "To what point did [the merit accomplished through] that voice endure to their credit?

    C.   "Up to: 'It came even to pass, when the trumpeters and singers were as one' (2 Chr. 5:13)."

11. A.   [Resuming from 9.D:] "'for your voice is sweet': this refers to the song[s sung in the temple rite].

    B.   "'...and your face is comely': this speaks of the offerings: 'And Solomon offered for the sacrifice of peace-offerings' (1 Kgs. 8:63)."

12. A.   [Supply: "And King Solomon offered the sacrifice of the oxen, twenty-two thousand" (2 Chr. 7:5)]:

B.   What are these oxen?

C.   "The four wagons and the eight oxen" (Num. 7:8).

13. A.   R. Elijah interpreted the verse to speak of the pilgrims who come up to celebrate the festivals:

B.   "'...my dove, in the clefts of the rock, in the covert of the cliff': these are the pilgrims who come up for the festivals: 'Three times in a year will all your males be seen' (Dt. 16:16).

C.   "'...let me hear your voice': this refers to the recitation of the Hallel-psalms [Ps. 113-188] in a beautiful choir.

D.   "When the Israelites recite the Hallel-psalms, their voice rises on high.

E.   "There is this proverb: 'Keep Passover in the house, and for Hallel break the roof.'

F.   "'...for your voice is sweet': this refers to the song.

G.   "'...and your face is comely': this refers to the priestly blessing."

We work through the remainder of the metaphorical possibilities of our base verse. The insertions are transparent, and the formal perfection of the whole therefore clear.

XXXI:iii

1. A.   Said R. Judah b. R. Simon in the name of R. Simeon b. Eleazar, "Why was Rebeccah childless [for so long]?

B.   "It was so that the nations of the world should not say, 'Our prayer has borne fruit.'

C.   "For they said to her, '"Our sister, be the mother of thousands of ten thousands" (Gen. 24:60.'

D.   "[Therefore she did not bear] until Isaac prayed in her behalf, and then she was visited [and got pregnant].

E.   "'And Isaac entreated the Lord for his wife' (Gen. 25:21)."

2. A.   R. Azariah in the name of R. Hanina b. R. Pappa said, "Why were the matriarchs childless [for so long]?

B.   "It was so that they [Simon:] should not put on airs towards their husbands by reason of their beauty."

3. A.   R. Huna and R. Jeremiah in the name of R. Hiyya b. R. Abba said, "Why were the matriarchs childless [for so long]?

B.   "It was so that the greater part of their lives should be spent without servitude."

4. A.   R. Hunai in the name of R. Meir: "Why were the matriarchs childless [for so long]?

B.   "It was so that their husbands should have a long time to enjoy their beauty.

C.   "For when a woman gets pregnant, she gets fat and clumsy.

D.   "You may know that that is the fact, for all the years that our matriarch, Sarah, was barren, she dwelt in her house like a bride in her bridal bower.

E.   "But when she got pregnant, her appearance changed: 'In pain you shall bring forth children' (Gen. 3:16)."

5. A.   R. Levi in the name of R. Shila of Kefar Tamarta and R. Helbo in the name of R. Yohanan: "Why were the matriarchs childless [for so long]?

B.   "It was because the Holy One, blessed be He, craved to hear their pleading.
C.   "He said to them, 'My dove, I shall tell you how come I have kept you barren. It was because I craved to hear your pleading.'
D.   "'...for your voice is sweet, and your face is comely.'"

The entire set is inserted only because of the concluding item. Otherwise there is not a single point of intersection.

32

Song of Songs Rabbah
to Song of Songs 2:15

2:15   *"Catch us the foxes,*
the little foxes,
that spoil the vineyards,
for our vineyards are in blossom."

XXXII:ii

1. A.   "Catch us the foxes, the little foxes, [that spoil the vineyards, for our vineyards are in blossom]":

    B.   When the other kingdoms are assigned metaphors, the metaphors pertain only to fire: "And I will set my face against them, out of the fire they have come fourth, and the fire shall devour them" (Ez. 15:7).

    C.   But when the Egyptians are assigned a metaphor, it is only that which is consumed by fire: "They are quenched as a wick" (Isa. 43:17).

    D.   When the other kingdoms are assigned metaphors, the metaphors pertain only to silver and gold: "As for that image, its head was of fine gold" (Dan. 2:32).

    E.   But when the Egyptians are assigned a metaphor, it is only lead: "They sank as lead" (Ex. 15:10).

    F.   When the other kingdoms are assigned metaphors, the metaphors pertain only to cedars: "Behold, the Assyrian was a cedar in Lebanon" (Ez. 31:3); "The tree that you saw, which grew" (Gen. 4:17); 'Yet I destroyed the Amorite before them, whose height was like that of cedars" (Amos 2:9).

    G.   But when the Egyptians are assigned a metaphor, it is only stubble: "It consumes them like stubble" (Ex. 15:7).

    H.   When the other kingdoms are assigned metaphors, the metaphors pertain only to beasts of pray: "And four great beasts came up from the sea, different from one another" (Dan. 7:3); "The first was like a lion" (Dan. 7:4).

    I.   But when the Egyptians are assigned a metaphor, it is only foxes: "Catch us the foxes, the little foxes."

	J.	[What follows is at 6.F and does not make sense here:] Guard them in the river.
2.	A.	Said R. Eleazar b. R. Simeon, "The Egyptians were clever, so they are given the metaphor of foxes.
	B.	"Just as a fox looks over its shoulder, so the Egyptians looked over their shoulders.
	C.	"They were saying, 'Now how shall we impose death upon them?
	D.	"'Shall we put them to death with fire? But has it not already been said, "For my fire will the Lord contend" (Isa. 66:16).
	E.	"'Shall we put them to death with the sword? "And by his sword with all flesh" (Isa. 66:16).
	F.	"'Let us put them to death with water, for the Holy One, blessed be He, has sworn that he will not again bring a flood on the earth: "For this is as the waters of Noah to me" (Isa. 54:9).'
	G.	"Said the Holy One, blessed be He, to them, 'By yours lives! Each one of you shall a drag into the flood: "He shall drag them to the power of the sword, they shall be a portion for foxes" (Ps. 63:11).'
	H.	"'He shall drag them to the power of the sword': this refers to the wicked, whom he dragged onto the [Simon:] dry bottom of the sea.' [Simon, p. 135, n. 7: Before the water returned. Thus he did not bring a flood upon them, but led them to the flood.]
	I.	"'...they shall be a portion for foxes': Said the Holy One, blessed be He, 'This portion will be reserved for the foxes.'"
3.	A.	Said R. Berekhiah, "The word for foxes is written out with all its vowels the first time, but the second time not.
	B.	"This refers to the foxes who went down to the bed of the sea."
4.	A.	Said R. Tanhuma in the name of R. Judah b. R. Simon, "It is written, 'He who makes a way in the sea' (Isa. 63:16).
	B.	"This is no big deal.
	C.	"'And a path in the mighty waters' (Isa. 63:16).
	D.	"This too is no big deal.
	E.	"But what really takes effort?
	F.	"'Who brings forth the chariot and horse, the army and the power' (Isa. 63:16)."
5.	A.	[Supply: "He who makes a way in the sea, and a path in the mighty waters, who brings forth the chariot and horse, the army and the power" (Isa. 63:16):]
	B.	Said R. Yudan, "[Simon, verbatim:] They entered in this order like the wild beasts at the games followed by the common spectator first and then by the nobility." [Simon, p. 136, n. 2: R. Yudan observes that in the verse just quoted chariot and horse are mentioned first, then the army, and finally the power , and it describes the order in which the Egyptians entered the sea, which may be compared to the procession at the games, when the wild beasts went first, the common spectators followed, with the aristocracy bringing up the rear.]
6.	A.	Said R. Hanan, "What did the proper and modest Israelite women do [when Pharaoh decreed death to the males]?
	B.	"They would take them and hide them in holes.

C. "So the wicked Egyptians would take their little babies and bring them into the Israelites' houses and pinch them, so the babies would cry.

D. "Then the Israelite baby would hear the voice of the other crying, and would cry with him.

E. "And they would then take them and throw them into the river.

F. "Thus: 'Catch us the foxes, the little foxes,' and guard them to throw them into the river."

G. And how many infants were there that they threw into the river?

H. Ten thousand: "Ten thousand, even as the growth of the field" (Ez. 16:7).

I. And R. Levi said, "Six hundred thousand, for so said Moses, 'The people, among whom I am, are six hundred thousand men on foot' (Num. 11:21)."

7. A. Now what did the Egyptians do?

B. They would bring their children from the schools and send them into the Israelites' bath houses, where they would see which Israelite woman was pregnant.

C. They would then make a note of them and go back and tell their fathers, "Thus and so has three months to go, thus and so, four months, thus and so, five months."

D. When the time had run out, they would take the babes from their breasts and cast them in the river: "Catch us the foxes, the little foxes."

E. What is written is not "seize," or "kill," but "catch,' meaning that they guarded them for the river.

The given here is that the foxes that spoil the vineyards are the Egyptians that mistreat the Israelites, and the rest follows. That accounts for the sense and, obviously, also the inclusion of No. 1. No. 2 goes over the same theme as No. 1. "Looked over their shoulders" means, examined the past for precedents. No. 3 carries forward a detail of No. 2. I assume that Nos. 4, 5 are included as part of a sustained interest in Isa. 63. Otherwise I see no reason for the insertion of the passage. No. 6 is then free-standing, reverting back to our base verse and the implicit meaning that the framers have assigned to it, that is, the Egyptians as foxes. No. 7 goes through the same process. The whole is not strongly cogent, but it also is not diffuse and haphazard. We now move from Egypt to Rome, the first to the last monarchy with which Israel must deal.

XXXII:ii

1. A. [Supply: "Catch us the foxes, the little foxes":]

B. R. Yudan and R. Berekhiah:

C. R. Yudan said, "'the little foxes' are Esau and his generals: 'Behold, I make you little among the nations' (Obad. 1:2)."

2. A. [=Gen. R. LXV:XI.1-2, with reference to Gen. 27:1: "When Isaac was old, and his eyes were dim, so that he could not see, he called Esau, his older son" – thus, "he called Esau his greater son."] Said

R. Eleazar b. R. Simeon, "The matter may be compared to the case of a town that was collecting a bodyguard for the king. There was a woman there, whose son was a dwarf. She called him 'Tall-swift' [Freedman]. She said, 'My son is "Tall-swift," so why do you not take him?'

B.　　　　"They said to her, 'If in your eyes he is "Tall-swift," in our eyes he is the smallest of dwarfs.'

C.　　　　"So his father called him 'great': '...he called Esau his great son.'

D.　　　　"So too his mother called him 'great': 'Then Rebecca took the best garments of Esau, her great son.'

E.　　　　"Said the Holy One, blessed be He, to them, 'If in your eyes he is great, in my eyes he is small: 'Behold, I make you small among the nations' (Obad. 1:2) [speaking of Edom/Esau/Rome]."

3.　A.　　[Genesis Rabbah's version:] Said R. Abbahu said R. Berekhiah, [Song: "And even if he is great, then:] "In accord with the size of the ox is the stature of the slaughterer.

B.　　　　"That is in line with the following verse: 'For the Lord has a sacrifice in Bozrah, and a great slaughter in the land of Edom' (Isa. 34:6)."

C.　　　　[Genesis Rabbah's version concludes:] Said R. Berekhiah, "The sense is, 'There will be a great slaughterer in the land of Edom. [Freedman, p. 587, n. 2: Since Esau is called great, his slaughterer, God, will likewise be great.]"

4.　A.　　"[Catch us the foxes, the little foxes,] that spoil the vineyards, [for our vineyards are in blossom]":

B.　　　　"that spoil the vineyards" refers to Israel: "For the vineyard of the Lord of hosts is the house of Israel" (Isa. 5:7).

5.　A.　　"...for our vineyards are in blossom":

B.　　　　"There is no cluster to eat, nor first-ripe fig which my soul desires" (Mic. 7:1).

6.　A.　　R. Berekhiah said, "'the little foxes': these are the four kingdoms:

B.　　　　"'There are four things that are little upon the earth' (Prov. 30:24).

C.　　　　"'...that spoil the vineyards': this refers to Israel: 'For the vineyard of the Lord of hosts is the house of Israel' (Isa. 5:7).

D.　　　　"'...for our vineyards are in blossom':

E.　　　　"Who is responsible that our vineyards are [Simon: merely] budding?

F.　　　　"'And I sought for a man among them, who should make up the hedge...but I found none' (Ez. 22:30),

G.　　　　"except for Noah, Daniel, and Job."

I give Nos. 2, 3 in the version of Genesis Rabbah, because the version before us does not make reference to Berekhiah at all. But the differences are not material. I take it that Nos. 4, 5 complete Yudan's exposition. Then No. 6 introduces Berekhiah, showing that Nos. 2, 3 are simply parachuted down for thematic reasons. Berekhiah wants to say that Israel's sin is what has made the vineyard less fruitful than it should be, and that is linked to the subjugation among the kingdoms, so would appear to be the intent of the whole.

33

Song of Songs Rabbah
to Song of Songs 2:16

2:16   *My beloved is mine and I am his,*
        he pastures his flock among the lilies.

XXXIII:i

1. A. "My beloved is mine and I am his":
    B. To me he is God, and to him I am the nation:
    C. To me he is God: "I am the Lord your God" (Ex. 20:2).
    D. and to him I am people and nation: "Attend to me, my people, and give ear to me, my nation" (Isa. 51:4).

2. A. To me he is father, and to him I am son:
    B. to me he is father: "For you are our father" (Isa. 63:6); "For I have become father to Israel" (Jer. 31:9).
    C. and to him I am son: "Israel is my son, my firstborn" (Ex. 4:22); "You are children of the Lord" (Dt. 14:1).

3. A. To me he is shepherd: "Give ear, shepherd of Israel" (Ps. 80:2).
    B. To him I am flock: "And you, my sheep, the sheep of my pasture" (Ez. 34:31).

4. A. To me he is guard: "He who guards Israel does not slumber nor sleep" (Ps. 121:4).
    B. To him I am vineyard: "For the vineyard of the Lord of hosts is the house of Israel" (Isa. 5:7).

5. A. He is for my against those who [Simon:] challenge me, and I am for him against those who spite him.
    B. He is for my against those who [Simon:] challenge me, for he hit the firstborn: "For I will go through the land of Egypt" (Ex. 12:12); "And it came to pass at midnight that the Lord smote all the firstborn" (Ex. 12:29).
    C. and I am for him against those who spite him, for I sacrificed [the lamb, which is] the god of Egypt.
    D. And thus: "And against all the Gods of Egypt I will execute judgments" (Ex. 12:12), and I sacrificed them to him: "Lo, if we sacrifice the abomination of the Egyptians before their eyes" (Ex.

		12:22); "They shall take to them every man a lamb, according to their fathers' houses" (Ex. 12:3).
6.	A.	He said to me, "Let not the mingled wine [which stands for the sanhedrin] be lacking": "Your navel is a rounded bowl, that never lacks mixed wine."
	B.	And I said to him, "You are my beloved, let your kindness never be lacking": "The Lord is my shepherd, I shall not want" (Ps. 23:1).
7.	A.	Said R. Judah b. R. Ilai, "He is my song, and I am his song.
	B.	"He praised me, and I praised him.
	C.	"He called me, 'my sister, my beloved, my perfect one, my dove,'
	D.	"and I said to him, 'This is my beloved and my friend.'
	E.	"He said to me, 'Behold, you are beautiful, my love; behold, you are beautiful; your eyes are doves' (Song 1:15),
	F.	"and I said to him, 'Behold, you are beautiful, my beloved, truly lovely' (Song 1:16).
	G.	"He said to me, 'Happy are you, Israel, who is like you' (Dt. 33:29),
	H.	"and I said to him, 'Who is like you, Lord, among the mighty' (Ex. 15:11).
	I.	"He said to me, 'And who is like your people, Israel, a nation unique on earth' (2 Sam. 7:23).
	J.	"And I declare his uniqueness twice a day: 'Hear Israel the Lord our God the Lord is unique' (Dt. 6:4)."
8.	A.	And when there is something that I need, I ask it only from his hand: "And it came to pass in the course of those many days that the king of Egypt died...and God heard their groaning...and God saw the children of Israel" (Ex. 2:23ff).
	B.	And when there is something that he needs, he asks it only from me and from my hand: "Speak to all the congregation of Israel, saying to them" (Ex. 12:3).
	C.	And when there is something that I need, I ask it only from his hand: "And when Pharaoh drew near, the children of Israel lifted up their eyes" (Ex. 14:10).
	D.	And when there is something that he needs, he asks it only from me and from my hand: "Speak to the children of Israel that they take for me an offering" (Ex. 25:2).
	E.	When I had trouble, I asked help only from him: "And the children of Israel cried to the Lord, for he had nine hundred chariots of iron, and he greatly oppressed the children of Israel" (Judges 4:3).
9.	A.	[Supply: "And the children of Israel cried to the Lord, for he had nine hundred chariots of iron, and he greatly oppressed the children of Israel" (Judges 4:3):]
	B.	What is the meaning of "greatly"?
	C.	With insults and blasphemy.
10.	A.	[Resuming from 8.E:] And when there is something that he needs, he asks it only from me: "And let them make me a sanctuary" (Ex. 25:8).

The reciprocity of the relationship is expressed in a variety of ways, Nos. 1-5 being perfectly formed throughout. The basic response then is to read the base verse as an assertion of the complete equality of the love.

XXXIII:ii

1. A. "...he pastures his flock among the lilies":
   B. R. Yohanan was punished with suffering from gallstones for three years and a half.
   C. R. Hanina came up to visit him. He said to him, "How're you doing?"
   D. He said to him, "I have more than I can bear."
   E. He said to him, "Don't say that. But say, 'The faithful God.'"
   F. When the pain got severe, he would say, "Faithful God," and when the pain became greater than he could bear, R. Hanina would come in to him and say something over him, and he restored his soul.
   G. After some time R. Hanina became ill, and R. Yohanan came up to visit him. He said to him, "How're you doing?"
   H He said to him, "How hard is suffering."
   I. He said to him, "Yes, but the reward is still greater."
   J. He said to him, "I don't want either them or their reward."
   K. He said to him, "Why don't you say that word that you said over me and restored my soul?"
   L. He said to him, "When I was up and about, I served as a pledge for others, but now that I am within, I don't need anybody else to serve as a pledge for me."
   M. He said to him, "It is written, 'he pastures his flock among the lilies':
   N. "the rod of the Holy One, blessed be He, draws near only to people whose hearts are as soft as lilies."
2. A Said R. Eleazar, "The matter may be compared to the case of a householder who had two cows, one strong, the other weak.
   B. "On which one does he place the burden? Is it not on the strong one?
   C. "Thus the Holy One, blessed be He, does not impose trials upon the wicked. Why not? Because they cannot endure: 'But the wicked are like the troubled sea' (Isa. 57:20).
   D. "Upon whom does he impose trials? Upon the righteous: 'The Lord tries the righteous' (Ps. 11:5); 'And it came to pass after these things that god tried Abraham' (Gen. 22:1); 'And it came to pass after these things that his master's wife cast her eyes on Joseph' (Gen. 39:7)."
3. A Said R. Yosé b. R. Hanina, "A flax-beater, when his flax is hard, does not beat it very much. Why? Because it will burst.
   B. "But if it is good flax, the more he beats it, the more it improves.
   C. "Thus the Holy One, blessed be He, does not impose trials upon the wicked, because they cannot endure.
   D. "But he imposes trials upon the righteous: 'The Lord tries the righteous' (Ps. 11:5)."
4. A Said R. Yohanan, "The potter, when he tests his furnace, does not test it with weak jars.
   B. "Why not? Because when he hits them, they will break.

C. "With what does he test his furnace? With strong jars, for even though he strikes them many times, they will not be broken.

D. "Thus the Holy One, blessed be He, does not impose trials upon the wicked. Upon whom does he impose trials? Upon the righteous: 'The Lord tries the righteous' (Ps. 11:5)."

The entire composition is parachuted down only because our base-text makes its appearance quite tangentially. The composition is coherent and makes its own point, completely autonomous of our document and its interests.

34

Song of Songs Rabbah to Song of Songs 2:17

2:17   *Until the day breathes*
        and the shadows flee,
        turn my beloved, be like a gazelle,
        or a young stag upon rugged mountains.

XXXIV:i
1. A.   "Until the day breathes":
    B.   R. Yudan and R. Berekhiah:
    C.   R. Yudan said, "[The meaning of 'until the day breathes' is that God says to Israel,] 'Until I bring a breathing space into the night of the kingdoms.
    D.   "'Did I not bring a breathing space into the night of the Egyptians, for there were to be four hundred years but I made them into only two hundred and ten.'
    E.   "'...and the shadows flee':
    F.   "[God continues,] 'Did I not remove from them two harsh shadows, the mud and the bricks?'"
2. A.   R. Helbo said, "'And also that nation' (Gen. 15:14): that refers to the Egyptians but also the four kingdoms."
    B.   R. Yudan said, "[Simon, verbatim:] [For four hundred years they would suffer] the condition of aliens, servitude, and affliction in a land that was not theirs, even when it offered hospitality."
3. A.   [Reverting to 1.F, Yudan continues,] "'...turn my beloved, be like a gazelle': [God says to Israel,] 'In the end I shall transform for you the Attribute of Strict Justice into the Attribute of Mercy,
    B.   "and hasten your redemption like [following Simon's emendation, dropping the word 'blood'] the gazelle or young hart.'"
4. A.   "...or a young stag [upon rugged mountains]":
    B.   R. Yosé b. R. Hanina said, "Like a young deer."
5. A.   [Reverting to 3.B, Yudan continues:] "upon rugged mountains":
    B.   "On account of the merit of the stipulations that I made with your patriarch, Abraham, between the pieces [the words for rugged

and pieces using the same consonants]: 'In that day the Lord made a covenant with Abram, saying' (Gen. 15:18)."

6. A   R. Berekhiah said, "'Until the day breathes': That is, 'until I make the day blaze,' as in these usages: 'I will blow upon you with the fire of my wrath' (Ez. 21:36), 'to blow the fire upon it' (Ez. 22:20).

     B.   "And what is the sense of, 'and the shadows flee'?

     C.   "This refers to the shadows of anguish and sighing.

     D.   "'...turn my beloved, be like a gazelle': [God says to Israel,] 'In the end I shall transform for you the Attribute of Strict Justice into the Attribute of Mercy, and hasten your redemption like the gazelle or young hart.

     E.   "'...or a young stag': a young deer."

7. A   "...upon rugged mountains":

     B.   R. Yudan said, "It is so that the kingdoms will receive [Simon, verbatim:] the punishment for their rapacity."

     C.   Said R. Levi b. R. Haitah, "When the kingdom [Simon, verbatim:] falls towards the thorn."

     D.   R. Berekhiah said, "Said the Holy One, blessed be He, 'Even if I held against them only what they did in Bethar [a word that uses the same consonants as rugged], my judgment will be executed on them."

8. A   And what did they do in Bethar?

     B.   Said R. Yohanan, "Caesar Hadrian killed in Bethar four hundred myriads of thousands of people."

The dispute-form announced in No. 1 is marred by a variety of obvious interpolations. Both authorities read the passage in an eschatological framework. We can follow Yudan at Nos. 1, 3, 5, and the message concerns the merit of the patriarchs. No. 6, Berekhiah, goes over pretty much the same ground, but focuses upon the wicked kingdoms. The two themes of course complement each other. For difficult passages I copy Simon verbatim, as indicated.

Part Three

PARASHAH THREE

Song of Songs Chapter Three

3:1   *Upon my bed by night*
I sought him whom my soul loves;
I sought him, but found him not;
I called him, but he gave no answer.

3:2   *"I will rise now and go about the city,*
in the streets and in the squares;
I will seek him whom my soul loves."
I sought him but found him not.

3:3   *The watchmen found me,*
as they went about in the city.
"Have you seen him whom my soul loves?"

3:4   *Scarcely had I passed them,*
when I found him whom my soul loves.
I held him and would not let him go
until I had brought him into my mother's house,
and into the chamber of her that conceived me.

3:5   *I adjure you, O daughters of Jerusalem,*
by the gazelles or the hinds of the field,
that you not stir up nor awaken love
until it please.

3:6   *What is that coming up from the wilderness,*
like a column of smoke,
perfumed with myrrh and frankincense,
with all the fragrant powders of the merchant?

3:7   *Behold it is the litter of Solomon!*
About it are sixty mighty men
of the might men of Israel,

3:8   *all girt with swords*
and expert in war,
each with his sword at his thigh,
against alarms by night.

3:9   *King Solomon made himself a palanquin,*

from the wood of Lebanon.
3:10   *He made its posts of silver,*
        its back of gold, its seat of purple;
        it was lovingly wrought within
        by the daughters of Jerusalem.
3:11   *Go forth, O daughters of Zion,*
        and behold King Solomon,
        with the crown with which his mother crowned him
        on the day of his wedding,
        on the day of the gladness of his heart.

35

Song of Songs Rabbah
to Song of Songs 3:1

3:1   *Upon my bed by night*
       I sought him whom my soul loves;
       I sought him, but found him not;
       I called him, but he gave no answer.

XXXV:I

1. A.   "Upon my bed by night":
    B.   Said R. Abba b. R. Kahana, "What is the meaning of the phrase, 'Upon my bed by night'?
    C.   "It means, 'in my sickness,' in line with the following usage: 'And he does not die, but stays in bed' (Ex. 21:18)."

2. A.   Said R. Levi, "Said the Community of Israel before the Holy One, blessed be He, 'Lord of the world, in the past, you would give light for me between one night and the next night,
    B.   "'between the night of Egypt and the night of Babylonia, between the night of Babylonia and the night of Media, between the night of Media and the night of Greece, between the night of Greece and the night of Edom.
    C.   "'Now that I have fallen asleep [Simon:] neglectful of the Torah and the religious duties, one night flows into the next.'"

3. A.   "Upon my bed by night":
    B.   Said R. Alexandri, "'When I fell asleep [neglectful] of the Torah and religious duties, one night flowed into the next.'
    C.   "'Upon my bed by night': that is, 'nights have come.'" [Simon, p. 143, n. 3: A play on words becased on the plural form, nights, implying that trouble follows on trouble, because I remain on my bed, asleep and heedless of my duties.]

4. A.   Another interpretation of the verse, "Upon my bed by night":
    B.   this refers to the night of Egypt.
    C.   "I sought him whom my soul loves":
    D.   this refers to Moses.
    E.   "I sought him, but found him not, I called him, but he gave no answer."

The amplifications are coherent with one another, translating the image into Israel asleep and neglectful of its duties, which accounts for the fact that former bleak periods alternated with bright ones, while nothing good has happened since the rise of Rome.

36

Song of Songs Rabbah
to Song of Songs 3:2

3:2   *"I will rise now and go about the city,*
       in the streets and in the squares;
       I will seek him whom my soul loves."
       I sought him but found him not.

XXXVI:I

1.   A.   "I will rise now and go about the city, in the streets and in the squares":

     B.   that is, in cities and towns.

     C.   "...I will seek him whom my soul loves":

     D.   that is Moses.

     E.   "...I sought him but found him not."

The glosses are light, the message coherent with the foregoing. The movement from verse to verse is now so swift that one wonders whether our compilers have simply run out of ideas.

37

Song of Songs Rabbah
to Song of Songs 3:3

3:3   *The watchmen found me,*
        as they went about in the city.
        "Have you seen him whom my soul loves?"

XXXVII:I
1. A.   "The watchmen found me":
    B.   this refers to the tribe of Levi: "Go to and fro from gate to gate"
            (Ex. 32:27).
    C.   "Have you seen him whom my soul loves":
    D.   this refers to Moses.

The established reading is repeated. In a moment we shall see that
the several verses are read as a group and that other implicit meanings
are exposed.

38

Song of Songs Rabbah to Song of Songs 3:4

3:4   *Scarcely had I passed them,*
        when I found him whom my soul loves.
        I held him and would not let him go
        until I had brought him into my mother's house,
        and into the chamber of her that conceived me.

XXXVIII:I

1. A.   "Scarcely had I passed them, when I found him whom my soul loves":
    B.   this refers to Moses.
    C.   "I held him and would not let him go until I had brought him into my mother's house":
    D.   this refers to Sinai.
    E.   "...and into the chamber of her that conceived me":
    F.   this refers to the tent of meeting.
    G.   For it was from then that the Israelites became liable for transgressing their instructions. [The words for "conceive" and "instruction" use the same consonants.] [Simon, p. 144, n. 1: Though they first received these teachings at Sinai, they were not liable for disobedience until they were amplified in the Tent of Meeting.]

The exposition of the verses with reference to Moses and the first redemption is now concluded. We now move to the second redemption, in the time of the Babylonians and Daniel.

XXXVIII:ii

1. A.   Another explanation of the verses, "Upon my bed by night I sought him whom my soul loves; I sought him, but found him not; I called him, but he gave no answer. 'I will rise now and go about the city, in the streets and in the squares; I will seek him whom my soul loves.' I sought him but found him not. The watchmen found me, as they went about in the city. 'Have you seen him whom my

soul loves?' Scarcely had I passed them, when I found him whom my soul loves. I held him and would not let him go until I had brought him into my mother's house, and into the chamber of her that conceived me":

B. "Upon my bed by night":

C. this refers to the night of Babylon.

D. "...I sought him whom my soul loves":

E. this refers to Daniel.

F. "...I sought him, but found him not."

G. "I will rise now and go about the city, in the streets and in the squares":

H. in the towns and cities.

I. "...I will seek him whom my soul loves":

J. this refers to Daniel.

K. "I sought him but found him not."

L. "The watchmen found me, as they went about in the city":

M. these are the Chaldeans.

N. "Have you seen him whom my soul loves":

O. this is Daniel.

2. A. So where had he gone?

B. One authority said, "To keep a fast."

C. The other authority said, "To keep a feast."

D. The authority who said, "To keep a fast," explained that he had gone to seek mercy on account of the destruction of the house of the sanctuary: "Now, therefore, O our God, listen to the prayer of your servant" (Dan. (9:17).

E. The authority who said, "To keep a feast," explained that it was to read the writing given to Belshazzar, "*Mene, mene, tekel upharsin*" (Dan. 5:25).

3. A. [Supply: "*Mene, mene, tekel upharsin*" (Dan. 5:25):]

B. R. Hiyya the Elder and R. Simeon b. Halafta:

C. R. Hiyya the Elder said, "What he saw were the letters in this order: MMTUS NNQFE EELRN. [Simon, p. 144, n. 3: By combining the first letters of each word one gets MNE, the second likewise, the third gives TKL, and UPHRSN consists of the rest.]"

D. R. Simeon b. Halafta said, "What he saw were the letters in this way: YTS YTS ASK PGHMT. [Simon, p. 144, n. 4: The words were written in the code that places the first letter of the alphabet with the last, the second with the penultimate, and so on.]"

E. Rabbis say, "It was in this form: ENM ENM LKT NSRFU [each word of the inscription reversed]."

F. R. Meir says, "He saw it just as it is given in the text: *Mene, mene, tekel upharsin.*

G. "*Mene:* 'God has numbered your kingdom and brought it to an end.'

H. "*Tekel:* 'you are weighed in the balance.'

I. "*Peres:* 'your kingdom is divided' (Dan. 5:26-28)." [This resumes at No. 27.]

4. A. At that time the Israelites gathered together with Daniel and said to him, "Our lord, Daniel, all of the bad and harsh prophecies that Jeremiah made have come upon us. But the one good prophecy

that he made for us, 'For after seven years are accomplished for Babylon, I will remember you and do my good word for you, bringing you back to this place' (Jer. 29:10), has not yet come about!"

B. He said to them, "Bring me the book of Isaiah."

C. He begin proclaiming it until he got to this verse: "The burden of the wilderness of the sea. As whirlwinds in the South sweeping on" (Isa. 21:1).

5. A. [Supply: "The burden of the wilderness of the sea. As whirlwinds in the South sweeping on" (Isa. 21:1):]

B. if "sea" then whence "wilderness"? And if "wilderness," whence "sea"?

C. But this refers to the four kingdoms, which are given the analogies of the wild beasts:

D. "four great beasts coming out of the sea, different from one another" (Dan. 7:3).

6. A. [Supply: "different from one another" (Dan. 7:3):]

B. R. Hanina said R. Yohanan [said], "'Different from one another':

C. "that is, the blows that they give are different from one another."

7. A. [Supply: "different from one another" (Dan. 7:3):]

B. If you enjoy sufficient merit, it will emerge from the sea, but if not, it will come out of the forest.

C. The animal that comes up from the sea is not violent, but the one that comes up out of the forest is violent.

D. So if you have sufficient merit, the nations will not rule over you.

8. A. Along these same lines: "The boar out of the wood ravages it" (Ps. 80:14):

B. The *ayin* is suspended in the word for "wood," meaning this: If you enjoy sufficient merit, it will come from the river, and if not, from the forest.

C. The animal that comes up from the river is not violent, but the one that comes up out of the forest is violent.

9. A. "The burden of the wilderness of the sea":

B. If you enjoy sufficient merit, it will emerge from the sea, but if not, it will come out of the forest. [I follow Simon's emended text.]

10. A. "As whirlwinds in the South sweeping on" (Isa. 21:1):

B. Said R. Levi, "Said R. Levi, "You have no more harsh whirlwind than the one that comes from the North and goes up and [Simon:] works havoc among the inhabitants of the South.

C. "And who is this? It is Nebuchadnezzar, who came up from the north and destroyed the house of the sanctuary, which is situated in the south."

11. A. "It comes from the wilderness" (Isa. 21:1):

B. Whence did he come?

C. R. Hanina said, "He came via the desolate wilderness: 'It comes from the wilderness, from a dreadful land' (Isa. 21:1)."

12. A. "A grievous vision is declared to me: (Isa. 21:1):

B. [=Gen. R. XLIV:VI.1, which begins: "After these things the word of the Lord came to Abram in a vision" (Gen. 15:1):] Prophecy is called by ten names:

C. prophecy, vision, exhortation, speech, saying, command, burden, parable, metaphor, and enigma.

D. And which of them is the most weighty?

E. R. Eleazar said, "It is vision, as it is said, 'A weighty vision is declared to me' (Isa. 21:2)."

F. R. Yohanan said, "It is speech, as it is said, 'The man, the lord of the land, spoke weightily with us' (Gen. 42:30)."

G. Rabbis say, "It is the burden, as it is said, 'As a heavy burden' (Ps. 38:5)."

13. A. "The treacherous dealer deals treacherously, and the spoiler spoils. Go up, Elam, besiege, Media" (Isa. 21:2):

B. The troubles brought by Elam have already been hidden [by those that came from others].

14. A. "...besiege, Media" (Isa. 21:2):

B. The trouble to be brought by Media has already been formed. [Simon, p. 146, n. 5: A double play on words: Elam is connected with the word for hidden or eclipsed, besiege is connected with the word for prepared, in existence, also with the word for trouble.]

15. A. "All the sighing thereof I have made to cease" (Isa. 21:2):

B. All the sighing on account of Babylon.

16. A. "Therefore my loins are filled with convulsion" (Isa. 21:1):

B. Said R. Simeon b. Gamaliel, "It is because they smelled some of the stench of the trouble that the kingdoms were bringing, that our ancestors became captious to begin with.

C. "Thus: 'And they journeyed from Mount Hor...to compass the land of Edom, and the soul of the people became captious because of the way' (Num. 21:1)."

17. A. Jeremiah said, "We get our bread at the peril of our lives" (Lam. 5:9).

B. Daniel said, "My spirit was pained in the midst of my body" (Dan. 7:15).

C. "Isaiah said, "Therefore my loins are filled with convulsion (Isa. 21:3)."

18. A. [Supply: "Therefore my loins are seized with convulsion, I am gripped by pangs like a woman in travail, too anguished to hear, too frightened to see" (Isa. 21:3)]

B. "Therefore my loins are seized with convulsion":

C. "We, who are swallowed up in their intestines for so many days, so many years, so many end-times, so many periods – what shall we say?"

D. "I am gripped by pangs like a woman in travail, too anguished to hear, too frightened to see."

E. "...too anguished to hear":

F. the sound of the blasphemy and offense of the wicked: "But you have lifted yourself up against the Lord of heaven and they have brought the vessels of his house" (Dan. 5:23).

G. "...too frightened to see."

H. the prosperity of the wicked one: "Belshazzar, the king, made a great feast" (Dan. 5:1).

19. A. [Supply: "Belshazzar, the king, made a great feast" (Dan. 5:1):]

B. What is the meaning of "great"?

	C.	R. Hama b. R. Hanina said, "It means, 'Greater than the one for his God.'
	D.	"He said to them, 'How much was the sheaf of first grain that you offered sifted?'
	E.	"They said to him, 'It was sifted through a sieve thirteen times.'
	F.	"He said to them, 'Mine is sifted fourteen times.'"
20.	A.	"My mind is confused, [I shudder in panic, my night of pleasure he has turned to terror]" (Isa. 21:4):
	B.	"My mind is confused":
	C.	this speaks of the court, which erred by one day in its calculations [of when the sheaf of first grain was brought].
21.	A.	"...I shudder in panic":
	B.	R. Phineas in the name of R. Joshua said, "'[Simon:] You have regaled yourself from my cup.'"
22.	A.	Another interpretation of the phrase, "I shudder in panic":
	B.	the mouth that speaks mockery.
21.	A.	Another interpretation of the phrase, "I shudder in panic":
	B.	it is because Israel has presumed to mock.
22.	A.	"...my night of pleasure he has turned to terror" (Isa. 21:4):
	B.	"The night that I had yearned for as occasion of redemption has been turned to terror."
23.	A.	"They set the table, [they light the lamps, rise up you princes, grease the shield]" (Isa. 21:5):
	B.	"They set the table":
	C.	they arrange the table.
24.	A.	"...they light the lamps":
	B.	they put up the lamp and light its branches.
25.	A.	"...rise up you princes":
	B.	this refers to Cyrus and Darius.
26.	A.	"...grease the shield":
	B.	take over the government.
27.	A.	Said Darius to Cyrus, "You rule before me."
	B.	Cyrus said to Darius, "Not so, for did not Daniel state, '*peres:* your kingdom is divided and given to Media and Persia' (Dan. 5:28) – Media first, then Persia.
	C.	"Accordingly, you rule before me."
	D.	Now when that wicked man Belshazzar] heard this [that Darius and Cyrus were going to take over the government,] he summoned his troops, saying, "Against every nation and kingdom that has rebelled against me let us march."
	E.	Said to him the Holy One, blessed be He, "Wicked one! Have you sent for everybody, or have you sent for me? By your life! Your downfall will come from no other place but from me!"
	F.	That is in line with this verse: "For neither from the east nor from the west...for God is judge, he puts down one and raises up another" (Ps. 75:7-8).
	G.	"He puts down" Belshazzar, and "raises up" Cyrus and Darius.
28.	A.	Cyrus and Darius were the gatekeepers of Belshazzar.
	B.	When he had heard about these writings, he said to them, "Whoever makes an appearance here tonight, even if he says to you, 'I am the king,' cut off his head."

C.   Now it is not the way of kings to leave their privy inside their chamber; rather [they put it] outside their chamber.

D.   All that night he had loose bowels.

E.   When he went outside, they did not realize it, but when he came back, they spied him out. They said to him, "Who goes there!"

F.   He said to them, "It is I, the king."

G.   They said to him, "And has not the king himself given orders as follows: 'Whoever makes an appearance here tonight, even if he says to you, "I am the king," cut off his head'?"

H.   What did they do? They took a branch of the candelabrum and broke his skull.

I.   That is in line with this verse: "In that night Belshazzar the Chaldean king was slain" (Dan. 5:30).

29. A.   What time was it that he was killed?

B.   R. Eleazar and R. Samuel b. R. Nahman:

C.   R. Eleazar said, "When sleep is sweet [at the beginning]."

D.   R. Samuel said, "[When the light is such that one can tell the difference] between a wolf and a dog."

E.   But they really do not differ.

F.   The one who said, "When sleep is sweet [at the beginning]," maintains that he writhed the entire day [emended to: night, to daybreak], [Simon:] to make up the full length of his reign].

G.   And one who said, "[When the light is such that one can tell the difference] between a wolf and a dog," says that he was drowsy all night [Simon:] to make up the full length of his reign].

30. A.   Said R. Benjamin b. Levi, "At an interval no greater than that between one cup and the next did one kingdom enter while the other expired: 'For in the hand of the Lord there is a cup, with foaming wine, and he pours out of it' (Ps. 75:9).

B.   "Therefore the prophet spites [Babylon], saying, 'Come down and sit in the dust, O virgin daughter of Babylon' (Isa. 47:1)."

31. A.   [Supply: "Come down and sit in the dust, O virgin daughter of Babylon" (Isa. 47:1):]

B.   That is to say, measure for measure.

C.   Elsewhere: "They sit on the ground and keep silence, the elders of the daughter of Zion" (Lam. 2:10),

D.   and here: "Come down and sit in the dust, O virgin daughter of Babylon [without a throne]" (Isa. 47:1).

32. A.   Said R. Hunia, "This is what Jerusalem said to the daughter of Babylon: 'You old whore! [Jastrow, cited by Simon, p. 149, n. 7:] What do you think of yourself? Is it that you are a virgin?

B.   "You are an old woman."

33. A.   "...sit in the dust without a throne" (Isa. 47:1):

B.   The merit that sustained that throne has been exhausted.

C.   And what was that merit?

D.   "At that time Merodach Baladan, the son of Baladan, sent" (Isa. 39:1).

34. A.   [Spelling out the story to which allusion has just now been made:] he was a sun-worshipper, and he would ordinarily eat at the sixth hour and sleep to the ninth hour.

B.	But, in the time of Hezekiah, king of Judah, when the sun reversed its course, he slept through it and woke up and found it was dawn.
C.	He wanted to kill his guards. He accused them, "You let me sleep all day and all night long."
D.	They said to him, "It was the day that returned [the sun having reversed its course]."
E.	He said to them, "And what god reversed it?"
F.	They said to him, "It was the God of Hezekiah who reversed it."
G.	He said to them, "Then is there a god greater than mine?"
H.	They said to him, "The God of Hezekiah is greater than yours."
I.	Forthwith he sent letters and a present to Hezekiah: "At that time Merodach-baladan, son of Baladan, king of Babylonia, sent letters and a present to Hezekiah [for he had heard that he had been sick and recovered]" (Isa. 39:1).
J.	And what was written in them?
K.	He wrote him, "Peace to King Hezekiah, peace to the city of Jerusalem, peace to the Great God!"
L.	But when the letters had been sent, his mind was at ease, and he said, "I did not do it right, for I greeted Hezekiah before his God."
M.	Forthwith he arose and took three steps and retrieved the letter and wrote another instead, in which he said, "Peace to the great God, peace to the city of Jerusalem, peace to King Hezekiah."
N.	Said the Holy One, blessed be He, "You have risen from your throne and taken three steps in order to pay honor to me. By your life, I shall raise up from you three cosmopolitan kings, who will rule from one end of the world to the other."
O.	And who are they? Nebuchadnezzar, Evil-Merodach, and Belshazzar.
P.	But when they went and blasphemed, the Holy One, blessed be He, crushed their eggs out of the world [exterminated them] and set up others in their place.
35. A	"And Hezekiah was happy about them and showed them his treasure house" (Isa. 39:2):
B.	What is the meaning of "his treasure house"?
C.	Said R. Immi, "It was the spoil that he had taken from Sennacherib, the booty that he had swiped from Sennacherib."
D.	R. Yohanan said, "He showed them a weapon that could swallow a weapon. [Simon: one kind of weapon better than another]."
E.	R. Simeon b. Laqish said, "Houses made of ivory poured out of wax he showed them. [Simon, p. 150, n. 2: carved with such skill as though cast in a mould]."
F.	R. Judah says, "Honey as hard as stone he showed to them."
G.	And R. Levi said, "[He said to them,] 'With this [ark of the covenant] we make war and conquer."
36. A	"Grasp the handmill and grind meal; [remove your veil, strip off your train, bear your leg, wade through the rivers; your nakedness shall be uncovered and your shame shall be exposed]" (Isa. 47:2-3):
B.	Said R. Joshua b. Levi, "Everybody grinds wheat, and you say, 'Grasp the handmill and grind meal'? [Who grinds meal?]

C.   "This is what Jerusalem said to the daughter of Babylon, 'If it were not that from above they made war against me, could you have overcome me? Had he not sent fire into my bones, could you have overcome me?

D.   "'You have ground ground meal, you have killed a dead lion, you have burned down a burned-out house.'"

37. A   Another matter concerning the verse, "Grasp the handmill and grind meal; [remove your veil, strip off your train, bear your leg, wade through the rivers; your nakedness shall be uncovered and your shame shall be exposed; I will take vengeance, and let no man intercede. Our redeemer, Lord of hosts is his name, is the Holy One of Israel]" (Isa. 47:2-4):

B.   In the past, others would grind for you, now ""Grasp the handmill and grind meal."

38. A   "...remove your veil":

B.   give up your separateness.

C.   This refers to the king, who had been located within seven screens.

39. A   "...strip off your train":

B.   [Simon:] breast the oncoming river.

40. A   "...wade through the rivers":

B.   In the past, you would cross in gold and silver carriages, now "bear your leg, wade through the rivers."

41. A   "...your nakedness shall be uncovered":

B.   measure for measure.

42. A   Just as elsewhere, "All those who honored her despise her, because they have seen her nakedness" (Lam. 1:8),

B.   so here: "your shame shall be exposed."

43. A   [Supply: "I will take vengeance, and let no man intercede. Our redeemer, Lord of hosts is his name, is the Holy One of Israel" (Isa. 47:4):]

B.   Said R. Joshua b. Levi, "Said the Holy One, blessed be He, 'I am going to bring punishment upon the daughter of Babylonia, and even if Daniel should pray for mercy for her, saying, "And break off your sins by almsgiving"'(Dan. 4:24), I shall not listen to him.'

C.   "Why not? 'I will take vengeance, and let no man intercede. Our redeemer, Lord of hosts is his name, is the Holy One of Israel.'"

The second metaphor speaks of Daniel and Babylonia, that is to say, the second redemption. But, as we see, the introduction of that theme triggers an avalanche of thematically related materials, none of them with any message pertinent to either our base verse or the implicit meaning intended for the base verse by the compilers. The basic principle of agglutination (we can hardly call it something so planned as conglomeration) is simply the exposition of verses deemed pertinent to the theme, beginning with No. 2. No. 3 then takes up the writing given to Belshazzar. Then through the device of having Daniel cite Isa. 21:1, we proceed to an extended amplification of that verse, showing how Isaiah spoke of the redemption of the Jews from

Babylonia. That runs from No. 4 through No. 5, then resumes at Nos. 10-18; 20-27. Then we revert to Dan. 7:3, and that is spelled out in its own terms, Nos. 6-7. The animals represented the four kingdoms are then worked out, Nos. 8, 9. These interpolations do not impede the course of the treatment of Isa. 21:1f. At No. 19 we move back to Belshazzar, now with a sizable account of the entire Babylonian dynasty that came to an end with him, Nos. 19ff. Belshazzar takes center stage at No. 28, and the exposition of the themes associated with him goes on through No. 30, 33-34. The interpolated expansions of prooftexts cited in connection with the Belshazzar-materials occupy Nos. 31-32. Hezekiah having been introduced, his materials are inserted, No. 35. I am not sure why Nos. 36-43, which work out Isa. 47:2-4, are tacked on; my best guess is that the pertinence lies in the curse upon Babylonia, which is to say, the theme of the end of the Babylonian dynasty with Belshazzar. In any event the run-on quality of the whole does not obscure the distinct and separate character of the parts, and we can readily see how various sets of materials have been joined together prior to insertion in this anthology on Babylonia. Obviously, we have long since forgotten the point at which we started and the purpose for which the entire discourse has been assembled. And yet, if we simply recall that at stake is the second redemption, we realize that there is not a line out of place!

39

Song of Songs Rabbah to Song of Songs 3:5

3:5   *I adjure you, O daughters of Jerusalem,*
by the gazelles or the hinds of the field,
that you not stir up nor awaken love
until it please.

Our compilation has no comment on this verse and appends nothing to it.

40

Song of Songs Rabbah
to Song of Songs 3:6

3:6   *What is that coming up from the wilderness,*
like a column of smoke,
perfumed with myrrh and frankincense,
with all the fragrant powders of the merchant?

XL:i
1.   A.   "What is that coming up from the wilderness":
      B.   The ascent [of Israel] was from the wilderness, the decline is from the wilderness.
      C.   the death is from the wilderness: "In this wilderness they shall be consumed and there they shall die" (Num. 14:35).
2.   A.   The Torah came from the wilderness, the tabernacle came from the wilderness, the sanhedrin came from the wilderness, the priesthood came from the wilderness, the Levitical caste came from the wilderness, the monarchy came from the wilderness:
      B.   "And you shall be to me a kingdom of priests" (Ex. 19:6).
      C.   So all the good gifts that the Holy One, blessed be He, gave to Israel are from the wilderness.
      D.   Said R. Simeon b. Yohai, "In the wilderness they took on the burden [of the priestly garb], in the wilderness they took off the same burden.
      E.   Prophecy is from the wilderness.
      F.   Thus the ascent was from the wilderness.
3.   A.   "...like a column of smoke":
      B.   Said R. Eleazar in the name of R. Yosé b. Zimra, "When the Israelites were wandering from [Simon:] stage to stage, the pillar of cloud would come down, and the pillar of fire would spring up,
      C.   "and the smoke of the woodpile would go up like two darts of fire, between the two staves of the ark, burning from before them snakes, scorpions, and adders.
      D.   "And the nations of the world would see and say, 'These are divinities, their deeds are only with fire.'

225

E.   "So fear of the Israelites fell upon them, terror and trembling: 'Terror and dread shall fall upon them' (Ex. 15:16).

F.   "The verse does not say 'has fallen' but 'shall fall,' meaning, from now on."

4.   A.   "...perfumed with myrrh":

B.   This refers to our father, Abraham.

C.   Just as myrrh is the best of all spices, so our father Abraham was the first of all the righteous.

D.   Just as the hands of anyone who picks up myrrh smart, so our father, Abraham, would punish and castigate himself with suffering.

E.   Just as myrrh emits its fragrance only in fire, so Abraham revealed his good deeds only in the fiery furnace.

5.   A.   "...and frankincense":

B.   this refers to our father, Isaac.

C.   For he was offered up upon the altar like a handful of frankincense.

6.   A.   "...with all the fragrant powders of the merchant":

B.   this refers to our father, Jacob.

C.   For his bed [offspring] was whole before him [the Holy One, blessed be He], and no blemish was found among them.

7.   A.   Said R. Tanhuma, "Just as the peddler's box has all kinds of spices, so the priesthood is from Jacob,

B.   "the Levitical caste and the monarchy likewise are from Jacob.

C.   "As to Isaac, our father Abraham gave him everything he had: 'Abraham gave all that he had to Isaac' (Gen. 25:5).

D.   "But the profits of Jacob came only from the dirt beneath his feet."

8.   A.   R. Yudan made two statements.

B.   R. Yudan said, "All of the profits that the Israelites make and all their success in this world are on account of the merit of that dirt of our father Jacob."

C.   R. Yudan made another statement: "All of the trade that the Israelites make and all their success in this world are on account of the merit of that dirt of our father Jacob."

9.   A.   R. Azariah made two statements.

B.   R. Azariah said, "All of the wars that the Israelites make and win in this world are on account of the merit of that dirt of our father Jacob."

C.   R. Azariah made another statement: "All of the Torah that the Israelites carry out in this world is on account of the merit of our father, Jacob."

10.   A.   R. Berekhiah and R. Simon in the name of R. Abbahu: "That dust did the Holy One, blessed be He, take and put under his throne of glory:

B.   "'The Lord in the whirlwind and in the storm is his way and the clouds are the dust of his feet' (Nah. 1:3)."

11.   A.   R. Berekiah in the name of R. Helbo said, "'And a man wrestled there with him' (Gen. 32:25):

B.   "From these words we do not know who ended up in the power of whom, the angel in the power of Jacob or Jacob in the power of the

		angel [for the word 'wrestle' uses the letters for the word for dirt. So the sense is that he was covered with dust.]
	C.	"But from the following, 'And he said, let me go, for the day breaks' (Gen. 32:27), the answer becomes clear.
	D.	"Said the angel to Jacob, 'Let me go, for my turn to give praises has come.'
	E.	"It follows that the angel ended up in the power of our father, Jacob."
12.	A.	In what form did he make his appearance to him?
	B.	R. Hama b. R. Hanina said, "He appeared to him in the form of the angel that served the wicked Esau: 'For since I have seen your face as one sees the face of a god' (Gen. 33:10).
	C.	"He said to him, 'Your face is like the face of your guardian angel.'"
	D.	"The matter may be compared to a king who had a savage dog and a tame lion. What did the king do?
	E.	"The king would take his lion and sick him against the son, saying, 'If the dog comes to have a fight with the son, he will say to the dog, "The lion cannot have a fight with me, are you going to make out in a fight with me?"'
	F.	"So if the nations come to have a fight with Israel, the Holy One, blessed be He, says to them, 'Your angelic prince could not stand up to Israel, and as to you, how much the more so!'"
13.	A.	R. Huna said, "He appeared to him in the form of a shepherd.
	B.	"This one had flocks and that one had flocks, this one had camels and that one had camels.
	C.	"He said to him, 'Bring yours across, and I shall bring mine across.
	D.	"Jacob brought his flock across, and then he checked to see whether he had forgotten anything behind. [Gen. R. LXXVII:I.2 adds:] Forthwith: 'And a man wrestled with him until the breaking of the day.'"
14.	A.	R. Hiyya the Elder, R. Simeon b. Rabbi, and Rabban Simeon b. Gamaliel were occupied in trading in silk in the area of Tyre. When they had gone out, they said, "Let us go and take up the example of our ancestor and see if we have left anything behind."
	B.	They went back and discovered that they had forgotten a bale of silk.
	C.	They said to him, "Where did this example come to you?"
	D.	They said, "It is from our father, Jacob, who went back, 'and a man wrestled with him until the breaking of the day.'"
15.	A.	Rabbis say, "He appeared to him in the guise of a bandit chief.
	B.	"This one had flocks and that one had flocks, this one had camels and that one had camels.
	C.	"He said to him, 'Bring mine across, and I shall bring yours across.'
	D.	"The angel brought our father Jacob's flock across in a flash, and then Jacob brought some across, came back, and found more to bring across, and came back and found still more to cross over.
	E.	[Gen. R. LXXVII:II.3:] "He said to him, 'You are a sorcerer.'"

F. Said R. Phineas, "When he realized this, he took a piece of wool and put it down his throat and said, 'Sorcerer, sorcerer, magicians do not succeed by night.'"

G. Said R. Huna, "At the end, he [the angel] said to him, '"Should I not tell him with whom he is involved?'

H. "What did he do? He took his finger and stuck it into the ground and the ground began to produce fire.

I. "He said to him, 'From this do you expect to frighten me? The whole of me is made up of such a substance: "And the house of Jacob shall be a fire" (Obad. 1:18).'"

16. A. Said R. Hanina b. R. Isaac, "Said the Holy One, blessed be He, to the angelic guardian of Esau, 'Why are you going up against him? He comes against you with five charms in hand, his own merit, the merit of his father, the merit of his mother, the merit of his grandfather, and the merit of his grandmother.

B. "'Take your measure against him, for you cannot withstand him even on the count of his own merit alone.'

C. "Forthwith: 'He saw that he could not prevail against him' (Gen. 32:6)."

17. A. Said R. Levi, "He saw through the Presence of God that he could not prevail against him.

B. "The matter may be compared to an athlete who was wrestling with a prince. He looked up and saw the king standing over him. He let himself be thrown.

C. "So when the angel saw the Presence of God standing above Jacob, he let himself be thrown beneath him: 'He saw that he did not prevail against him.'"

D. Said R. Levi, "He saw through the Presence of God that he could not prevail against him."

18. A. "...he touched the hollow of his thigh, [and Jacob's thigh was put out of joint as he wrestled with him]" (Gen. 32:25):

B. He touched the righteous men and women, prophets and prophetess, who are destined to arise from him and his children.

C. And who were these? For example, the generation that would survive the repression [after the war against Hadrian].

19. A. "...and Jacob's thigh was put out of joint as he wrestled with him" (Gen. 32:25):

B. R. Eliezer and R Berekhiah:

C. R. Eliezer said, "He flattened it."

D. Berekhiah in the name of R. Assi said, "He cut it open like a fish."

E. R. Nahman b. R. Jacob said, "He separated it, as in this verse: 'Then if my soul was separated [using the same word as 'put out of joint] from her' (Ez. 23:18)."

20. A. "...perfumed with myrrh and frankincense, with all the fragrant powders of the merchant":

B. R. Yohanan interpreted the verse to speak of the incense of the house of Abtinas.

C. This was one of the eleven kinds of incense that they would put into it.

21. A.   R. Huna interpreted the verse ["perfumed with myrrh and frankincense, with all the fragrant powders of the merchant"] in light of the following:

B.   "'And the Lord said to Moses, take for yourself sweet spices stacte and onycha and galbanum sweet spices' (Ex. 30:34):

C.   "'sweet spices': two.

D.   "'...stacte and onycha and galbanum: now we have five.

E.   "'...sweet spices': this cannot mean only two, since we have said spices, thus 'of each shall there be a light weight' means five, matching the other five, ten in all.

F.   "'...with pure frankincense': this eleven."

22. A.   [Supply: "'And the Lord said to Moses, take for yourself sweet spices stacte and onycha and galbanum sweet spices' (Ex. 30:34):]

B.   In this connection sages investigated and came up with the fact that suitable for the incense are only these eleven spices.

23. A.   It has been taught on Tannaite authority [with reference to the following passage of the Mishnah: But these were remembered dishonorably: the members of the household of Garmu did not want to teach others how to make the show bread; the members of the household of Abtinas did not want to teach others how to make the incense; Hygras b. Levi knew a lesson of singing but did not want to teach it to anyone else; Ben Qamsaw did not want to teach others how to write (M. Yoma 3:11A-E):

B.   [In the version of T. Kippurim 2:6-7, 2:5, 2:8 verbatim, omitting reference to variations in Song of Song Rabbah:] The members of the house of Abtinas were experts in preparing the incense for producing smoke, and they did not want to teach others how to do so.

C.   Sages sent and brought experts from Alexandria, in Egypt, who knew how to concoct spices in much the same way.

D.   But they were not experts in making the smoke ascend [in the way in which it ascended for the others].

E.   The smoke coming from the incense of the house of Abtina would ascend straight as a stick up to the beams and afterward would scatter in all directions as it came down. But that of the Alexandrians would scatter as it came down forthwith.

F.   Now when the sages realized this, they said, "The Omnipresent has created the world only for his own glory: 'The Lord has made everything for his own purpose' (Prov. 16:4) [so we might as well pay the tariff]."

G.   Sages sent to [the members of the house of Abtinas], but they declined to come until the sages doubled their wages.

H.   "They had been receiving twelve manehs every day, and now they went and got twenty-four," the words of R. Meir.

I.   R. Judah says, "They had been getting twenty-four every day. Now they went and got forty-eight."

J.   Sages said to them, "Now why were you unwilling to teach others?"

K.   They said to them, "The members of father's house knew that the Temple is destined for destruction, and they did not want to teach others their art, so that people would not burn incense before an idol in the same way in which they burn incense before the Omnipresent."

L. And in this matter, they are remembered for Good: a woman of their household never went out wearing perfume at any time,

M. and not only so, but when they would marry into their household a woman from some other place, they made an agreement that she not put on perfume,

N. so that people should not say, "Their women are putting on perfume made up from the preparation of the incense for the Temple."

O. This they did to carry out the following verse, "And you shall be clear before the Lord and before Israel" (Num. 32:22).

24. A. Said R. Aqiba, "Simeon b. Luga told me, 'A certain child of the sons of their sons and I were gathering grass in the field. Then I saw him laugh and cry.

B. "'I said to him, "Why did you cry?"

C. "'He said to me, "Because of the glory of father's house, which has gone into exile."

D. "'I said to him, "Then why did you laugh?"

E. "'He said to me, "At the end of it all, in time to come, the Holy One, blessed be He, is going to make his descendants rejoice. [Song of Songs Rabbah's version: Because it is stored away and kept for the righteous in the time to come, and because in the end he will make his children rejoice – may it speedily come.]"

F. "'I said to him, "Why? [What did you see that made you think of this?]"

G. "He said to me, "A smoke-raiser in front of me [made me laugh]."

H. "'I said to him, "Show it to me."

I. "'He said to me, "We are subject to an oath not to show it to anyone at all."'

J. "They say that not many days passed before that child died."

K. Said R. Yohanan b. Nuri, "One time I was going along the way and an old man came across me, with a scroll in his hand containing a list of spices. I said to him, 'What is that you have in your hand?

L. "He said to me, 'I am a member of the house of Abtinas. At the beginning, when the house of father was discreet, they would give their scrolls containing the prescriptions for frankincense only to one another. Now take it, but be careful about it, since it is a scroll containing a recipe for spices.'

M. "When I came and reported the matter before R. Aqiba, he said to me, 'From now on it is forbidden to speak ill of these people again.'"

25. A. The members of the house of Garmu were experts in making show bread and they did not want to teach others how to make it.

B. Sages sent and brought experts from Alexandria, in Egypt, who were expert in similar matters but were not experts in removing it from the oven.

C. The members of the house of Garmu would heat the oven on the outside, and the loaf of bread would be removed on its own on the inside.

D. The experts from Alexandria did not do so.

E.   And some say that this made it get moldy.
F.   And when the sages learned of the matter, they said, "The Holy One, blessed be He, has created the world only for his own glory: 'Everyone that is called by my name and whom I have created for my glory' (Isa. 43:7) [so we might as well pay the tariff]."
G.   They sent for them, but they would not come until they doubled their former salary.
H.   "They had been receiving twelve manehs every day, and now they went and got twenty-four," the words of R. Meir.
I.   R. Judah says, "They had been getting twenty-four every day. Now they went and got forty-eight."
J.   Sages said to them, "Now why were you unwilling to teach others?"
K.   They said to them, "The member of father's house knew that the Temple was going to be destroyed, and they did not want to teach others how to do it, so that they should not be able to do it before an idol in the way in which it is done before the Omnipresent."
L.   And on account of this next matter they are remembered with honor:
M.   For a piece of clean bread was never found in the hands of their sons or daughters under any circumstances, so that people might not be able to say about them, "They are nourished from the show bread of the Temple."
N.   This was meant to carry out the following verse: "You shall be clean before the Lord and before Israel."

26. A.   All the others found an answer, but Ben Qamsar did not find an answer to what they said.
B.   They said to them, "Why do you not wish to teach?"
C.   They kept silent and did not reply.
D.   Because they wanted to increase their own glory and diminish the glory owing to heaven, therefore their own glory was diminished, while the glory of heaven was increased.
E.   Not only so, but they have no issue or descendant in Israel.
F.   To the others applies the verse, "The memory of the righteous is for a blessing," but with regard to these, "But the name of the wicked shall rot" (Prov. 10:7).

27. A.   On this basis, Ben Azzai said, "Yours do they give back to you,
B.   "by your name they will call you,
C.   "in your place they will seat you.
D.   "There is no forgetting before the Omnipresent,
E.   "and no man can touch what is designated for his fellow."

28. A.   Hugram b. Levi knew a certain mode of singing, but he did not want to teach it to others.
B.   They say of Hugram b. Levi that when he opened his mouth to sing, he would put one thumb into his mouth and the other into the ground, with his fingers between his moustaches, and raise his voice in song.
C.   And he could imitate the sound of every kind of musical instrument.
D.   So his fellow Levites willy-nilly would turn around to look at him.

29. A.   Phineas was the dresser.
B.   He once helped a general to dress and got a fee.

The pertinent materials speak of Israel in the wilderness, a predictable allusion, once we remember that God speaks here. But the point is not God's; it is simply the narrator's observation that the wilderness is where the Israelites got whatever good things they ever had. That is worked out at Nos. 1-3. At No. 4 we revert to another predictable theme, the patriarchs, and ask the second clause of the verse to tell us about them. Nos. 4-7 complete that proposition. The reference to "dirt", 7.D, accounts for the addition of Nos. 8-9, 10, and what happens then is predictable too. Since the words for "dirt" and "wrestle" use the same consonants, we forthwith invoke the exposition of Gen. 32:25ff., and that matter, pretty much as we find it at Genesis Rabbah (ad loc.) is inserted whole at Nos. 11-19. We return to our base verse's reference to myrrh and frankincense, and Yohanan's reference to the incense-makers of the Temple, the house of Abtinas, provides for our compilers the occasion to take over and insert whole the entire discussion of that matter attached to M. Yoma 3:11 at T. Kippurim 2:5-8. The differences in the versions of Tosefta and Song of Songs Rabbah need not detain us; I give Tosefta's version.

XL:ii

1. A.   "What is that coming up from the wilderness":
    B.   The passage speaks of Elisheba, daughter of Amminadab [and wife of Aaron].
    C.   They say: Elisheba, daughter of Amminadab witnessed five occasions for rejoicing on a single day.
    D.   She witnessed her brother-in-law as king, her brother as prince, her husband as his priest, her two sons as prefects of the priesthood, and Phineas, her grandson as priest anointed for war.
    E.   But when her two sons entered [the sanctuary] to make an offering, they emerged burned, so her joy was turned to mourning.
    F.   Forthwith she turned into pillars of smoke [thus: "What is that coming up from the wilderness like a column of smoke"].
2. A.   When R. Eleazar b. R. Simeon died, his generation recited in his regard: "What is that coming up from the wilderness like a column of smoke, perfumed with myrrh and frankincense, with all the fragrant powders of the merchant."
    B.   Why "with all the fragrant powders of the merchant"?
    C.   For R. Eleazar b. R. Simeon was learned in Scripture, Mishnah, liturgy, and poetry.

No. 1 seems to me rather strange, though the general thematic framework is sustained; No. 2 of course is available for use anywhere the base verse appears, even though it is completely out of phase with the program of our compilers overall. It is a mark that the compilers have a dual purpose: collect and amass pretty much anything said about the verses on which they compile materials, but also, demonstrate a few fundamental propositions.

41

Song of Songs Rabbah
to Song of Songs 3:7-8

3:7   *Behold it is the litter of Solomon!*
       About it are sixty mighty men
       of the mighty men of Israel,
3:8   *all girt with swords*
       and expert in war,
       each with his sword at his thigh,
       against alarms by night.

XLI:I

1. A.   "Behold it is the litter of Solomon! About it are sixty mighty men of the mighty men of Israel [all girt with swords and expert in war, each with his sword at his thigh, against alarms by night] (Song 3:8)":

   B.   R. Bibi in the name of R. Eleazar b. R. Yosé interpreted the verse to speak of the priestly blessing:

   C.   "'Behold it is the litter': behold it is the clans [a word that uses the same letters as litter]: 'the oaths of the tribes' (Hab. 3:9).

   D.   "'...of Solomon': of the king to whom peace belongs.

   E.   "'About it are sixty mighty men': this refers to the sixty letters that make up the words for the priestly blessing.

   F.   "'...of the mighty men of Israel': for they [the blessings] strengthen Israel.

2. A.   "'...all girt with swords [and expert in war, each with his sword at his thigh, against alarms by night]'":

   B.   Said R. Azariah, "These are blessed through [Simon:] the strength [of the Divine Name]: 'The Lord bless you...the Lord make his face to shine...the Lord lift up' (Num. 6:24-6).

   C.   "'...and expert in war': for they make war against all manner of visitations that there are in the world.

   D.   "'...each with his sword at his thigh against alarms by night': for if someone sees in his dream a sword cutting into his thigh, what is he to do?

	E.	"Let him go to the synagogue and recite the Shema and say the Prayer and listen to the blessing of the priests, answering after them, 'Amen,' and nothing bad will happen to him.
	F.	"Therefore Scripture admonishes the sons of Aaron: 'In this way you shall bless the children of Israel' (Num. 6:23)."
3.	A.	R. Simlai interpreted the verse to speak of the priestly watches [who take turns in conducting the actual rite in the Temple, through the year in sequence]:
	B.	"'Behold it is the litter': behold it is the clans [a word that uses the same letters as litter]: 'the oaths of the tribes' (Hab. 3:9).
	C.	"'...of Solomon': of the king to whom peace belongs.
	D.	"'About it are sixty mighty men': this refers to the twenty-four priestly watches, the twenty-four Levitical watches, and the twelve divisions [1 Chr. 27].
	E.	"'...of the mighty men of Israel': who guard Israel.
4.	A.	"...all girt with swords [and expert in war, each with his sword at his thigh, against alarms by night]":
	B.	Said R. Zeira and R. Judah in the name of Samuel, "This refers to the disciples of sages who teach the priests how to conduct the slaughter of the sacrificial beast and the laws governing the tossing of the blood, the receiving of the blood, and the taking up of the handful of the meal-offering."
	C.	R. Isaac in the name of R. Ammi said, "This refers to those who examine the blemishes on the beasts that have been declared holy and who receive their salary from the Temple treasury."
5.	A.	R. Gidul b. R. Benjamin in the name of R. Yosé: "There were two judges of civil cases in Jerusalem, and they would take their salary from the Temple treasury."
	B.	Samuel said, "Women would weave the curtain [for the Most Holy Place], and they would take their salary from the Temple treasury."
	C.	R. Huna said, "From the fund for the upkeep of the building."
	D.	The latter regarded the curtain as classified with the building, the former as classified with the offerings.
6.	A.	"'...and expert in war': for they would teach the priests how to conduct the liturgy.
	B.	"'...each with his sword at his thigh, against alarms by night': for they would admonish them at the time that they conducted the slaughter of the sacrificial animal not to render any of the sacrifices an abomination [by forming the improper intention to eat their share of the beast at the wrong time, that is, too late, or to toss the blood at the wrong place], and not to invalidate any of the offerings through leaving over the meat for too long."
7.	A.	R. Yohanan interpreted the verse to speak of the Sanhedrin:
	B.	"'Behold it is the litter': behold it is the clans [a word that uses the same letters as litter]: 'the oaths of the tribes' (Hab. 3:9).
	C.	"'...of Solomon': of the king to whom peace belongs.
	D.	"'About it are sixty mighty men': this refers to the sixty men of the people of the land: 'And sixty men of the people of the land who were found in the city' (2 Kgs. 25:19).

E.   "'...of the mighty men of Israel': this refers to the eleven men cited here, 'And the captain of the guard took Seraiah, chief priest, and Zephaniah, second priest, and the three keepers of the door, and out of the city he took an officer [and five men of those who had access to the king' (2 Kgs. 25:18)."

8. A.   "...he took an officer":
   B.   This refers to the head of the court.
   C.   And why is he called "an officer"?
   D.   Because he officiates over the law [the words for officer and officiate or adjudicate use the same consonants].

9. A.   "...and five men of those who had access to the king" (2 Kgs. 25:18):
   B.   lo, eleven in all.
   C.   And when Jeremiah says, "seven" (Jer. 52:25), the intent is to add to the count the two scribes of the judges, who sit in their presence.

10. A.   [Continuing 7.F:] "of the mighty men of Israel': they acquit the Israelites through strength [Simon: of argument]."

11. A.   "...all girt with swords":
    B.   R. Meir and R. Yosé:
    C.   R. Meir says, "For all of them were as sharp as a sword in the study of the law, so that if a case should come to them, the law should not be unclear to them."
    D.   R. Yosé says, "In the time of reaching a judgment, all of them would give and take in argument concerning how to produce a judgment, subject to the fear of the punishment of Gehenna [should they err]."
    E.   R. Menahem, son-in-law of R. Eleazar b. R. Abona in the name of R. Jacob b. R. Abina: "If a woman comes before you to the school house to ask you a question concerning the determination of the blood on her rag [that is, whether it is menstrual blood or of some other sort] and concerning her status as a menstruant, you should regard her as though she herself had come forth from your loins and not look upon her, but should be subject to the fear of the punishment of Gehenna."

12. A.   Rabbis interpret the verse to speak of the Israelites who came forth from Egypt:
    B.   "'Behold it is the litter': behold it is the clans [a word that uses the same letters as litter]: 'the oaths of the tribes' (Hab. 3:9).
    C.   "'...of Solomon': of the king to whom peace belongs.
    D.   "'About it are sixty mighty men': this refers to the sixty myriads who came forth from Egypt from the age of twenty years and onward.
    E.   "'...of the mighty men of Israel': this refers to the sixty myriads who came forth from Egypt from the age of twenty years and below.
    F.   "'...all girt with swords and expert in war, each with his sword at his thigh, [against alarms by night]':
    G.   "For when Moses said to them, 'Thus has the Holy One, blessed be He, said to me [Simon:] in one word: "No uncircumcised person shall eat of it" (Ex. 12:48), forthwith each one of them took his sword on his thigh and circumcised himself."

13. A.   Who circumcised them?

B.   R. Berekhiah said, "Moses was circumcising them, Aaron was doing the trimming, and Joshua gave them to drink."

C.   Some say, "Joshua did the circumcising, Aaron did the trimming, and Moses gave them to drink.

D.   "So it is written, 'At that time the Lord said to Joshua, Make knives of flint and again circumcise the children of Israel the second time' (Josh. 5:2).

E.   "Why a second time? Because he was the one who had done it the first time.

F.   "Forthwith: 'Joshua made knives of flint and circumcised the children of Israel at Gibeat-haaralot' (Josh. 5:3)."

G.   What is the meaning of "at Gibeat-haaralot"?

H.   R. Levi said, "On this basis we learn that they made it a hill of foreskins."

The program of the whole carries us through the following situations that are evoked by our metaphor of the litter of Solomon: the priestly blessing, the priestly watches, the sanhedrin, and the Israelites coming out of Egypt. The first three are coherent, the sanhedrin being part of the Temple structure; the relevance of the fourth is not equivalently clear, introducing as it does a different class. The structure of all four however seems to me uniform, with the obvious secondary expansions and clarifications; but most of these fit in quite well. A few, e.g., Nos. 5, 8, 9, impede progress, and No. 11 is out of phase as well. No. 13 is tacked on; it fits better at Chapter Twelve. We now proceed to a completely different reading of our base verse.

XLI:ii

1. A.   It has been taught on Tannaite authority:

    B.   Before someone sins, he is paid awe and fear, and creatures fear him. But once he has sinned, he is subject to awe and fear, and he fears others.

    C.   You may know that this is so, for so said Rabbi, "Before the First Man sinned, he heard the sound of the Divine Speech while standing on his feet, and he was not afraid.

    D.   "But once he had sinned, when he heard the sound of the Divine Speech, he was afraid and he hid: 'I heard your voice and I was afraid' (Gen. 3:10); 'And the man and his wife hid themselves' (Gen. 3:8)."

2. A.   Said R. Aibu, "At that moment Adam's stature was diminished and reduced to a hundred cubits."

3. A.   R. Levi said, "Before the First Man sinned, he heard the sound of the Divine Speech in a mild way.

    B.   "But once he had sinned, when he heard the sound of the Divine Speech, it was fierce [Simon: it came to him like a fierce wild thing].

    C.   "Before the Israelites sinned, they saw [Simon:] seven fiery partitions pressing on one another, but they were not afraid nor did they tremble or concern themselves.

D. "But once they had sinned, even upon the face of the mediator [Moses] they could not gaze: 'The skin of Moses's face sent forth beams' (Ex. 34:35); 'And they were afraid to come near him' (Ex. 34:30)."

4. A. R. Phineas and R. Abun in the name of R. Hanin said, "Even the mediator himself felt with them [the impact of] that transgression.

B. "Of the period before the Israelites sinned what is written? 'Kings of armies flee, they flee' (Ps. 68:13)."

5. A. [Supply: "'Kings of armies flee, they flee" (Ps. 68:13):]

B. R. Aibu said, "What is written here is not 'angels of armies flee,' but 'kings of armies flee,' meaning, kings of the angels.

C. "Who might they be?

D. "This refers to Michael and Gabriel.

E. "For they could not gave upon the face of Moses.

F. "But once they had sinned, even upon the face of the quite ordinary angels they could not gaze: 'For I was afraid of the anger and displeasure' (Dt. 9:19)."

6. A. [Continuing the discourse left off at 3.D:] "Concerning the time before that tragic event [involving Bath Sheba] happened to David, it is written, 'The Lord is my light and my salvation, whom shall I fear' (Ps. 27:1).

B. "But afterward [Ahitophel could say], 'I will come upon him while he is weary and weak-handed and I will frighten him' (2 Sam. 17:2).

C. "Before Solomon sinned, he ruled male and female singers: 'I got myself male and female singers and the delights of mortals' (Qoh. 2:8), [Simon:] baths, and male and female demons who used to heat them.

D. "But once he had sinned, he appointed for himself sixty mighty men of the mighty men of Israel and set them up to guard his bed: 'Behold it is the litter of Solomon! About it are sixty mighty men of the mighty men of Israel all girt with swords and expert in war, each with his sword at his thigh, against alarms by night,'

E. "because he feared the spirits."

Now we see the difference between an exegesis of a verse and a propositional composition that makes use of a verse. XLI:i has focused upon our base verses, and XLI:ii refers in passing, in developing and proving its general proposition concerning the effects of sin, to our base verse, among many others. The order is a fairly standard one for our document, first the exegesis, then the proposition, but that is not so rigid a matter of ordering types of discourses as is the case in Leviticus Rabbah and Pesiqta deRab Kahan, not to mention Genesis Rabbah. The proposition, of course, is beautifully articulated, and the formal discipline is readily discerned. No. 4 is completed at No. 5 and forms a single thought, but because of the intervention of a different attribution, I have distinguished the one from the other. A good case can be made for the opposite parsing.

42

Song of Songs Rabbah to Song of Songs 3:9

3:9 *King Solomon made himself a palanquin,*
from the wood of Lebanon.

1. A. "King Solomon made himself a palanquin, [from the wood of Lebanon]":

    B. R. Azariah in the name of R. Judah b. R. Simon interpreted the verse to speak of the tabernacle:

    C. "'palanquin' refers to the tabernacle.

2. A. Said R. Judah b. R. Ilai, "The matter may be compared to the case of a king who had a little daughter. Before she reached maturity and produced the signs of puberty, he would see her in the marketplace and speak with her quite publicly, whether in an alleyway or in a courtyard.

    B. "After she grew up and produced the signs of puberty, the king said, 'It is not [Simon:] becoming for my daughter that I should speak with her in public. So make her a pavilion, and when I have to speak with her, I shall speak with her in the pavilion.

    C. "So: 'When Israel was a child, then I loved him' (Hos. 11:1).

    D. "In Egypt they saw him in public: 'For the Lord will pass through to smite the Egyptians' (Ex. 12:23).

    E. "At the Sea they saw him in public: 'And Israel saw the great work' (Ex. 14:31).

    F. "...and the children pointed at him with their finger, saying, 'This is my God and I will glorify him' (Ex. 15:2).

    G. "At Sinai they saw him face to face: 'And he said, the Lord came from Sinai' (Dt. 33:2).

    H. "When the Israelites stood at Mount Sinai and received the Torah and said, 'All that the Lord has spoken we shall do and obey' (Dt. 24:7), so becoming for him a nation complete in all ways,

    I. "then said the Holy One, blessed be He, 'It is not becoming for my children for me to speak with them in public. Make me a

239

tabernacle, and when I have to speak with them, I shall speak with
them from within the tabernacle: 'But when Moses went in before
the Lord that he might speak with him' (Ex. 34:34)."

3. A.   "King Solomon made himself a palanquin":
    B.   he is the king whose name is peace.
    C.   "...from the wood of Lebanon":
    D.   "And you shall make the boards for the tabernacle of acacia-
          wood, standing up" (Ex. 26:15).

The established metaphorization of the cult and priesthood now
continues in a cogent way, so that the reading of the larger passage
remains consistent. I assume No. 3 continues No. 1, with a sizable, quite
relevant interpolation inserted. The exegesis of this verse continues in
Chapter Forty-Three.

43

Song of Songs Rabbah
to Song of Songs 3:10

[3:9	King Solomon made himself a palanquin, from the wood of Lebanon.]
3:10	He made its posts of silver, its back of gold, its seat of purple; it was lovingly wrought within by the daughters of Jerusalem.

XLIV:I

1. A. "He made its posts of silver":
   B. this speaks of the pillars: "The hooks of the pillars and their fillets shall be of silver" (Ex. 27:10).
   C. "...its back of gold:
   D. "And you shall overlay the boards with gold" (Ex 26:29).
   E. "...its seat of purple":
   F. "And you shall make a veil of blue and purple" (Ex. 26:31).

2. A. "...it was lovingly wrought within by the daughters of Jerusalem":
   B. R. Yudan said, "This refers to the merit attained through the Torah and the merit attained through the righteous who occupy themselves with it."
   C. R. Azariah in the name of R. Judah in the name of R. Simon said, "This refers to the Presence of God.

3. A. One verse of Scripture says, "So that the priests could not stand to minister by reason of the cloud, for the glory of the Lord filled the house of the Lord" (1 Kgs. 8:11).
   B. And another verse of Scripture says, "And the court was full of the brightness of the Lord's glory" (Ez. 10:4).
   C. How are these two verses to be harmonized?
   D. R. Joshua of Sikhnin in the name of R. Levi: "To what is the tent of meeting comparable? To a cave open to the sea.
   E. "When the sea becomes stormy, it fills the cave.
   F. "The cave is filled, but the sea is undiminished.

G. "So the tent of meeting was filled with the splendor of the Presence of God, while the world was undiminished of the Presence of God."

4. A. When did the Presence of God come to rest on the world?
B. On the day on which the tabernacle was raised up: "And it came to pass on the day that Moses had made an end" (Num. 7:1).

We continue the exposition of the base verse in terms of the tent of meeting, that is, reading Song 3:9-10 together as a single problem in interpretation. No. 1 works out the basic theme, and the rest is simply a secondary amplification of details.

XLIII:ii

1. A. [Supply: "King Solomon made himself a palanquin, from the wood of Lebanon. He made its posts of silver, its back of gold, its seat of purple; it was lovingly wrought within by the daughters of Jerusalem":]
B. R. Yudan b. R. Ilai interpreted the verses to speak of the ark:
C. "'...a palanquin': this is the ark."

2. A. [Supply: "a palanquin":]
B. What is a palanquin?
C. A litter.

3. A. The matter may be compared to the case of a king who had an only daughter, who was beautiful, pious, and gracious.
B. Said the king to his staff, "my daughter is beautiful, pious, and gracious, and yet you do not make her a litter? Make her a litter, for it is better that the beauty of my daughter should appear from within a litter."
C. So said the Holy One, blessed be He, "My Torah is beautiful, pious, and gracious, and yet you do not make an ark for it?
D. "It is better that the beauty of my Torah should appear from within the ark."

4. A. [Reverting to 1.C:] "'King Solomon made himself': the king to whom peace belongs.
B. "'...from the wood of Lebanon': 'And Bezalel made the ark of acacia-wood' (Ex. 37:1).
C. "'He made its posts of silver': these are the two pillars that stand within the ark, which were made of silver.
D. "'...its back of gold': 'and he overlaid it with pure gold' (Ex. 37:2)."

5. A. "'...its seat of purple':
B. R. Tanhuma says, "This is the veil that adjoined it."
C. R. Bibi said, "This refers to the ark-cover, for the gold of the ark-cover was like purple."

6. A. "'...it was lovingly wrought within by the daughters of Jerusalem":
B. R. Yudan said, "This refers to the merit accruing to the Torah and those who study it."
C. R. Azariah said in the name of R. Yudah in the name of R. Simon, "This refers to the Presence of God."

7. A. Said R. Abba b. Kahana, "'And there I will meet with you' (Ex. 25:22):

	B.	"This serves to teach you that even what is on the other side of the ark cover the space was not empty of the Presence of God."
8.	A.	A gentile asked R. Joshua b. Qorha, "Why did the Holy One, blessed be He, speak from within the bush and not from any other tree?"
	B.	He said to him, "Had he spoke with him from the midst of a carob or a sycamore, you would have asked the same thing, and would I have had to answer you?
	C.	"Nonetheless, to turn you away with nothing is not possible.
	D.	"It serves to teach you that there is no place in the world that is empty of the Presence of God,
	E.	"for even from within the bush did he speak with him."

The ark now takes its place, the natural next step after the tent of meeting. The basic point is completed at No. 6, and the rest is a secondary expansion on the general theme of the ark, how it was made and so forth.

XLIII:iii

1.	A.	[Supply: "King Solomon made himself a palanquin, from the wood of Lebanon. He made its posts of silver, its back of gold, its seat of purple; it was lovingly wrought within by the daughters of Jerusalem":]
	B.	Another interpretation of "a palanquin":
	C.	this refers to the house of the sanctuary.
	D.	"King Solomon made himself":
	E.	this refers in fact to Solomon.
	F.	"...from the wood of Lebanon":
	G.	"And we will cut wood out of Lebanon" (2 Chr. 2:15).
	H.	"He made its posts of silver":
	I.	"And he set up the pillars of the porch of the Temple" (1 Kgs. 7:21).
	J.	"...its back of gold":
	K.	So we have learned on Tannaite authority: The entire house was overlaid with gold, except the backs of the doors.
	L.	Said R. Isaac, "That teaching on Tannaite authority applies to the second building, but as to the first building, even the back parts of the doors were covered with gold."
2.	A.	We have learned: Seven kinds of gold were in it: [Simon:] good gold, pure gold, chased gold, beaten gold, gold of *mufaz*, refined gold, gold of *parvayim*.
	B.	Good gold: that is meant literally, "And the gold of that land is good" (Gen. 2:12).
	C.	In this regard R. Isaac said, "It is good to have in the house, good to take on a trip."
	D.	Pure gold: for they would put it into the furnace and come out undiminished.
	E.	R. Judah in the name of R. Ammi: "A thousand bars of gold did Solomon put into the furnace a thousand time, until they yielded a single bar."
	F.	But lo, said R. Yosé b,. R. Judah on Tannaite authority, "There was the case that the candlestick of the Temple was heavier than that

of the wilderness by the weight of one Gordian *denarius,* and it was passed through the furnace eighty times, until it lost the excess."

G. But to begin with it lost dross, and thereafter it lacked only the smallest volume.

H. beaten gold:

I. for it was drawn out like wax.

J. Hadrian had an egg's bulk of it.

K. Diocletian had a Gordian *denarius's* volume of it.

L. This government today has none of it and never had any of it.

M. chased gold: it bears that name because [Simon:] it made all the goldsmiths shut up their shops.

N. Lo, it is written, "Seven thousand talents of refined silver, with which to overlay the walls of the houses" (1 Chr. 29:4):

O. now was it silver? And was it not gold? And why call it silver?

P. It was to shame everyone who owned gold.

Q. And from it were made all of the utensils, the basins, pots, shovels, snuffers, bowls, forks, spoons, censers, and *potot.*

R. R. Isaac of Magdala said, "'*Potot*' are pivots."

S. R. Sima said, "It refers to a cup under the hinge."

T. This teaches you that the sanctuary was not lacking even the most minor thing.

U. Gold of *mufaz:*

V. R. Patriqi, brother of R. Derosah in the name of R. Abba b. R. Bunah said, "It was like sulphur flaring upon in the fire."

W. R. Abun said, "It is so called by reason of the country in which it originates, which is Ufaz."

X. Refined gold:

Y. The household of R. Yannai and the household of R. Yudan b. R. Simeon:

Z. The household of R. Yannai said, "They cut it into the size of olives and feed it to ostriches, and they defecate it in refined condition."

AA. The household of R. Yudan b. R. Simeon said, "They buried it in dung for seven years and it would come out refined."

BB. Gold of *parvayim:*

CC. R. Simeon b. Laqish said, "It was red, like the blood of a bullock."

DD. Some say, "It produces fruit."

EE. For when Solomon built the house of the sanctuary, he made with it every kind of tree, and when the trees produced fruit, the ones in the Temple did too, and the fruit would drop from the trees and be gathered and was saved for the upkeep of the Temple.

FF. But when Manasseh set up an idol in the Temple, all the trees withered: "And the flower of Lebanon languishes" (Nah. 1:4).

GG. But in the age to come, the Holy One, blessed be He, will bring them back: "It shall blossom abundantly and rejoice, even with joy and singing" (Isa. 35:2).

3. A. "...its seat of purple":

B. "And he made the veil of blue and purple and crimson and fine linen" (2 Chr. 3:14).

4. A. "...it was lovingly wrought within by the daughters of Jerusalem":

B.   R. Yudan said, "This refers to the merit attained through the
        Torah and the merit attained through the righteous who occupy
        themselves with it."

C.   R. Azariah in the name of R. Judah in the name of R. Simon said,
        "This refers to the Presence of God."

From the ark we move on to the sanctuary, with predictable results;
primary is the object chosen as metaphor, secondary is the expansion of
the verses that are used to amplify the connection. That the framers
have nothing new to say, once they have selected their basic object for
metaphorization, is shown at the end, which is repeated verbatim.
That shows that the motivation derives not from the base verse but
from the basic plan.

XLIII:iv

1. A.   [Supply: "King Solomon made himself a palanquin, from the wood
            of Lebanon. He made its posts of silver, its back of gold, its seat of
            purple; it was lovingly wrought within by the daughters of
            Jerusalem":]
    B.   Another interpretation of "a palanquin":
    C.   this refers to the world.
    D.   "King Solomon made himself":
    E.   the king to whom peace belongs.
    F.   "...from the wood of Lebanon":
    G.   for [the world] was built out of the house of the Most Holy Place
            down below.

2. A.   For we have learned on Tannaite authority:
    B.   When the ark was removed [after 586], there remained there a
            stone from the days of the earlier prophets, called foundation-
            stone [Shetiyyah].
    C.   Why was it called foundation-stone [Shetiyyah]?
    D.   For upon it the world was based [the word based uses the same
            consonants as the word for foundation, Shetiyyah].
    E.   That is in line with this verse: "Out of Zion the perfection of beauty
            God has shined forth" (Ps. 50:2).

3. A.   "He made its posts of silver":
    B.   this refers to the chain of genealogies.
    C.   "...its back of gold":
    D.   this speaks of the produce of the earth and of the true, which are
            exchanged for gold
    E.   "...its seat of purple":
    F.   "Who rides upon heaven as your help" (Dt. 33:26).
    G.   "...it was lovingly wrought within by the daughters of Jerusalem":
    H.   R. Yudan said, "This refers to the merit attained through the
            Torah and the merit attained through the righteous who occupy
            themselves with it."
    I.   R. Azariah in the name of R. Judah in the name of R. Simon said,
            "This refers to the Presence of God."

It is not surprising move from the Temple to the natural world, since the Temple and its cult are understood to correspond to the world beyond the walls, which focus within; there the produce of nature is offered to the supernatural. So the symbolism moves on a steady course. The next move is from this world upward to God.

XLIII:v

1. A.   [Supply: "King Solomon made himself a palanquin, from the wood of Lebanon. He made its posts of silver, its back of gold, its seat of purple; it was lovingly wrought within by the daughters of Jerusalem":]

    B.   Another interpretation of "a palanquin":

    C.   this refers to the throne of glory.

    D.   "King Solomon made himself":

    E.   the king to whom peace belongs.

    F.   "...from the wood of Lebanon":

    G.   this is the House of the Most Holy Place above, which is directly opposite the House of the Most Holy Place down below,

    H.   as in the following usage: "The place...for you to dwell in" (Ex. 15:17),

    I.   that is, directly opposite your dwelling place [above].

    J.   "He made its posts of silver":

    K.   "The pillars of heaven tremble" (Job 26:11).

    L.   "...its back of gold":

    M.   this refers to teachings of the Torah: "More to be desired are they then gold, yes, than much fine gold" (Ps. 19:11).

    N.   "...its seat of purple":

    O.   "To him who rides upon the heaven of heavens, which are of old" (Ps. 68:34).

    P.   "...it was lovingly wrought within by the daughters of Jerusalem":

    Q.   R. Berekhiah and R. Bun in the name of R. Abbahu: "There are four proud [creatures]:

    R.   "The pride of birds is the eagle.

    S.   "The pride of domesticated beasts is the ox.

    T.   "The pride of wild beasts is the lion.

    U.   "The pride of them all is man.

    V.   "And all of them did the Holy One, blessed be He, take and engrave on the throne of glory: 'The Lord has established his throne in the heavens and his kingdom rules over all' (Ps. 103:19).

    W.   "Because 'The Lord has established his throne in the heavens,' therefore: 'his kingdom rules over all.'"

The conclusion is truly triumphant, as we now succeed in holding together within the single metaphor earth with Heaven. The palanquin has stood for each of the principal components of the world of sanctification, in nature, cult, and supernature. All is made explicit. The love, then, is cosmopolitan: King Solomon's palanquin is all of reality, which loves, and is loved by, God.

44

Song of Songs Rabbah
to Song of Songs 3:11

3:11   *Go forth, O daughters of Zion,*
        and behold King Solomon,
        with the crown with which his mother crowned him
        on the day of his wedding,
        on the day of the gladness of his heart.

XLIV:I
1. A.   "Go forth, O daughters of Zion":
    B.   the daughters who are distinguished for me by the mode of hair, circumcision, and show-fringes. [The words for distinguished and Zion use the same consonants.]
2. A.   "...and behold King Solomon":
    B.   the king who created his creatures in wholeness [the words for whole and Solomon use the same consonants],
    C.   He created sun and moon in their fullness,
    D.   stars and planets in their fullness.
    E.   Bar Qappara said, "Adam and Eve were created at the age of twenty years."
3. A.   "King Solomon":
    B.   On the king to whom peace belongs.
4. A.   Another explanation of the phrase, "Upon King Solomon":
    B.   upon the king [meaning, God} who brought peace between his works and his creatures.
    C.   How so?
    D.   He made peace between fire and our father Abraham.
    E.   He made peace between the sword and Isaac,
    F.   He made peace between the angel and Jacob.
5. A.   Another interpretation of the phrase, "Upon King Solomon":
    B.   upon the king [meaning, God} who brought peace among his creatures.
6. A.   It was taught on Tannaite authority by R. Simeon b. Yohai: "The firmament is made of snow and the heavenly creatures of fire.

B.   "The firmament is made of snow: 'and over the heads of the living creatures there was the likeness of a firmament, like terrible ice' (Ez. 1:22).

C.   "...and the heavenly creatures of fire: 'As for the likeness of the living creatures, their appearance was like coals of fire' (Ez. 1:13); 'And the living creatures ran and returned as the appearance of a flash of lightning' (Ez. 1:14).

D.   "But this one does not extinguish that, and that does not extinguish this.

E.   "Michael is the angelic prince of ice, and Gabriel is the angelic prince of fire.

F.   "But this one does not extinguish that, and that does not extinguish this."

G.   Said R. Abin, "It is not the end of the matter that he makes peace between one angel and another, but even within a single angel, half of whom is made up of fire and half of ice, the Holy One, blessed be He, brings peace within."

7. A.   There are five aspects in which [in Scripture this power of God to make peace is illustrated,] and these are they:

B.   "His body also was like the beryl and his face as the appearance of lightning" (Dan. 10:6), yet the one does not do injury to the other, and the other does not do injury to the one.

C.   One verse of Scripture says, "Who lays the beams of your upper chambers in the water" (Ps. 104:3), and another says, "For the Lord your God is a devouring fire" (Dt. 4:24), and also, "His throne was fiery flames" (Dan. 7:9), yet the one does not do injury to the other, and the other does not do injury to the one.

D.   Said R. Yohanan, "'He makes peace in his high places' (Job 25:2):

E.   "The firmament is made of water, the stars of fire, , yet the one does not do injury to the other.

F.   "The sun has never behold the defect of the moon [Simon, p. 172, n. 1: the hollow of the moon's crescent is never turned to the sun, as this would give offense to her]."

G.   Said R. Jacob of Kefar Hanan: "'Dominion and fear are with him' (Job 25:2).

H.   "'Dominion' is Michael, 'fear,' Gabriel.'

I.   "'...with him': they make peace in him."

J.   Said R. Levi, "You have no planet that rises out of turn before the other.

K.   "You have no star that sees what is above it, but only what is below it, like a man descending a ladder, who cannot see what is behind him."

L.   Even among the plagues that he brought on Pharaoh he made peace:

M.   "There was hail, fire flashing up amidst the hail" (Ex. 9:24).

8. A.   [Supply: "There was hail, fire flashing up amidst the hail" (Ex. 9:24).]

B.   R. Judah, R. Nehemiah, and Rabbis:

C.   R. Judah said, "The cup of hail was filled with fire, but this did not extinguish that, nor did that extinguish this."

D.   Said R. Hanin, "That statement of R. Judah suggests that it was like a fully-ripened pomegranate, in which every pip can be seen through [the skin]."

E.   R. Nehemiah said, "The fire and the hail mingled with one another."

F.   Said R. Hanin, "That statement of R. Judah suggests that it was like light in a glass, the water and oil are mixed but the fire goes on burning, but this did not extinguish that, nor did that extinguish this."

G.   And rabbis said, "It kept going out and kindling again so as to carry out the will of its creator."

9. A.   Said R. Aha, "The matter may be compared to the case of a king who possessed two crack platoons.

B.   "They bore a grudge against one another.

C.   "But when they saw that the battle of the king was going against him, they made peace with one another so as to make war for the king.

D.   "So fire and water bore a grudge against one another, but when they saw the war of the King of kings, the Holy One, blessed be He, which he fought against the Egyptians, they made peace with one another and did battle for the Holy One, blessed be He, against the Egyptians.

E.   "Thus: 'so there was hail and fire flashing up amid the hail' (Ex. 9:24) – a miracle."

Now our base verse speaks of God, whom the daughters of Zion – the Israelites – are now to behold and admire. This requires our reading "Solomon" in accord with the consonants that yield wholeness, on the one side, and peace, on the other. No. 2 expresses the former, Nos. 3ff., the latter. This yields a variety of secondary amplifications. Through No. 5 our base verse predominates, and from that point onward we call upon thematically relevant, but exegetically indifferent, materials, all of them underlining the same fact about God.

XLIV:ii

1. A.   "...with the crown with which his mother crowned him":

B.   Said R. Yohanan, "R. Simeon b. Yohai asked R. Eleazar b. R. Yosé, saying to him, 'Is it possible that you have heard from your father [Yosé b. R. Halafta] the meaning of the phrase, "with the crown with which his mother crowned him"?'

C.   "He said to him, 'Yes.'

D.   "He said to him, 'And what was it?'

E.   "He said to him, 'The matter may be compared to the case of a king who had an only daughter, whom he loved exceedingly, calling her "My daughter."

F.   "'But he loved her so much that he called her, "My sister," and he loved her so much that he called her, "My mother."

G.   "'So did the Holy One, blessed be He, exceedingly love Israel, calling them, "My daughter." That is shown in this verse: "Listen, O daughter, and consider" (Ps. 45:11).

H.   "'Then he loved them so much that he called them, "My sister," as in this verse, "Open to me, my sister, my love" (Song 5:2).

I.   "'Then he loved them so much that he called them, "My mother," as in this verse, "Listen to me, my people, and give ear to me, my nation" (Isa. 51:4), and the word for "my nation" is written "my mother."'"

J.   R. Simeon b. Yohai stood up and kissed him on his head and said, "If I had come only to hear from your mouth this explanation, it would have sufficed."

2. A.   [Supply: "with the crown with which his mother crowned him":]

B.   Said R. Hanina b. R. Isaac, "We have made the rounds of the entire Scripture and have not found evidence that Bath-Sheba made Solomon her son a crown, and yet you say, 'with the crown with which his mother crowned him'!

C.   "But just as a crown is studded with precious stones and pearls, so the tent of meeting was marked off with blue and purple, crimson and linen."

3. A.   R. Joshua of Sikhnin taught in the name of R. Levi: "When the Holy One, blessed be He, said to Moses, 'Make me a tabernacle,' Moses might have brought four poles and spread over them [skins to make] the tabernacle.

B.   "But this is not how the Holy One, blessed be He, did it. Rather, he took him above and showed him on high red fire, green fire, black fire, and white fire. He then said to him, 'Make me a tabernacle like this.'

C.   "Moses said to the Holy One, blessed be He, 'Lord of the ages, where am I going to get red fire, green fire, black fire, or white fire?'

D.   "He said to him, 'After the pattern which is shown to you on the mountain' (Ex. 25:40)."

4. A.   Said R. Abun [Pesiqta deRab Kahana I:III.10: R. Berekhiah in the name of R. Levi], "[The matter may be compared to the case of] a king who had a beautiful icon.

B.   "He said to the manager of his household, 'Make me one like this.'

C.   "He said to him, 'My lord, O king, how can I make one like this ?'

D.   "He said to him, 'You in accord with your raw materials and I in accord with my glory.'

E.   "So said the Holy One, blessed be He, to Moses, 'See and make.'

F.   "He said to him, 'Lord of the world, am I god that I can make something like this?'

G.   "He said to him, 'After the pattern which is shown to you on the mountain' (Ex. 25:40)."

5. A.   R. Berekhiah in the name of R. Bezalel: "The matter may be compared to the case of a king who appeared to his household manager clothed in a garment covered entirely with precious stones.

B.   "He said to him, 'Make me one like this.'

C.   "He said to him, 'My lord, O king, how can I make one like this [Pesiqta: where am I going to get myself a garment made entirely of precious stones]?'

D. "So said the Holy One, blessed be He, to Moses, 'Make me a tabernacle.'

E. "He said to him, 'Lord of the world, can I make something like this?'

F. "He said to him, 'See and make.'

G. "He said to him, 'Lord of the world, am I god that I can make something like this?'

H. "He said to him, 'After the pattern which is shown to you on the mountain' (Ex. 25:40)."

6. A. [Supply: "...of acacia trees, standing up" (Ex. 26:15):]

B. What it says is not, "set up acacia trees," but rather, "acacia trees standing up."

C. It is like the ones that are stationed in the council above.

7. A. [Continuing No. 5, supply, "He said to him,] 'Moses, if you make what belongs above down below, I shall leave my council up here and go down and reduce my Presence so as to be among you down there.'

B. "How so?

C. "Just as up there: 'seraphim are standing' (Isa. 6:2), so down below: 'boards of shittim-cedars are standing' (Ex. 26:15).

D. "Just as up there are stars, so down below are the clasps."

E. Said R. Hiyya bar Abba, "This teaches that the golden clasps in the tabernacle looked like the fixed stars of the firmament."

8. A. "...on his wedding day":

B. this refers to the day of Sinai, when they were like bridegrooms.

C. "...on his day of joy":

D. this refers to the words of the Torah: "The precepts of the Lord are right, rejoicing the heart" ()Ps. 19:9).

9. A. Another interpretation of the phrase, "on his wedding day, on his day of joy":

B. "...on his wedding day" refers to the tent of meeting.

C. "...on his day of joy" refers to the building of the eternal house.

D. [Pesiqta deRab Kahana concludes with its base verse: Therefore it is said, "On the day that Moses completed the setting up of the Tabernacle, he anointed and consecrated it" (Num. 7:1).]

The exposition of the concluding unit, borrowed, as the earlier ones, from Pesiqta, continues to link the passage of Song of Songs to the tabernacle. There is nothing that Pesiqta has not supplied, though some of the wordings are slightly different. The point our compilers wish to make, however, allows them to take over whole what others have made up for their own purposes, and that is the indicative trait of this compilation and its companions.

Index

Brown Judaic Studies

140001	*Approaches to Ancient Judaism I*	William S. Green
140002	*The Traditions of Eleazar Ben Azariah*	Tzvee Zahavy
140003	*Persons and Institutions in Early Rabbinic Judaism*	William S. Green
140004	*Claude Goldsmid Montefiore on the Ancient Rabbis*	Joshua B. Stein
140005	*The Ecumenical Perspective and the Modernization of Jewish Religion*	S. Daniel Breslauer
140006	*The Sabbath-Law of Rabbi Meir*	Robert Goldenberg
140007	*Rabbi Tarfon*	Joel Gereboff
140008	*Rabban Gamaliel II*	Shamai Kanter
140009	*Approaches to Ancient Judaism II*	William S. Green
140010	*Method and Meaning in Ancient Judaism*	Jacob Neusner
140011	*Approaches to Ancient Judaism III*	William S. Green
140012	*Turning Point: Zionism and Reform Judaism*	Howard R. Greenstein
140013	*Buber on God and the Perfect Man*	Pamela Vermes
140014	*Scholastic Rabbinism*	Anthony J. Saldarini
140015	*Method and Meaning in Ancient Judaism II*	Jacob Neusner
140016	*Method and Meaning in Ancient Judaism III*	Jacob Neusner
140017	*Post Mishnaic Judaism in Transition*	Baruch M. Bokser
140018	*A History of the Mishnaic Law of Agriculture: Tractate Maaser Sheni*	Peter J. Haas
140019	*Mishnah's Theology of Tithing*	Martin S. Jaffee
140020	*The Priestly Gift in Mishnah: A Study of Tractate Terumot*	Alan. J. Peck
140021	*History of Judaism: The Next Ten Years*	Baruch M. Bokser
140022	*Ancient Synagogues*	Joseph Gutmann
140023	*Warrant for Genocide*	Norman Cohn
140024	*The Creation of the World According to Gersonides*	Jacob J. Staub
140025	*Two Treatises of Philo of Alexandria: A Commentary on De Gigantibus and Quod Deus Sit Immutabilis*	David Winston/John Dillon
140026	*A History of the Mishnaic Law of Agriculture: Kilayim*	Irving Mandelbaum
140027	*Approaches to Ancient Judaism IV*	William S. Green
140028	*Judaism in the American Humanities*	Jacob Neusner
140029	*Handbook of Synagogue Architecture*	Marilyn Chiat
140030	*The Book of Mirrors*	Daniel C. Matt
140031	*Ideas in Fiction: The Works of Hayim Hazaz*	Warren Bargad
140032	*Approaches to Ancient Judaism V*	William S. Green
140033	*Sectarian Law in the Dead Sea Scrolls: Courts, Testimony and the Penal Code*	Lawrence H. Schiffman
140034	*A History of the United Jewish Appeal: 1939-1982*	Marc L. Raphael
140035	*The Academic Study of Judaism*	Jacob Neusner
140036	*Woman Leaders in the Ancient Synagogue*	Bernadette Brooten
140037	*Formative Judaism: Religious, Historical, and Literary Studies*	Jacob Neusner
140038	*Ben Sira's View of Women: A Literary Analysis*	Warren C. Trenchard
140039	*Barukh Kurzweil and Modern Hebrew Literature*	James S. Diamond

Brown Studies on Jews and Their Societies

Brown Studies in Religion